/

Inspiring Generations

INSPIRING GENERATIONS

150 Years, 150 Stories in Yosemite

YOSEMITE CONSERVANCY
Yosemite National Park

YOSEMITE
CONSERVANCY.

yosemiteconservancy.org

Library of Congress Control Number: 2013945036

Cover and book design by Nancy Austin

ISBN 978-1-930238-45-9

Printed in the United States of America by Worzalla.

2 3 4 5 6 – 17 16 15 14

Manufactured using recycled paper and soy inks.
All materials are from sustainable sources.

FSC
www.fsc.org
MIX
Paper from
responsible sources
FSC® C002589

CONTENTS

FOREWORD

THE MUSE OF YOSEMITE . . .

We had just emerged from the Wawona Tunnel when someone hollered from the back of the car, "Stop here!" It was late and everyone was tired, but the Valley's iconic sights (Bridalveil Fall, Half Dome, El Capitan) filled the windshield and commanded our attention. An approaching sunset painted the sky with a broad palette of colors. The scene was jaw-dropping. Yosemite was showing off.

Earlier in the day, we hiked the western boundary of the park with our new congressman. It was warm and sunny and the breeze blew lightly, to the point where you had to hold onto your map. Along the way, we discussed some of Yosemite's complex history, its current pressures, as well as how vital Yosemite National Park is to California, the U.S., and the world.

But now we were at Tunnel View—and the heart of Yosemite Valley lay before us—unobstructed, magnificent, completely available—just as it has always been and just how it should always be. This was the first time our new congressman had seen the Valley this way, and as we drifted among the visitors and the majesty soaked in, I overheard him say, "Wow, this . . . is . . . really amazing." A smile stretched across his face as the charm of Yosemite took hold. In that short moment, the magic of the Valley had reenergized and inspired him, as well as the people next him, and everyone there—just as it has done for visitors for over 150 years.

Each day, this glacier-carved Valley high in the Sierra Nevada—with its meandering snow-fed rivers, spectacular waterfalls, gigantic sequoia trees, towering granite cliffs, historic landmarks, and extraordinary animals—astounds, mesmerizes, and enchants people from around the globe. Its preservation embodies every element of the conservation movement and is a testimony to America's commitment "to conserve the scenery and the natural and historic objects and the wildlife therein . . . unimpaired for the enjoyment of future generations."

As a young boy, our family camped in Yosemite Valley. We hiked the trails, plunged into the icy Merced, and gathered to watch the now historic firefall from Glacier Point. One of my earliest Yosemite memories is being held by my mother in Stoneman Meadow as a bear passed too close. These types of experiences have become the fabric of my life, and I am forever privileged to have had so much time in such an incredible place.

Inspiring Generations is a collection of memories and experiences about one of the most beloved places on earth. Each author pays a tribute of respect, admiration, and awe for what is an international symbol of scenic beauty, recreation, and conservation of spectacular resources. In the pages of this book are stories of love, adventure, discovery, rejuvenation, and inspiration. They are a slice of Yosemite National Park. In these stories, you will hike the John Muir Trail, float the Merced River, smell an alpine flower, hear a songbird, revisit traditions, and reenergize your spirit—just as our new congressman did during his visit. Yosemite is a muse for the soul, and that muse reverberates in the stories and experiences shared within *Inspiring Generations*.

Don Neubacher, Superintendent
Yosemite National Park

Don Neubacher has been the superintendent of Yosemite since 2010.
Prior to this, he has worked at Golden Gate National Recreation Area,
Point Reyes National Seashore, and Glacier Bay National Park.

ACKNOWLEDGMENTS

Yosemite Conservancy profoundly thanks the four hundred individuals who, because of their love for Yosemite, set their memories on paper as part of the story contest that became this book. All four hundred stories now reside in the Yosemite National Park archives. From the original four hundred submissions, one hundred fifty were chosen by a team of volunteer readers who, without identification of authors, read, ranked, and categorized each story. A special thanks go to Suzanne Gladstone, Nancy Rice, Jack Slocombe, Leslie Strayer, Jeannie Tasker, and Lynn Upthagrove for hours of reading and conference call discussions to ensure the integrity of their mission. Volunteer projects require champions who believe in their project enough to make it a reality. Thank you to Jeannie Tasker and Kassandra Hardy for being the champions of this book.

1

INSPIRING
GENERATIONS

What Auntie Brought

Carol Eve Ford

In the mid-1950s, a few days before our much-anticipated annual camping trip to Yosemite, Daddy sat my three brothers and me down. "How would you kids feel about Auntie joining us this year? She loves Yosemite, and she's asked to go along."

We looked at each other as if he'd just said something in Russian. The thought of Auntie in Yosemite—camping—was incongruous! "Auntie," our grandmother's older sister, was ancient: a bent, squarish little octogenarian with flat-brimmed straw hat, silver-white hair, wire-rimmed glasses, always a midcalf-length dress, nylons with seams, sturdy lace-up shoes, and block heels.

"Sure," we shrugged, mystified.

She was the first to comment on the glorious aroma of the pines as we ascended the foothills. She didn't approve of whistling or honking in the tunnel, believing it could bring the mountain down on us, but as soon as we came out into the stunning first view of the Valley, she was home!

"Ah, Tis-se'-yak!" she breathed. "Good, old, faithful—Tis-se'-yak! Some call it Half Dome, but the Indians called it O-o-ld Tis-se'-yak!"

"Bridalveil Fall! Look how the breeze BLOWS her veil, children!" Her voice was as light and promising as a bride's veil wafting in the breeze.

"EL, Capitan! Mag-NI-ficent—EL, Capitan!" she announced regally, every syllable a fanfare—as if the "Capitan" were entering the royal ballroom in full dress uniform.

As we drove up the Valley, she greeted every outcropping and waterfall as old friends, gesturing reverently with her arthritic hands, bowing forward to take it all in through the windshield.

"The mighty Merced!" she pronounced reverently. "The Mighty, Clear, Emerald, Merced!"

"Thr-r-ree Brothers, boys! Thr-r-ree Brothers!" she trilled happily. It was both greeting and inside joke. We had three brothers, too.

"Oh, look back, children!" she intoned as if we had entered a vast, holy sanctuary. "Cath-e-dral Spi-ires!"

Every year, no matter how much water was in Yosemite Falls, she proclaimed it "the best I've EVER seen it! The most beautiful, BOOMing falls IN the world! Just look at that cataract!"

She pointed with outstretched hand: "See that thin finger of rock there, boys? The Lost Needle! Some call it Lost Arrow!"

"Rr-r-oy-al Arch-es! Rr-r-oy-al Arch-es!" She sang rolling her r's in pure delight.

By the time we reached Camp 11, all the familiar rock formations and bodies of water had been acknowledged. We wondered how Auntie would camp. After all, she was really old! Would she sleep on the ground, as we did, in a pup tent on a sighing, shifting, seeping air mattress? In a sleeping bag? Surely not!

That first year, we watched as Daddy, taking Auntie's instruction, set up her camp in the exact manner we did it every year after that. For Auntie, there was a right way to do everything; camping was no exception.

First Daddy hefted Auntie's tent to a spot she had found that was absolutely flat and level, facing the creek. It was what they called an umbrella tent, and it weighed a ton! Dark brown waxed canvas fabric, heavy metal frame, floor, awning, net window. Far from a pup tent, it was a walk-in affair.

Once it was up, Auntie had Daddy haul in two army cots with massive wooden frames, canvas surfaces, and lots of potential for pinching little fingers, so we weren't allowed to help. One cot went on the right, one on the left of the doorway.

Next we lugged her two large leather suitcases in and laid them on the right-hand cot. She made up the other cot like a real bed with sheets, blankets, pillow, and pillowcase. Her tent was like a bedroom, with her sturdy suitcases acting as a dresser.

Next we unpacked two folding chairs, similar in bulk to the cots, and put one outside her door, facing the creek, the other between the cots, under the net window. Meanwhile she hung a whisk broom, small pan, and wooden spoon inside the tent near the door and asked us kids to go find two solid stumps that we could roll over near her "front porch."

"What are the pan and spoon for?" we asked.

"To shoo the bears away," she said matter-of-factly.

We set the stumps to the right and left of her doorway. She placed a huge white metal enamel basin on each stump. One was for washing her hands and face. That one had a hand towel and a soap dish with a bar of soap on it. The other was for washing out articles of clothing in the evenings. She hung the washed clothing modestly on the "umbrella" structure inside her tent so they'd be fresh and dry the next morning.

Auntie did not backpack or fish, but she enjoyed eating trout, and she strolled the Valley floor contentedly in her sturdy shoes. She soaked her bare white feet in the cold Merced, and waded, bent and interested in the gold-flecked sand of El Capitan beach. She pointed out ouzels, jays, majestic pines, chipmunks, owl's clover, and shooting stars. She marveled at the vastness of the granite. When the bears came in at night, she whacked her pan with her spoon and emitted a no-nonsense "SHOO!" to which the bears responded appropriately with a sheepish "Oops sorry ma'am" kind of look as they lumbered back into the woods.

At the time, I thought she did all of these things because she was old and didn't know how to camp. But this was how people had camped in Yosemite for a hundred years. Auntie had ridden her horse in the Valley as a young woman. She referred to John Muir fondly, as if he were a revered old friend. Maybe he was. I never asked her about these things. I knew only that she and I agreed: Yosemite was the best place in the universe.

My Daughter, One of Them

Guy Cottle

A BRIEF LOOK UPWARD, toward the heavens, stirs my heart, quickens my pulse. I worry, but the moment passes. She will be fine. My eyes return to the trail and find her there as well—my daughter, Tee, just ahead.

My daughter is a half-pint child again, bouncing along, jumping from rock to rock. We are three days out from the trailhead at White Wolf Lodge and about fourteen miles into the Grand Canyon of the Tuolumne. Tigger bounced, too, that day. He was tied to the top of her backpack. His fur-bare stuffed-animal head flopped up and down with each step—as if in crazed agreement with the experiment my daughter and I shared.

Then as now, gray walls soared, one to each side in a narrowing corridor. The granite stone barriers, one hundred million years in the making, reached upward, pinching the blue sky for a piece of eternity. Earth has surely forgotten the geothermal conception, the muscled push to the surface by tectonic plates, the scouring of character by water and ice.

Or can a parent forget?

Our experiment, a first-ever backpacking trip that lasted five days, tested our legs, challenged our fortitude, and pushed our ability to "keep on keeping on" to new limits. Tee was just past ten. I was just past self-imposed midlife shambles—a divorce from the woman I loved, a change of career. It was our first time together—just us—since our family had fallen. We walked, played, and talked as friends, as equals in an adventure, but my intent was parental. My heart set to fill her heart with reassurance, to connect her thoughts firmly to the forever of family.

A river large enough to nourish nearly one million people in San Francisco crashed, weaved, stormed, and fell into tranquil contemplation. The sounds echoed back and forth in the corridor before escaping upward to the sky. The quiet echoed, too. We watched in awe as trees larger than diesel trucks jostled and sometimes spiked out of the water. We left footprints in the mud. We theorized one day, if the mud hardened into stone, future archeologists would try to reconstruct our lives. Like they did with the footprints of Lucy, an original human parent who lived in Africa millions of years ago.

No matter how tired we were, or how late the day, I often looked ahead to see my child pretending that brown dirt was yellow hot lava. She jumped from rock to rock to avoid the danger. "It's fun, Dad. Try it," she called, almost missing the next rock as she turned to look back. We both knew that yellow lava is hotter and more perilous than red. She had learned the fact at school. She taught the colors to me.

The canyon spoke in a language layered to all senses. The river crackled, the wind whistled through crevices in the rocks, limbs knocked together, fingers caressed granite. Odors filled the air: moss, pine, decaying wood. Grass tall enough to tickle our chins. Boulders broken into crumbs and pieces by ancient falls. All became one, a unified message in a multisensory language. We were immersed in the language of Earth.

I listened, struggled to know, but I was as a newborn child who loves the cadence of a dinner table conversation but lacks connection to the specifics of meaning. I wondered if my daughter felt it, too.

"Tee," I called. "Wait. Just stand still."

She stopped.

"Do you feel it?"

She paused.

"Yeah," she said, "feels like Christmas Eve."

We were tired much of the time, hungry most of the time, and exhilarated all of the time. Fully alive. Connected to ourselves, the moment, each other. Everything about our experience was driven by the larger time line of our place in the canyon—beneath the stars, next to the fire at night, sitting with hungry bellies while food cooked. Everything would outlast us, perhaps even our footsteps in the mud. We were less than a blink; our species, less than breath.

One morning, near the end of our backpacking trip, my daughter and I rose to find small black dots moving near the top of one of the cliffs. They looked like gnats from the distance, but the binoculars told us that we were seeing rock climbers.

"They are trying to escape eternity," I said.

"I'm going to do that one day," she answered.

And the memory passes. I am alone again, hiking the same trail. Now as then, I see the small black specks moving near the top of the cliffs. One of them is her: my daughter grown up. Fully immersed, climbing into the future.

Bierstadt Paints Yo-semite Falls

Daniel Williams

STONE WATER AND FIRE
a meadow green as grass
and a looking glass pool
at the base of the falls
Water in all of its glory
gray mists above the rims
the flow of it over the cliff
pure white as cotton
mixture of water and sky
first the Upper and then
the Lower
I would that the blood of
Fredericksburg could be
washed by this mighty flow
that the nation that stands
divided even as this
divides the face of stone
could find the glory and power
of this white purity with which
to bind its wounds
These trees I've included are
fine old sentinels, catchers of
first light in their crowns
givers of lovely scent and shade
in the heat of every day
It is their branches which we burned
at night, the yellow snap of their flames

the popping of the resin knots and the
spark showers skyward
stand off a ways and you can see the
powerful orange dome of fire in all that
pristine darkness the faces of Williams
Ludlow and Perry shining as if disembodied
and circling the coals each of us a spirit
of art serving the god that is this miraculous
Valley this Yo-semite home to this waterfall
this darkness and this luminous light

———◆———

"There are two kinds of enjoyment of scenery, as of
everything else. The one is the enjoyment of beauty and
grandeur, heightened by novelty; the other is the enjoyment
of the same mellowed and hallowed by association. The
one affects more the imagination, the other the heart."

—Joseph LeConte, 1903

Yosemite Environmental Living Program

Carolyn Boster (eleven years old)

I've had two major memorable trips to Yosemite. These special times were with my wonderful fourth-grade teacher, Marlene Bergstrom, also known as Miss B. This very dedicated lady has taken each of her classes on a three-day, two-night adventure every year for the past twenty-three years. I went in 2010 as a fourth grader in her class, and I also had the good fortune to go again in 2011 as a fifth grader. Every year Miss B selects a chosen few to go for a second time, and I was one of them! The second time was the best. Mostly because the weather was unseasonably warm for the middle of May, and we got to stay longer than any other class that has gone on this trip. The first year I went, also in May, we all about froze in the snow, rain, sleet, and ice. The first day and a half of the trip are spent at the Pioneer Yosemite History Center in Wawona. There, students reenact the days before Yosemite became a national park. The next day and a half are spent camping and hiking in Yosemite Valley. The last day we hike to the top of Vernal Fall.

The first day of our trip, we experienced the Environmental Living Program in Wawona in the southern part of the Park. Back at school Miss B had assigned each of us an historical character to "become." Each of these characters were part of a group. These groups were: the Early People, the Artisans, the Transportationists, the Guardians, and the Living Services. Each group spent the day moving through rotations. These were different stations that re-created a picture of the life in the 1800s before Yosemite became a national park. All of what I'm about to describe I did in costume. This was a skirt, a long-sleeved blouse, a hat, and even the right shoes. Miss B wanted everything to be very authentic! These rotations included blacksmithing, where we made a dinner bell. Preparing part of dinner and chopping wood with a real ax were others.

We also shopped in a general store that stocked candy, old-fashioned toys, and other period things. We bought these things with Curry Cash we had earned back in the classroom. Fancy "high tea" was still another rotation. There was real china that we had to be very careful not to break. Yet another was going out in the meadow and creating an art project. The last station was meeting and riding with Buckshot in his horse and wagon. This was my favorite.

When the day was over we had dinner, which was meatloaf, mashed potatoes, and vegetables that we all had made. For dessert we feasted on homemade ice cream. We made that, too. After we ate, we sang songs while sitting by the campfire. Next we went to our cabins and rolled out our sleeping bags to get ready for sleeping. We went to the gray barn after we got our cabins ready. In this old building we square-danced. This was easy because we had been practicing at school before we went. It was really exciting to dance in the place Miss B had been preparing us for. The day was full and fun, but I was ready for bed!

The next day, we ate a breakfast that the Living Services group got up an hour early to make for us. It was eggs, potatoes, muffins, and bacon. Yum! After our meal we held a town meeting, which included showing the art we made in the meadow the first day and talking about why we thought the meadow was important. Next there was a controversial meeting about whether we should keep the meadow the way it was or modernize it. When the meeting was over, we packed everything and took a bus down to the Valley.

When we arrived in the beautiful Yosemite Valley we ate lunch by the Swinging Bridge. As we finished, we took a hike around the Valley. Remember, we were all still in our costumes. We visited the Yosemite Cemetery where many of the characters we "became" were buried. We went to the Valley Visitor Center, the Yosemite Museum, and the Yosemite Chapel. There we had a "wedding" in which two members of our group got to be the bride and groom. Our hike led us to Curry Village where we showered and got out of our costumes and into regular clothes. Boy did that feel good!! After everyone was clean, we went to our campsites and had dinner. We had hamburgers and hotdogs. It was the best meal ever!

That night—the end of day two—we went on a night hike to prepare us for the big hike the next day to the top of Vernal Fall. We, meaning the kids, had no idea where we were headed. It turned out to be the famous Ahwahnee. The whole class got to tiptoe through the lobby and the first floor. What a beautiful place. Maybe when I'm older I can actually stay there! When we hiked back to camp it was the end of our second day! Sleeping wasn't hard at all that night. We were all so tired we didn't care where we slept.

The sun was up and it was our third and last day in wonderful Yosemite. There was much to do to prepare for hiking to the top Vernal Fall. We had to pack our bags and sleeping bags, make our lunch for the top of the fall, pack our backpacks, and be ready for the BIG hike. The hike was the toughest walk I've ever loved. So many stairs to climb! I was so glad Miss B had us run laps and do "step-ups" on benches for several weeks before our trip. We took the Mist Trail to the top. I now know why it is called the Mist Trail. There was so much water coming off the fall that it almost felt like it was raining. Good thing we had rain ponchos to help keep us dry. When we made it to the top we gobbled up our lunch and saw the fall drop into the Merced River. After many photos we headed back down the John Muir Trail. This route has mostly winding switchbacks. When we got back to the bottom my legs were shaking because I had used so many new muscles.

We were done with the hike and our three-day adventure was over. The bus was coming to take us back to school. Or so we thought. We waited and waited. . . . No bus. So Miss B and the parents had to figure out why. Turned out the bus was due to arrive the next day! Hurray, our trip was extended!! This was a first. No other Miss B class has ever had an extended trip. We were all so lucky. We had dinner at a restaurant in the Yosemite Lodge and watched a film in an outdoor theater about hiking in Yosemite. We took another night hike, this time to the base of Yosemite Falls. The adults worked things out, and the bus finally arrived at ten-thirty that night.

What a great time I had in Yosemite with Miss B and her fourth-grade class. I will never, ever forget it! I go to Yosemite at least five times a year with my family. I've hiked Vernal Fall twice, and I've hiked North Dome and Sentinel Dome. Because of all of these wonderful memories, Yosemite National Park is one of my favorite places on Earth.

During the Spring of 2001

Linda Glick

At the age of eighty, my mother moved to Sonora in the fall of 1998 to live close to my husband and me and our two children. We had relocated to Sonora during the summer of that same year. We love living in Sonora, and one of the reasons is its close proximity to Yosemite National Park. Yosemite has always been one of our most favorite places to visit. My mom was raised in New York and took the subway everywhere, so she never learned to drive. My parents moved from New York to Los Angeles back in the late 1940s, and since Mom didn't like to travel, she really didn't know much about Yosemite. In fact, there were only two reasons Mom would agree to go on a long car drive: either we were visiting family or the destination had a casino. She was never fond of long car rides, most especially if there were a lot of curves in the road or a high elevation. After my mother moved to Sonora, I began in earnest my quest to finally get her to Yosemite. Off and on I would bring up the idea of taking her, and she would always decline and say she wasn't interested.

One day during Easter break in 2001, I had promised my kids (ages fourteen and ten at the time) I would take them to Yosemite for the day. My mother happened to be in my Expedition with us on an unexpected quick trip to Modesto to pick up my brother from out of town, and he had agreed to go to the park with us after we picked him up. My mother, upon hearing our intent to go to Yosemite on our way back home, demanded to be taken back to her apartment first. I told her that in no way was I going to drive an extra hour to take her back home when for years I had wanted her to see the park, so in a sense she was being held captive, and she was very annoyed with me. All along the drive up to Groveland and past the entrance gate, all she did was complain and complain. She complained about the winding roads, complained that we have trees in Sonora, why must I take her somewhere else where all she was seeing were trees! I would glance in my rearview mirror at my daughter's face, which clearly showed her exasperation at all her Grandma's complaining, and so it went for over an hour. I soon totally doubted myself for making this decision to force her to go with us; maybe I should have just taken her back to her apartment.

Then we finally made our way down into the Valley floor, and when we cleared the tunnel and had that spectacular unobstructed view of the granite cliffs, I looked at my mother who sat in the front seat and I could see that her jaw had literally dropped open, and for a moment she was totally speechless. She was looking in awe and wonder, and I so wish I could have taken her picture at that very moment. Finally, as I was driving I glanced at her again and all she could say was, "Linda, how did this happen?" I believe those were her exact words, and at the same time I saw that tears were starting to drip down her face. I just replied, "God and Mother Nature."

The rest of the day, my mom never uttered one more word of complaint; she was all smiles. We drove straight to The Ahwahnee and I asked the man at the entrance to the hotel if he might know of a wheelchair we could borrow while we were at the hotel. He replied, "sure, one moment." Well, that sealed the deal for my mother, since she was also disabled. We had a wonderful lunch at The Ahwahnee, and my mom had the most remarkable trip to Yosemite and told all her neighbors about it when she returned. We drove her all around as much as we could before heading back home, and then on the drive home she commented on how quick it was to drive back to Sonora and please could I take her to Yosemite again. Wow. We never did make it back before she passed away two years later, but I will forever hold that day close to my heart. I did it. I got my mom to Yosemite for the first time in her life at the age of eighty-two, and not only that, she loved it and I have some cherished pictures of us at The Ahwahnee with my mom in the wheelchair to prove it. Wonders never cease.

My Yosemite Vacations with My Mom

Kim Dalton

As my children have grown and moved out of the house, my relationship with my mom has now taken center stage. In 2010, I surprised my mom on her birthday with a minivacation for just the two of us. In deciding where to go, we both realized we hadn't been to Yosemite in a very long time, so we targeted it as our vacation destination. This was our first trip together since I was a teenager; now in my fifties and my mom in her eighties, I realized it was finally time to get to know her and enjoy our time together.

In the spring of 2010, we traveled from Southern California to Oakhurst and then down into the Valley. What magnificent sights bombarded our senses! The majesty of the mountains, the stark contrast of colors, the wildlife and the pure nature was overwhelming . . . and the fresh air and the voluminous sound of the waterfalls! As we drove through the Valley, my mom started relaying her experiences as a young child with her parents (during the early 1930s). I had no idea what a wealth of sweet history awaited me. In my midfifties, I was finally past the stage of self-absorption and raising children, and was able to thoroughly enjoy hearing and appreciating her experiences as a child. She recanted their long drive from Los Angeles into the Valley and the many twists and turns in their 1925 Ford. She pointed out the campsite where she and her Swedish parents and friends stayed for many years, and I heard about how one morning, she fell in the small, slow-moving creek and her mom panicked because her little child of five years old didn't know how to swim (it wasn't dangerous). She told me many stories of their campfires and ghost stories, and how the adults would weave and sing around the campfire. Their cooking over the ancient Coleman stoves and cleanup now sounds like such an effort and so time-consuming. I'm sure they would have loved having paper plates and utensils back then to make camping a bit easier, but they had the small plastic tubs and had to heat the wash water over the campfire to wash the dishes. My mom's family and friends would play card games by the lantern at night. I heard about the walks through the forest and the noisy camping neighbors who would stay up late. My mom named all her friends that were vacationing with them—what a memory! Most special and unexpected to me was giving her the opportunity to reminisce about her early days.

When our vacation was winding up and we were driving out of Yosemite Valley, my mom related how after World War II, when she was a teenager, she and a girlfriend hitchhiked out of part of the Valley. A young soldier drove by and picked them up, and took them where they needed to go. While driving, I started yelling, "Mother, what? That's dangerous! Why would you do such a thing?" I guess back then it was safe. When we got back to our hotel in Oakhurst, we feasted on our gourmet dinner from the grocery store's frozen section, heated in our hotel's microwave, all of three dollars each. We created our own little memory.

In the spring of 2011, we once again traveled to Yosemite. We were planning to choose another vacation location but Yosemite called us and drew us back again. We were not disappointed. It turns out the winter of 2011 had a tremendous snowfall and in May 2011, the falls were spectacular and at their zenith. My mom waited below while I ventured up on the slippery path into the heavy sprays of Bridalveil. What an exhilarating experience, but more exhilarating was once again, listening and absorbing more memories from my mom.

My mom and I discovered we are excellent travel partners and we enjoy being in each other's company. We didn't travel in 2012, but where will we go this year in 2013? Maybe Yosemite again! I wouldn't be surprised.

I am sure there are many stories like ours; I hope so.

Christmas Moment

Steven Gadecki

MY STORY BEGINS when my mother bought me an L.L.Bean backpack when I first started attending Broome Community College (BCC) in Binghamton, New York. Little did I know at the time that this backpack would become the catalyst for the next fifteen years of my life and last me through college, Habitat for Humanity, one year with AmeriCorps, hiking one hundred and four mountains, exploring two new countries and twelve new states, one cross-country move from New York to California, fourteen National Parks, ten years at my current job, and the introduction to my wife, which led to the birth of my son. When the backpack had finally worn out I was standing at the garbage ready to throw it away. I then started to remember everything that I had experienced with it, and to simply toss it away felt too final. So I sat down and wrote a letter of all my memories and sent it back to L.L.Bean.

After a couple months they wrote back to me saying that they appreciated my letter, and that they've included my backpack into the official archives at L.L.Bean headquarters. I was happy that it had a "final resting spot" and found out later that the archive is a serious deal. It actually houses the founder's boots. That backpack was with me when I first explored Yosemite, and more importantly, during the greatest gift my father could have given me in the park.

In college, I eventually graduated from BCC and transferred to SUNY Plattsburgh, New York. While I was there, I didn't have a car, so I took full advantage of the weekend hiking trips that the college would take to the Adirondack Mountains of northern New York. Gaining access to some of my most beloved hiking ground with the college's help really broadened my scope on patience and balance. After graduating, I spent a year with AmeriCorps working at the Traumatic Brain Injury (TBI) center in Plattsburgh. Then I moved out to California, bought my first car, and began my next chapter.

When I visited Yosemite for the first time it was like a living dream. I had grown up seeing images of the park my whole life and then, there I was, standing in front of El Capitan, looking upon Half Dome, and witnessing Yosemite Falls. I would visit the park many times over the next twelve years and embark on some defining hikes (Half Dome, Hoffmann, Dana, and El Cap). However none of these compared to the time my brother and I took my parents to Yosemite for Christmas.

Until then my parents hadn't visited California since their honeymoon. So there was much anticipation on how special this trip would be.

We started in Los Angeles and spent our time driving up the coast to San Francisco where we picked up my brother. From there we trekked over to Yosemite as the sun set. By the time we made it into the park it was too dark for my parents to grasp the grandeur of anything, but the excitement was there. It was cold when we pulled up to The Ahwahnee and a man bundled up in a long coat greeted us with a warm "Welcome!" The warmth and mystique of the lodge enveloped us as we entered, and though we were weary from the road, we were just in awe of our surroundings.

The next morning I opened up the door from our room to a massive deck that was above the dining hall. There they were, right in front of me, without any obstruction: Yosemite Falls! I gave out a "WOOT" and heard a door open behind me. My father came out from his room and we realized that the entire deck, which could easily hold fifty people comfortably, was ours. That day my brother, father, and I spent most of our time hiking around Lower Yosemite Fall. Back on the deck, my mother was totally content writing her letters while taking in the magnificent views.

Christmas Eve has always had a special presence to it, but that night when we attended the Bracebridge Dinner, it brought me back to my youth. Giddy with that overwhelming feeling of knowing that tomorrow is Christmas. When I look back, I can't remember a time when I had slept so peacefully.

Christmas morning was like a cloud just floating over the reality of the world, and it seemed as if Yosemite was our own private park. After the magical morning of opening presents and laughing, we slowly packed up for checkout. I had just put my backpack on and headed out to the deck for one more look around, when my father came out to join me. As we stood there looking at the falls, he turned to me and said; "Never in my life did I think I would see Yosemite. Thank you." At that moment, I don't know if it was the Christmas-morning feeling or the power of his words, but high emotion swept right over me. It truly was the best gift I could have received.

Yosemite's Magic

Rebecca Waddell

THE MAGIC OF Yosemite captured me the instant I took my first step on the pine-needle-strewn Valley floor. I was five years old that first trip and nothing has stopped me from returning every year. However, my history with Yosemite began long before I was born.

It is really no wonder that I am drawn to the granite-monolith-guarded paradise. I am the fourth generation of my family to have the privilege of falling under Yosemite's spell. For sixty-two years, the women in my family have been camping with their children and loving Yosemite. From the towering trees to the coolness of the river, we return year after year to see it all.

Since my great-grandmother has passed on, each summer sees four generations camping together. Like my ancestresses before me, I bring my children to Yosemite so they can also grow up loving the waterfalls and hiking trails that are so dear to me. Though things have changed over the years, the innate beauty of the Valley never fails to stop me in my tracks and make me fall madly in love with Yosemite all over again.

As I have grown, Yosemite has taught me many life lessons. I saw my first moonbow and ate my first s'more in Yosemite. Rafting down the Merced taught me basic hydrodynamics and cold tolerance. Hiking Half Dome taught me to endure and persevere. Sleeping under the stars taught me to dream big even when I feel small. Overall, I have learned to love and respect the natural word in all its glory and power.

I have seen fire, flood, politics, and rockfalls reshape my beloved Valley. With these things, I have borne joyful witness to the preservation efforts like meadow boardwalks and the Lower Yosemite Fall Project. These measures will allow many more generations to carry on enjoying the unspoiled splendor of Yosemite National Park.

Five Generations

Linda Petsche

I AM AT THE midpoint of five generations in my family who have regularly visited Yosemite Valley; my grandparents, my parents, my children, and my grandchildren.

My first visit to Yosemite was in 1950 when I was just five months old. My dad liked to tell the story of how he walked over to the cafeteria early in the morning to ask someone to heat a bottle of milk. They were staying in the old cabins in the Lodge area, 32C, where they had honeymooned in 1948. For many years, my sister and I had our picture taken in front of that cabin. We managed to get one last one for posterity after the flood that forced the razing of those cabins.

Growing up in the San Francisco Bay Area meant a long drive, but my family visited often when I was a child. I remember walking out to Mirror Lake when it was a lake, watching the firefalls, and feeding the deer, before we knew better. My dad often reminisced about a hike he and his mother took in 1936, when he was seventeen years old. They climbed the Four Mile Trail to Glacier Point and back. They were wearing street shoes, carried no water, and did it in a day . . . a LONG day!

As a young adult, I continued visiting the park, hiking, backpacking, cross-country skiing, snowshoeing, and photographing the breathtaking sights. When my children were born, we introduced them to the park. Starting with bicycle rides around the Valley when they were toddlers, they learned to love hiking, camping, cross-country skiing, sledding, and snowshoeing.

Over my sixty-two years of visiting, I've had an opportunity to watch the transition as the park grew and expanded its traffic areas. Then, happily, I've seen the rebirth and rejuvenation of the habitat, as parking areas were returned to their natural state.

For nearly thirty years, now, I have gone to Yosemite to celebrate my birthday in January. I love the quietness of winter in the Valley. The past six years, my kids and grandkids have joined us. Sledding and playing in the snow, or climbing on the big rocks when there isn't any snow, picnicking near the Ahwahnee Meadow and hanging out with family. They know that Gramma's birthday means a trip to Yosemite. For me, it doesn't get much better than that!

—◆—

"The nation behaves well if it treats the natural resources as assets which it must turn over to the next generation increased, and not impaired, in value."

—Theodore Roosevelt, 1910

An Odd Tale

Robert H. Boyer

We are all quite proud of our Lodges
And the wonderful work that they do,
So I feel free to brag about some history
That just might surprise all of you.
With the help of our membership rolls
That takes me back in time,
I'll share some historic accomplishments
Of your Brothers of Lodge Thirty-Nine.
The splendor of Yosemite Valley
Is a subject still talked about but yet
The first printed word of its beauty
Was published by Brother Holmes in the Mariposa Gazette.
So vivid was its grandeur described
Anxious visitors were lured without fail;
To accommodate these avid tourists
The three Mann brothers built a toll trail.
Brothers Abel, Milton, and Houston
Of this trail-building enterprise,
Guided Galen Clark to the Mariposa Big Trees
A marvel to everyone's eyes.
Their toll trail from Mariposa to Yosemite
Was not an easy trick.
It was accomplished in very challenging country
In eighteen fifty-six.
Brother George Coulter was so impressed by their venture
Its success hailed with pride,
With the aid of other admirers
Built a similar trail on the north side.

To accommodate these early travelers
They built a hotel on the Valley floor.
Yosemite's scenic grandeur became world famous
And hordes beat a path to its door.
A clientele of genteel travelers
Dressed in their raiment so fine,
Prompted our Washburn brothers
To establish their first famous stage line.
This stage line increased tourism
And caused their business to thrive,
So they constructed the beautiful Wawona Hotel
In eighteen seventy-five.
Meanwhile back in Mariposa
Support business began to expand.
To maintain frontier law and order
The Odd Fellows again took command.
Brother Crippen, the county's second sheriff
And four more who have worn that badge,
Were brothers whose names appear
On the rolls of Mariposa Lodge.
And the brother who is our chief law enforcer
I'm proud to say
Is a descendant of our early day members
Who give us protection today.
Travel to Yosemite
For the last hundred thirty-six years,
No matter how accomplished—
Owes thanks to our Odd Fellow peers.
Today's highways that enter from the west
Follow those pioneer trails,
They've witnessed such historic happenings
It's worth a ransom to hear all their tales.

The eastern route over Tioga Pass
So steep, picturesque, and winding,
Starts from the little town
Named after Brother Leroy Vining.
Yosemite's visitors are counted in millions
And they hail from near and far,
And they've traveled by every conveyance
Stagecoach, horseback, train, ship, and car.
Every level of society had made
This pilgrimage of splendor to see;
Yes, even Brother Schuyler Colfax
Who wrote the Rebekah Degree.
We haven't always claimed the credit through the years
That maybe we should,
The rewards that we have considered
Is being a part of this Brotherhood.
These historic facts you've been exposed to
You can share on down the line,
And that our romance with beautiful Yosemite is continuing
Here, in Mariposa Lodge number Thirty-Nine.

The Day I Discovered Ashes

Rebecca Waddell

I GLORIED IN THE warmth of the pine-scented mountain air. It was the first time I had visited Yosemite Valley, the first time I camped. I'd never experienced the beauty of that place and as I return yearly, I've never failed to be awed by the majesty of the granite-rimmed wilderness.

My first trip, we camped in Upper Pines, though I can't remember which site. There was a small stream running right through our campsite. After gaining my mother's permission, my brothers and I donned our swimsuits and played in the clear cold water. When I got too cold, it was time to take a break to warm up from the icy water. I stepped out of the stream onto a patch of spongy, grayish dirt.

In my five years of life, I couldn't remember a substance that felt so soft, almost silky. The temptation was too much, and I plunged my hands deep into my new discovery. The incinerated wood turned my skin the color of a foggy sky, as I spread the ashes all over my arms and legs.

While I enjoyed the soft touch of the smooth gray dust, my mom began to laugh. In her adult ignorance, she failed to realize how wonderful it felt to rub ash all over her limbs. She let me indulge in my discovery until the water on my skin combined with the ashes to form a delightful gray paste. My mom allowed me to display the extent of my new skin tone before she took me over to the cool stream to wash me off.

The warm summer evening made the water feel refreshing despite the lateness of the day. We laughed together as I was cleaned up. Finally, we sat down to a fire-grilled dinner on the day I discovered ashes.

Each year since that first camping trip, my mom took us back to Yosemite. I have hiked to the top of Vernal Fall more times than I can count on my fingers. I've stood at the bottom of Yosemite Falls and, to this day, never fail to be impressed by the sheer beauty of the cascading water. Half Dome is more of a beloved friend than a granite monolith keeping watch over the Valley. One year I climbed up his back just to see from his point of view. Yosemite is a place more dear than Grandma's house, and I look forward to each visit the way I anticipate my next breath. I simply need it to stay alive.

This summer, as I return to Yosemite with my mom and my two daughters, I wonder how long it will be before they discover ashes. My youngest is five now. I can only hope we have a nice wet winter so that I, too, will have a convenient stream right in our campsite.

Never Too Old to Backpack

Michelle Bachman

IT ALL STARTED in July of 1991, with my brother asking my sixty-two-year-old dad to go on a backpacking trip to Yosemite. Sixteen years later would be our last backpacking trip, due to my dad's passing, but those sixteen summers were the most memorable times for my brother, sister, and me. The bond we developed with our dad by backpacking at Yosemite, along with the beauty of this natural wonder, will stay with us for the rest of our lives. Here are a few excerpts from my dad's sixteen stories about our adventures.

BEARS

Our first encounter with bears was about to occur. There was a group of people camped about twenty yards away from us. I heard them talking very excitedly and the clatter of pots and pans being hit together. Then someone said, "He's just sitting there!" I knew that they were talking about a bear. Then I heard someone say, "He took a swing at me!" Sam was sound asleep, so I awoke him and told him that there was a bear in the camp. He said, excitedly, "Zip up the door! If he can't see us, maybe he will leave us alone." I hurriedly zipped up the door, and we lay there quietly and very fearful. Finally, things quieted down, but it was difficult to go back to sleep, as we were frightened that a bear might molest us. I thought to myself, "Why do I come here?" My answer, as I smiled, was, "for the beauty and peacefulness."

SWIMMING IN THE RIVER AT DUSK

At the halfway mark from Half Dome we came to an underground spring. We purified water and refilled our canteens. When we returned to our camp it was 5:00 p.m., and the temperature had cooled off. It was kind of foolish to go into the water that late, but we did it anyway. We hiked through the forest upstream from our camp. We stripped down to our shorts and stepped into the icy water. It was difficult to get used to the freezing water, and when we got out we were shivering from the cold. We passed a solitary camper who was lying on top of his sleeping bag. It was obvious that we had been in the water, as our T-shirts and shorts were soaked and stuck to our bodies. As we passed the camper he uttered in a thick German accent: "You guys are crazy!"

"Yeah, we are," I replied.

ONE FOOT IN FRONT OF THE OTHER

We rose early on this day, as we knew it was going to be the longest stretch of our journey, 9.2 miles to Little Yosemite Valley, our next stop from Lake Merced. Along the trail, we met a sole backpacker named Rob. He had driven his car to Tuolumne Meadows, parked it there, and made his way down to Merced Lake by way of the trail that passed by Tenaya Lake. Since he had a bear canister with him, he could stop wherever he liked for camping, and did so. Rob had been introduced to backpacking by his father, who had taken him when he was a boy. Rob had an interesting philosophy about backpacking. He said, "You just put your left foot forward, and then you bring your right foot forward, and you just keep going!" This was our motto when our body ached from the day's hike or sleeping on the hard ground, and we even starting using it in our everyday life. If you just put one foot in front of the other, you actually move!

AGE

Last year we were on a bus going to Yosemite Falls. I told my children that this was my last backpacking trip. As soon as I had said this, the bus driver made an announcement on the speaker. "See that man walking?" she said. "He is eighty years old, and he has just taken up backpacking." We all laughed at the irony. "I guess that I have a few more years to backpack," I said.

Among a group of hikers coming down the trail I spotted a man with a white chin beard. He looked like he might be seventy years old. Maybe someone near my age was hiking. I stopped him. A group of hikers stopped with him. Discreetly, I asked, "How young are you?"

A young woman in the group asked me, "How old are you?"

"I asked him first," I replied.

He spoke, "I was born in 1917."

The young woman responded, "You are eighty-seven years old!"

Then I told him, "I'm just a youngster of seventy-five years old."

He said, "You will have to keep backpacking for many more years."

My reply was in jest. "Why did I have to meet you?"

My knowledge of backpacking has evolved from the first trip sixteen years ago. Back then, I had thought that I was too old for backpacking at age sixty-two. On that first trip we had heavy camping sleeping bags, canteens, an ax, a shovel, a large stove, large cans of propane for the stove, lanterns, large cans of food, and bottled drinks. When I tried on my backpack, at that time, it was so heavy that I became dizzy and might have fainted, except one of the straps broke from the weight of the load. We named this backpack "The Monster" since it hung down below my knees.

During the following years we changed to lightweight sleeping bags. Water bottles replaced canteens. We eliminated cans and bottles. Instead, we used trail mix, dried fruit, and jerky. We brought mats to sleep on. The stories of our backpacking adventure in Yosemite sound like it was more misery than fun. Would I go again? Yes, definitely! Memory is a funny thing. The pain is soon forgotten, and only the good memories remain. And, remember, you are never too old to start backpacking!

In loving memory of our dad, Al Bachman

Yosemite and Half Dome—
The Tradition Continues

Tom Larsen

YOSEMITE KEEPS CALLING US BACK, generation after generation. As children, my mom and grandma would take my brother and me to Yosemite to camp. We would camp in the house tents, which were at Curry Village. This was back in 1957.

As we got older, mom bought a tent, and we would camp each year. There wasn't much better than the beautiful nights, the Merced River close by, and the soft nature of a campfire, with singing, storytelling, and s'mores.

The highlight of the night was the firefall, a spectacle I will never forget, and having the privilege of seeing this beautiful sight, night after night, year after year, as we camped at Yosemite. The song that was sung, the echo you could hear as the Valley floor called out to the top of Glacier Point, made a memory never to be forgotten.

Now I have three children, and one of our first camping trips had to be to Yosemite. I told my children of the fun we had at Yosemite, and especially about the firefall, which they could not believe. When they became teenagers, Yosemite was still a cool place to go. I wanted to make a real memory for them, so my two teenage daughters, and two of their best friends, packed our backpacks, made reservations, and hiked Half Dome. This is and was the experience of a lifetime. Nothing can compare. I wanted to really enjoy Half Dome and Little Yosemite Valley, so we took three days and two nights to make this hike. We took our time, camped at Little Yosemite Valley the first night. We enjoyed the night culture around the campfire, where we met people from around the world. These were memories that are never to be forgotten.

We were surrounded by bears the entire night. There is an unspoken communication between the bears and campers, which we could feel that night. I knew we had nothing to worry about.

The next morning we got up, had dad's terrific breakfast, and we headed out for the cables. Finally, there they were. Just like the many pictures I saw, but looking much steeper. We put on our gloves and walked to the top.

The beauty of the park from up there, and the unbelievable feeling of climbing Half Dome, was almost too much to take in all at once. All four of us walked over to the Diving Board, and walked out on it, to have our pictures taken. It was a picture of a lifetime, a picture never to be forgotten, and a picture that will be in the hearts of the Larsen family for generations to come.

My children are grown now, and they have children of their own. And the calling of Yosemite continues. Each year, my daughter and I, and her four children, have to go to Yosemite. (My two other children live out of state.) It may be only for a day or two, with busy lifestyles and professional careers, but we must go. And we do.

And now the magic happens. As my daughter and I, and her four children, enter Yosemite Valley, we drive to a clearing where you can see the first view of Half Dome from the Valley floor. We stop the car, we get out, and my daughter points to Half Dome. Then she says, "See that beautiful dome in front of us? They call it Half Dome. And see that little point sticking out to the left of it? Dad and I stood on the point." The children can't believe that old grandpa climbed that rock. As the children "ooh and ahh," I stand there with a tear in my eye. I'm thinking back on days that seemed like only yesterday, and I wonder where the time has gone but am so grateful that we climbed Half Dome.

Then the call of Yosemite comes in strong and right on cue. My eight-year-old grandchild says, "I want to climb Half Dome, Grandpa, and stand where you and Mom stood." I said to Brock, "You will, my son, you will."

And the tradition continues, as we visit the most beautiful park in the world, Yosemite. I thank my Heavenly Father, for giving the world such a beautiful blessing and gift.

"The Half Dome [is] perfectly inaccessible, being probably the only one of all the prominent points about the Yosemite which has never been, and will never be, trodden by human foot."

—Dr. Josiah D. Whitney, head of the Geologic
Survey of California, 1869

The Direction of Inspiration

Garrett Radke

SUMMER 1989:

As he sat in the nook of a tree overlooking the South Fork of the Merced River, the boy might well have been the only person in the Wawona Campground that evening. Yosemite was a magical place unlike any he had ever seen, and it took only the smallest use of his imagination to transport him into another world. It was a world of mystery and astonishment filled with giant trees, magnificent rock formations, and a deep and abiding sense of wonder and adventure.

As he looked down at the water rushing along its way, he was no longer a six-year-old boy only yards from his campsite; he was the old man the ranger had talked about at the campfire program the night before: the man who wandered in the mountains and climbed trees in thunderstorms. The hundreds of ladybugs he could see on the banks of the river were little people far below his perch at the top of one of the great trees, looking down upon the Valley beneath him.

Then he was sitting on a horse amid the Mariposa Battalion, discovering this world for the first time. . . . He was at the top of the great waterfall, looking down at the little chapel across the meadow they had driven by in the Valley that morning. . . . He was a peregrine falcon like the one they had seen in the museum, flying over the Valley looking for something to eat. . . .

"Garrett, dinner!" someone called from the Valley below. . . . And suddenly he was back on his branch alongside the river and his mother was there next to him, reaching out to help him down to join the rest of the family at their nearby campsite.

Though he had to walk to dinner instead of swooping down to capture it, unlike when he was at home, he didn't have to leave the majestic realm of his imagination behind when he returned to the "real world." Here, in this place, a magnificent world surrounded him wherever he went, often exceeding even the wildest manifestations of his whimsy.

As the boy and his mother arrived at the table, he glared at his sister. The previous night she had woken them all by imitating a bear in their tent. His parents had explained that she hadn't made the noises on purpose, that it was because of something called her "tonsils" that she made those sounds in her sleep. He wasn't sure he believed that, though, and figured she had done it to annoy him.

When dinner was finished, the boy and his sister made sure all the leftover food and dishes were safely packed in the bear box like the ranger had showed them. Their mom approved, proclaiming, "We don't want any real bears to come visit us tonight!"

"What do you think the ranger is going to talk about at the campfire tonight?" the boy asked.

"Well I don't know," his mother responded. "I suppose we better go and find out!"

"Yay!" the boy exclaimed in reply. "I love the campfire program!"

"I know you do." His mother smiled. "What would you like the ranger to talk about?"

The boy thought a moment and said, "Something new. I want to learn about something I don't already know."

"That sounds like a great idea," his mom replied. "There are always new things to learn in a national park."

"What's a national park?" the boy asked.

"Everything around you," his mom began. "All of this is a national park."

"Is this the only one?" he asked.

"No it isn't," his mom said. "There are lots of national parks, and each one is different. But every park is someplace special that has been set aside and protected so that people like us can come and enjoy them."

"Who protects them?"

"Why, we all do." His mom smiled. "But especially the park rangers. That's their job—to protect the park and help us to better understand it."

"The rangers get to live here in the park and tell other people about how special it is?"

"They sure do."

"Then I want to be a park ranger," the boy declared.

JANUARY 14, 2012:

Twenty-two and a half years later a man stood on the steps of that same little chapel he had looked down on in his imagination as boy. As he gazed across the meadow at Yosemite Falls he remembered what it had been like to stand at the top in real life when he had hiked up the trail several years before. His eyes followed the line of the granite walls surrounding him, and he thought fondly of the many times he had come back to this place since that first visit with his family.

But this time was different from any of the others. This time he looked at the cathedral around him through different eyes. He was no longer only a visitor to national parks: he was one of their protectors. It had not been easy and had taken a lot of perseverance, but three years previously, more than nineteen years after that conversation with his mother in the Wawona Campground, he had accepted his first position as a national park ranger.

As his eyes turned in the direction of Bridalveil Fall he reached down and took the hand of the woman standing next to him. Eleven months earlier he had asked her to marry him along the banks of the Rose River in Shenandoah National Park. Now, as his eyes took in her white dress illuminated by the rays of the setting sun, he thought about all that had happened between that first visit and this moment. He smiled as he pulled his new wife close, reflecting like that old man of the mountains who said, "When we try to pick out anything by itself, we find it hitched to everything else in the Universe."

NOTE ON THE STORY:

This is actually an entirely true story. I really did come to Yosemite with my family at the age of six, stay in the Wawona Campground, and frequently visited that tree by the river. My sister really did keep us up with bearlike sounds because of enflamed tonsils. I really was that nerdy as a six-year-old, really did get excited about the ranger programs, was very conscientious about food and bear boxes, and really had conversations with my parents like the one described above. I really did tell my parents I wanted to be a park ranger at the age of six, and conversations like the one at Wawona actually did inspire me to want to be a park ranger.

I have now been a ranger for four years and have worked at Wind Cave, the National Mall, and Shenandoah. I am currently a member of the interpretive media team for the sesquicentennial of the Civil War.

I have visited Yosemite many times since that first visit as a child, and in January 2012 I really did marry my wife in the chapel, and subsequently had a reception at The Ahwahnee.

———◆———

"Probably you will laugh at me, but I want to be a ranger."

—Claire Marie Hodges, first woman ranger in
Yosemite and the National Park Service, 1918

Yosemite Inspires the World

Robert Bennet Forbes

WHEN I WOKE up in my tent I could hear the sound of the creek, and I heard chickadees calling. The familiar sound of chickadees in nearby conifers had always been a friendly part of my camping experiences. I stretched in my sleeping bag and looked forward to another day of exploring a fantastic mountain environment. The big difference from all my previous nature outings was that these chickadees were in China. On this morning our group would encounter no less than four species of Asian chickadees in the local pines and firs. These forests were much like those of our Sierra Nevada—except that the understory plants included a small bamboo. This was a great adventure of the familiar and the exotic in Yosemite's sister national parks in China.

A group of Yosemite Conservancy members had traveled to China for two weeks to visit Yosemite's two sister national parks. We came to hike, to explore the natural history of China's mountains, and to meet with Chinese rangers to learn about Yosemite's foreign sisters. We had already spent a few days hiking the astonishing mountain trails of Huangshan Mountains National Park in eastern China and were now far to the west in Sichuan to see a very different park.

Yosemite's two sister park partnerships were formalized in 2006. Both nations' park managers believe they have things to learn from each other in terms of resource protection and visitation. The genesis of the national park idea in Yosemite in 1864 means that we have a lot to share with the ancient civilization of China, which didn't have national parks until 1982. Chinese parks do not have nonprofit partners like Yosemite Conservancy; that's one element of American creative genius that we hope will inspire a Chinese knockoff.

At Jiuzhaigou Valley we stayed in a small hotel right at the park entrance. We had dinner in an adjacent restaurant that was built over a river and had a glass floor! For breakfast, our group leaders got us into the park's own dining room to share breakfast with employees who graciously accommodated Americans joining them. We had coffee, toast, and granola while the staff had steamed buns, rice porridge, and spicy pickles.

No visitors drive their cars into Jiuzhaigou. Everyone walks through the entrance and boards a bus. The buses go up both arms of the Y-shaped valley that extends up into the Min Mountains. Coniferous forests reached up to tree line, and snowy peaks went up to over fourteen thousand feet. What people come to see at Jiuzhaigou is the remarkable water on display. These mountains are limestone and the runoff carries a tiny amount of calcium carbonate. The rock and the water combine in startling ways: unearthly colored lakes and waterfalls that are completely different from those of Yosemite.

Our first stop was Mirror Lake. We all know and love Mirror Lake, the shallow basin in Tenaya Creek, hidden at the foot of Half Dome and popular with families for a summertime dip. Our sister Mirror Lake in Jiuzhaigou was quite different: it was many times the acreage of Yosemite's, it doesn't dry up in late summer, and its deep waters reflect steep mountain slopes, but no cliffs. We walked from here and discovered that while Jiuzhaigou has perhaps forty miles of trails (compared to Yosemite's eight hundred miles), every inch of them is a nicely made wooden boardwalk. China has a vast pool of inexpensive labor for building and maintaining this kind of infrastructure. Yosemite's trail work goes into keeping access relatively wild, while China's park management has engineered access for the 1.5 million visitors who almost all just walk short distances between bus stops that serve lakes and waterfalls. Almost no Westerners visit here.

With park rangers accompanying us we walked where only a few Chinese visitors have, learned much more about the birds and plants that we saw, and about how the park manages resources and crowds. In our several days at Jiuzhaigou, we experienced the special treat of getting overnight access to a side valley that had been opened to only a few Westerners. We walked up past an old Tibetan village and a famed Buddhist shrine, while our supplies were trucked up to our campsite at the road's end. Ranger Jack Li led our group on the hike, identified tracks and signs from local wildlife, and kept us on the faint path up-valley. Jiuzhaigou has giant pandas but we didn't see them. One treat in communicating with rangers whose English was limited was to discover the value of Latin plant names for easy understanding; we share many families and genera between our mountain parks. We had a deluxe camp meal prepared for us in the ranger cabin and spent a comfortable night in tents near a gentle creek.

No lights, no traffic, no other people around for miles—this was the wild China we'd wanted to see, and this was our national park ideal beyond the infrastructure. Despite the numerous differences between Yosemite and China's parks, the similarities were more significant. The commonalities include:

- A ranger and management staff that's committed to park stewardship and visitor experiences
- A national pride in natural heritage
- Complicated challenges of balancing use with preservation
- Beautiful landscapes fully worthy of international recognition and global inspiration

John Muir visited China, and though he never got to our sister parks, I'm sure he'd have appreciated them as much as we did. We all felt fortunate to explore an exotic place that expanded on what Yosemite meant to us. Those who preceded us in history gave us a genuine gift in the idea of preserving beautiful landscapes for the public. To experience for ourselves how Yosemite has inspired the world was a great privilege. It reinvigorates us to think about what gifts we can send ahead from 2014 into the world of the future.

Family Beginnings in Yosemite

Christine Johnson

THERE WAS ALWAYS a feeling of something drawing me toward Yosemite, only I didn't quite realize why. Besides the majestic scenery, wildlife, and intriguing history, something kept bringing me back. It began for me in the summer of 1995 when my parents, grandmother, and childhood best friend left on a journey in a borrowed motor home to Yosemite National Park. It was my first visit, a graduation gift from Mom and Dad, along with a new tent and a lifetime of memories. On that visit I learned that my grandmother, Teola L. Johnson, had worked in Camp Curry in 1947. She told us about a picture of her family by the Wawona Tree taken in the thirties. We also took her back to visit Camp Curry where she had worked.

I wasn't able to return again until I had an opportunity at work to lead a youth backpacking/caravan trip to the Mammoth Lakes area in 2004. Twenty kids ages twelve to seventeen, some of whom claimed, "My parents made me come!"

On the final day of our caravan, I drove them about an hour and a half from our campsite into Yosemite Valley. Along our route I pulled into a turnout where you could see Half Dome in the distance. All of the counselors jumped out of the vans excitedly with their cameras ready to capture the moment. The campers just sat there, looking confused as to why all the adults had the look of young children at their favorite theme park. After coaxing them out of the van, their mood soon changed when they looked out into a postcard-perfect view. We spent the afternoon walking through the village and then near a meadow. We took photos in the meadow of our campers in their natural habitat posing as wild animals!

This particular caravan was normally a six-day trip. I had asked my boss to add a day to our itinerary so we could have time for a visit into Yosemite. About six months after the trip, I was called into his office and he told me that some of the parents of the campers from my caravan had called to let him know that their kids loved the trip and that the addition of Yosemite was a hit. Apparently, the same campers who had complained were still talking about it and how much fun they had.

I continue to make it into the Valley at least once every year. But it wasn't until a recent conversation with my grandma that I answered why I feel I am still drawn there. I asked her about how she had met my grandpa while working in Camp Curry, a story I vaguely remembered hearing as a child. Here is her story in her words: "In the 1930s as a child I went with my parents and my brother to Yosemite in the summer, for two weeks. We visited the Indians and Maggie made acorn patties; at night we would go to the campfire meetings and watch the firefall. I can still remember my dad singing or whistling.

"In May of 1947, I turned twenty-one. I saw in the paper they were hiring in Yosemite for the summer. Two of my girlfriends and I decided to go. I went first. My dad drove me to the train station, which I took to Merced, California. Once there, I got on a big two-story bus that took me up to Camp Curry. My friends came up in a few days and my Dad brought my car up to me later. One friend and I worked in housekeeping, cleaning the cabins in Curry Village, and the other worked in the cafeteria. It was so beautiful up there; when we arrived, patches of snow were still on the ground. Everyone was happy and it was a great place to work. We went to campfire every night and watched the firefall.

"After almost a month, we decided to go to a dance one night, and at the last song, they were playing 'Goodnight Sweetheart,' a boy asked me to dance. His name was Bill, and he had a southern accent. He was from Tennessee. He told me he was the ambulance driver for the hospital. Since we were both working up there, we saw each other almost every day. Sometimes at night I would put pillows under my blankets, because they had bed checks; Bill and I would sneak out and drive down the mountain to a little bar called The Flats.

"One day I was riding my bike and fell and hurt my back. When I went to the hospital they said I shouldn't work anymore and I would have to go home. Bill asked me to marry him and I said yes. We watched the firefall one more time, and the next day we both took a bus to Reno, Nevada, and got married at the courthouse. That was sixty-five years ago.

"Our family used to go camping every summer as my three sons and daughter were growing up. Mike, my oldest, joined the Marines during the war in Vietnam; he made one more trip to Yosemite and saw the last firefall. We sure miss it.

"Then Bill passed away due to a heart attack after thirty-six years of marriage. We had four children, six grandchildren, and five great-grand-children; some of them still go up there to visit the beautiful place where we all began."

Working on Five Generations

Anne Jones

As a young child growing up in Michigan, I heard lots of stories about Yosemite, as it was near and dear to my parents' hearts. They both grew up in California and spent the summers camping in the Valley. My grandfather was a schoolteacher in Los Angeles but worked as a carpenter in the summertime on the construction of The Ahwahnee. My father roamed the valleys all summer, exploring the high country. My mother would camp with her parents along the Merced River, having driven up from Santa Barbara with mattresses strapped on their car's roof. They both loved it and felt it was the most special of places.

My immediate family visited several times as I was growing up. Each time we entered the Valley through the tunnel, my heart would stop in wonder at the magic that seemed to pull me there. I always went away from our trip promising myself that I would come back. It was a promise I have been able to keep. Not only did I introduce my children to the Valley as often as I could (it is a lot easier when you live in California) but now that they are grown, we have been able to have a few family reunions there. We gather from Kentucky, Tennessee, North Carolina, and, of course California, to explore, wonder, and be in awe of the majesty and beauty of the place. We hiked through the Mariposa Grove and marveled at the trees. Their enormous height almost strains your neck as you gaze up their massive trunks. Yet, somehow they seem barely anchored in the earth, holding on by what we later termed "Sequoia Toes."

The next generation has arrived and we plan on introducing him to the Valley next year.

I have also brought in a photography group from the greater Cincinnati area for a five-day workshop. They were overwhelmed with the magnificent views. While we were there a storm developed, dropping snow at the higher elevations and leaving small windows of photography opportunities through the swirling clouds. We couldn't have ordered anything more dramatic and were able to capture extraordinary images, which I have hanging on my wall in my house. We ventured up to the Mariposa Grove, where the snow sat upon the previous burned, now blackened, logs that lay scattered about. This is pure magic.

Am I coming back? Absolutely. I hope to make it back every other year for the remaining years of my life.

My license plate in Kentucky reads: YOSMTE. It is my happy, soul-satisfying refuge from the world.

My Lifetime Connection

Jeanne Herrick

LAST NOVEMBER I had a special birthday. I turned sixty-two and headed for Yosemite with my "boyfriend" (I like to use the term "boyfriend" because it makes me feel younger), Billy, to collect my Senior Pass. I consider the Senior Pass one of the few rewards of aging, and the best bargain to be had for ten dollars, because it will allow me free admission to all of the national parks and monuments and half-price camping for the rest of my life, which I am hoping will be for a very long time. Billy is a few years younger than I, and an avid camper and hiker, so I joke that the pass is a form of insurance that he will keep me around for a while and take me camping on a regular basis—at the very least until he qualifies for a pass of his own.

While in the Valley, we enjoyed three days of snow and sun. We were fortunate to have been able to book a room at the Lodge at Yosemite Falls and took advantage of the free bus system to get around, as well as using our feet, to hike to Mirror Lake, around Happy Isles, and up and down the length of the Valley. We took our meals at the cafeteria with the exception of a birthday brunch celebration at The Ahwahnee on our last day in the Valley. The Ahwahnee is one of my favorite spots on the planet, and I always pretend that I am actually staying there as I warm up by the fire, read in a comfy chair, and sip wine or a hot drink from the bar. Only one time did I get in trouble by spreading my wet clothing and soaked hiking socks out in front of the fire on one of the Hearst castle–sized massive hearths. Since then, I have tried to behave myself out of fear of being thrown out as an imposter.

I have been coming to Yosemite my whole life. My parents were campers and had five children so we definitely didn't stay in fancy hotels or resorts on vacation—we camped at Yosemite, Big Sur, Standish-Hickey, and Richardson Grove in Northern California, and at the beach in Carpinteria—the town my folks eventually moved to in retirement. On one later Yosemite trip, after I was married and had three kids of my own to bring camping, I remember the ranger at a campfire taking a survey as to who had been coming to Yosemite the longest. I won the prize in being able to raise my hand when he asked if anyone had been coming for more than forty years. And that was quite a few years ago! Additionally, I scattered a few of my late husband's ashes near the site of the old wooden cabins where we stayed for his parent's sixtieth anniversary celebration about twenty years ago, cabins that were washed away in the flood.

The point of this story you might ask?

While on my birthday weekend in Yosemite, I saw a large photograph of a family in the late 1800s posed by Yosemite Falls. I noticed it partly because I remembered a similar one that I had at home in a family album compiled by my late husband's mother, Mary. At the time, I didn't think much about it because Yosemite Falls is, of course, the natural spot to have your portrait taken, both then and now. On returning home and seeing the same photo in an article in my *Yosemite Conservancy* magazine, I dug out the family album and was astounded to realize that it was not just a similar photo, it was the exact same photo, complete with empty chair on the far right—a portrait of my husband's family, the Roths from Strathmore, a small town in the Central Valley. In addition, I had all the information regarding the photo as to when it was taken—in June of 1887, who the photographer was, and the names of all the persons in the photo, dutifully recorded by Grandma Mary who was quite a historian in her younger days. Those pictured were Aunt Barbara Roth who lived to be over one hundred, Senator and Mrs. Meany with their son, Senator John Roth, and Mrs. John Roth. The photo was taken, Mary wrote, by a Mr. Gustav Fagersteen, who I assume was an early Yosemite portrait photographer.

I was thrilled to find that Yosemite had used a portrait of my late husband's ancestors to accompany the article on Yosemite's early visitors. I have now inserted the magazine article next to my copy of the photo in the family album, where it occupies a place of honor, a further reminder of my family's connection to Yosemite and its heritage.

"On the south side of the valley, our attention was first attracted by a magnificent waterfall, about seven hundred feet in height. It looked like a broad, long feather of silver, that hung depending over a precipice; and as this feathery tail of leaping spray thus hung, a slight breeze moved it from side to side, and as the last rays of the setting sun were gilding it with rainbow hues, the red would mix with the purple, and the purple with the yellow, and the yellow with the green, and the green with the silvery sheen of its whitened foam, as it danced in space."

—James Mason Hutchings in the first published
description of Yosemite Falls, 1855

Being Charlie's Mom

Debbie Hoffman

A MOTHER AND SON relationship is always evolving; from dependent to independent, affectionate to angry to loving, challenging to accepting, talkative to quiet, embarrassing to proud. So it has been with my son Charlie and I. But within the ups and downs of growth between us is a memory that will always bring a smile. In August of 2009, we took our first backpacking trip together—a fifty-mile, five-day loop in northern Yosemite.

Yosemite was already a place we both loved. It had been special to me as a young adult, having spent two months backpacking in the park learning natural history via a college course. I then brought my children to Yosemite each spring, hoping to pass along the joy of the Mountains. Charlie was now twenty-one and it had been years since we'd even taken a hike together.

Charlie borrowed a backpack, chose a bivy sack instead of a tent, had a down sleeping bag and rain jacket already, brought no extra clothes, and relied on me to deal with cooking supplies, water treatment, first aid, bug spray, bear canisters, and most of the food. I brought more than I needed, not having learned yet what I could live without to lighten the load.

Starting outside Yosemite at Twin Lakes, near Bridgeport, gave us the easiest access to a less traveled area of the park—our primary goal: Matterhorn Canyon. Day one started with us talking while we hiked, me stopping for numerous pictures of wildflowers, and lunch at Barney Lake. When we finally reached our 2,200-foot elevation gain, camping amid a colony of mosquitoes didn't bother us much. Charlie's boots were causing blisters, and would get worse throughout the trip. He didn't complain much, just looked for as many opportunities to go barefoot as he could.

On day two we climbed our first pass and entered Yosemite. We had a little company at the top of that pass—mules and a packer. I thought they had to be tied together, but these guys were all loose and on their own. One of them took a look down the other side (at 10,470 feet) and decided to turn around and graze up at the top for a while. It was quite an effort on the part of the packer to get the mule on track. Of course we had to wait off to the side of the trail, with Charlie forced to listen to my lecture on why there shouldn't be stock on the trails!

Then, down into the pristine Piute Creek drainage with Sawtooth Ridge to the north of us. Charlie decided I was either too slow for him or stopped to take pictures too often—in ten minutes he was way ahead and in twenty I lost sight of him. A couple hours later, I was becoming distracted wondering how long before I'd see him next? Suddenly there he was; sound asleep, barefoot, laying in a fetal position on a large, flat rock next to the trail, using his backpack as a pillow and the warmth of the sun as a blanket, as peaceful as a baby!

Day three started with a gorgeous, peaceful morning. As was the routine each day, I would be out of the tent boiling water for coffee around 6:00 a.m. and Charlie would sleep until the sun was on his face. Mentally, we were gearing up to climb Burro Pass; anticipating our first sights of Matterhorn Peak and Canyon. Charlie breezed up the pass, while I stuck to a slower pace, constantly turning around to catch the views of the Valley and peaks behind us. With a little break together at the top for pictures, our first moments looking down Matterhorn Canyon were breathtaking! Charlie was energized and ready to cover some ground; he told me he wanted to see how far we could go today—push ourselves!

The canyon was stunning; high peaks and walls on each side, winding Matterhorn Creek, green meadows of tall grass and wildflowers everywhere. The gardens of wildflowers were amazing—giant ten-foot stalks of deep blue larkspur, tiger lilies glowing orange in the sun, rein orchids, bluebells, monkshoods, columbine, mule's ear, penstemon, heather, pennyroyal, paintbrush . . . endless! Walking at a decent pace between flower gardens and stream crossings, a couple of backpackers traveling the opposite direction stopped and asked, "Are you Charlie's mom?" I mumbled, "yeah," with a confused look on my face. "He wanted us to let you know that he just finished his lunch break and isn't going to stop again until Benson Pass." I smiled at Charlie's networking efforts, had a little conversation, and kept walking. That's progress; I have a general idea when we'll meet up next!

As I approached Benson Pass, hoping Charlie would be waiting, the weather was changing—clouds coming in fast and very windy. Up ahead, there he was, asleep on the ground with his jacket on. Together we walked another two miles to camp at Smedberg Lake; first order of business, gathering wood and getting a fire going to warm up!

Instead of waking up to sunshine on day four, we had a light dusting of snow on the ground, on my tent fly, and on Charlie's bivy. The clouds were dark and the wind was blowing pine needles into my coffee! We got off to a quick start as the snow began falling again. Charlie's reaction to the snow: "We did thirteeen miles yesterday, let's walk faster and do fifteen today!" Staying together, we rambled through the fifteen miles, passing Benson Lake, up to Seavey Pass, through serene Rancheria Creek Canyon, Kerrick Meadow, and finally to Peeler Lake for the night. We enjoyed our last campfire the following morning and arrived back to the car around noon.

It's wonderful how the Yosemite backcountry brings two people closer than ever! Nowhere to hide, pretend, no reason to misrepresent; just walking, eating, drinking water, sleeping, and keeping your eyes open to treasure the beauty!

—◆—

"Then the sun shone free, lighting the pearly gray surface of the cloud-like sea and making it glow. Gazing, admiring, I was startled to see for the first time the rare optical phenomenon of the 'Specter of the Brocken.' My shadow, clearly outlined, about half a mile long, lay upon this glorious white surface with startling effect. I walked back and forth, waved my arms and struck all sorts of attitudes, to see every slightest movement enormously exaggerated. Considering that I have looked down so many times from mountain tops on seas of all sorts of clouds, it seems strange that I should have seen the 'Brocken Specter' only this once. A grander surface and a grander stand-point, however, could hardly have been found in all the Sierra."

—John Muir, reminiscence of an ascent of Half Dome, 1912

A Tradition Continued

Liz Tyree

HALF DOME CAN be seen from a distance
Its granite stature gives dominance
To hikers making the eight-mile feat
Climbing famed Tis-se'-yak without defeat.
In '36, my father of fourteen years was just a lad,
And climbed to the top of Half Dome with his dad.
To Glacier Point without a rail,
He snapped a picture of the grand hotel,
And dangled his feet overlooking trails.
A trip would not be complete
Without a drive in a Model T
Through the California redwood tree.
In '58, it was my first trip
To walk a trail without a slip.
Pitched a tent by the river high,
Crossed a swinging bridge and sighed.
From Glacier Point fell a firefall
Of red-hot cinders in a ball.
Half Dome's reflection in a lake
Gave its name to Mirror Lake.
Bears and raccoons roamed the night
Raiding trash cans with delight.
In '68, to capture one more thrill,
Dad returned with his two girls.
It was an all-day feat to the top.
Going up the Mist Trail we could not stop.
To see that granite monolith in view
Fearlessly, knew what we had to do.

Clouds overhead and rain a threat,
Loafers for shoes we tugged on the cable,
Pulling ourselves up as we were able
And conquered the top at four o'clock.
In '96, the sisters returned to Yosemite
To carry on Dad's legacy.
Three families climbed to the summit,
Gratified to say they had done it!
Yosemite brings families to unite,
To camp and hike or ride a bike.
In awe its natural wonders do unfold,
A tradition to continue remains untold.

2

YOSEMITE ADVENTURES

Skin Tracks

David Lo

Two miles an hour was the goal as we left for Ostrander Ski Hut in Yosemite's backcountry in January 2011. At that pace, we would ski and snowshoe the ten miles in five hours and arrive at the hut in the afternoon, with plenty of time to enjoy the nearby bowls. For the first four miles, the four of us did stay on that pace, enjoying the groomed trail. However, as we left the groomed and headed off into the backcountry proper, I found myself more anxious about the safety of my partners and our ability to get to the hut before dark. We had slowed down dramatically, as the backcountry offered up icy, rutted snow, due to a dry January. Without much experience skiing in ungroomed conditions, much less icy ones, Peter, a tall sixty-one-year-old peace activist, fell repeatedly. Hearing every fall behind me compelled me to stop and look back with anticipation of a twisted knee or worse. After several slow miles of falls, rest stops, and careful skiing, Jonathan, a twenty-two-year-old snowshoer, and I decided to take some of Peter's pack to help with pace. We were way off the five-hour pace; sunset was soon approaching.

At one of the rest stops, I thought about how it was that I found myself with my three inexperienced partners on this long-awaited trip to Ostrander. As the sole backcountry skier of us four, I had wanted to visit the historic hut, meet the equally venerable hutkeeper, and ski the surrounding ridges and bowls for at least ten years. However, I couldn't convince anyone that the ten-mile journey was worth it. Now that I was forty-one years old, Ostrander seemed to be a hut that I would reach one day solo, perhaps when my kids were grown.

My Ostrander fortunes changed unexpectedly in December when I found out that my friend Peter had also been dreaming of visiting the hut. He had first met Howard Weamer, the hutkeeper, and his wife through activism in the 1970s, when Howard first started his annual winter job. Lack of experience and partners had prevented Peter from visiting his friend. As we talked, we realized excitedly that with each other and my experience backcountry skiing in the Sierra, we could make a trip to Ostrander happen.

Ostrander hut was built in 1941 by the Civilian Conservation Corps, hewn from local granite and timbers. This was when all skiing was back-country skiing, before the dominance of the ski lift. With two-foot-thick granite walls, three-deep bunks, and a long communal table, the hut has an ambience of history, natural beauty, and toughness.

During our planning and training, two unemployed twenty-some-things joined our adventure. Ruth, Peter's daughter, was an athletic for-mer basketball player. Like her father, Ruth had skied before, but never with a pack in the backcountry. Jonathan, a recent college grad, had become enthralled with Yosemite and was excited to visit the park for a second time. As he had never cross-country skied or backpacked before, we decided to strap his enthusiasm to snowshoes instead.

As the trip started to approach the seven-hour mark, my worry, impa-tience, and consequent irritability mounted. I looked back at Peter and Ruth yet another time, in anticipation of another fall, further delaying our now arduous ski-in. Instead, I saw father and daughter singing Bob Dylan songs, Peter's favorite, while gingerly following the tracks of my climbing skins. Listening to them, it was clear that they were still enjoy-ing being together, under the soft light of the setting winter sun. Here I was, the experienced skier of the group, carrying unnecessary worry and irritability, wanting to rush to a goal. Singing Dylan in the Yosemite, alone with friends and family, sliding our skis over the shadows of burnt trees, was a much better way to go.

We did get to Ostrander safely that night, after eight-plus hours. The next afternoon, when we decided to read a bit on the hut's balcony, Jon-athan pulled out a thick tome written by firebrand Princeton professor

Cornel West. I gently chastised him for packing such a heavy book, all the while delighting in finding out what really matters to him; certainly not the conventions of going light, but a marriage of race politics and the Sierra.

That night, a group of middle-aged friends arrived in the early afternoon. They had skied in faster than the two-mile-an-hour pace I had hoped for ourselves. They were expert skiers who came to Ostrander annually. The ten miles and the nearby steeps seemed to be enjoyable, but of little challenge for them. I was struck by their ability to find time in their adult lives, their ready and willing friends, and their skill. Yet would I exchange my three partners for entry into their group?

Not for that moment, maybe never. We didn't have the latest skis, the lightest books, or the fastest pace. But to see this classic backcountry ski trip through their singing, their personal histories, and their whims, I realized that how we arrived at Ostrander WAS the adventure. Peter and I had waited and dreamed many years to arrive at Ostrander. Jonathan had just learned about Ostrander a month ago. The unique connections that formed our group and the challenges in our ski-in mirrored the natural world of our adventure: never predictable, moments of thrill and grandeur, as well as the ordinary and prosaic. Yosemite is many things to many people. The soaring cliffs and waterfalls rightfully capture our attention. But it is also rutted skin tracks, burnt trees, pinecones floating on snow, and green moss on the common lodgepole pine.

Late May of 1874

Gail Perlee

In late May of 1874 my great-grandfather J. K. Smedley traveled with three companions to Yo-Semite Park. They took the train from Sacramento to Milton, picked up a rented carriage and guide, and proceeded along Rock Creek Canyon through Oak Grove, across the Salt Springs Valley, over Bear Mountain, past what is now Copperopolis, and into Altaville (now part of Angels Camp). From there they headed up Murphy's Grade Road to spend the night in Murphy's Hotel.

Next morning they went to see the Calaveras Big Trees, returning to Murphy's for another night before continuing on to Yosemite. At Big Trees Great-Grandfather was impressed with the "house" built over the Big Stump, and how four sets of dancers could dance the Cotillion on it!

In the morning they drove through Vallecito to the Pendola Ferry (later, Parrotts Ferry), where they waited several hours to cross the Stanislaus River, as the weather had been warm and snowmelt had caused the river to run faster than usual. Once across the river they passed through Columbia into Sonora and after a short rest, set out again, as Great-Grandfather was insistent on spending the night at Priest Station atop what was then Rattlesnake Hill (later, Old Priest Grade).

Their route from Sonora took them through Jacksonville (now under Don Pedro Lake) and across the Tuolumne River at Stevens Bar ferry to reach the bottom of Rattlesnake Hill at 10:00 p.m. There, they took turns riding in the carriage as they worked their way up the steep hill—arriving at Priest's at midnight, where the owners rose from their beds to fix them a fine meal before they retired for the night. Talk about hospitality!

Early the next morning they were off to Yosemite—stopping to take a drink from a bubbling brook in First Garrote (now Groveland). From there they passed a breathtaking view of the Tuolumne River Canyon, crossed the south fork of the river through a covered bridge above (now) Rainbow Pool, and on up Hardin Hill.

At Hodgdon's (now the Big Oak Flat Entrance to the park), they must have taken a road above the Mariposa Grove of Giant Sequoias rather than going through the grove because he didn't mention a thing about the trees in his journal, yet Great-Grandfather was very descriptive about everything else along the way, and looking at old maps of the park, there was an upper route to what is now Crane Flat—known then as Gobin's.

At Gobin's they headed for Tamarack Flat, where they exchanged their carriage for horses and mules to complete their journey into the Valley, and he exclaimed about the view of the Valley and trail from Moran Point. (Quite steep and rugged I gather from his description!) The Big Oak Flat Road into the Valley, suitable for wagons and carriages, was completed in July of 1874—less than two months after my great-grandfather made his journey. Why he didn't wait till then, I'm not sure. Perhaps he wanted to avoid the crowds.

When they reached the Valley, the snowmelt had rendered the Merced River nearly impassable, but they forded it on mule and horseback to reach Hutchings' hotel, where they would stay for the duration of their visit in the Valley. Strangely, he never mentioned in his journal the room of the hotel built around a tree, so perhaps they stayed in the hotel's Cedar Cottage.

From Hutchings' they sallied forth each day to visit various points in the park, including Vernal Fall, where Great-Grandfather signed Register Rock, then up the zigzags to Nevada Fall and Snow's La Casa Nevada below Liberty Cap, where the group took lunch that first day. That evening they converged on Cosmopolitan House (a sort of spa and saloon), where they enjoyed a cool mint julep before dinner. In fact, they visited Cosmopolitan House twice more before they left the Valley!

Early the second morning they went to view the sunrise over Mirror Lake, and in his journal my great-grandfather expounded on the sheer beauty of the experience. After breakfast the group rode up to Glacier Point, stopping at Union Point to carve their initials in a tree (tsk!). He acknowledged the famous Overhanging Rock at Glacier Point and the dangerous shenanigans some folks tried on it, but he and his companions abstained from such foolishness.

All too soon it was time to leave for home, and he mentions riding on a sled at Tamarack Flat on their return trip because it had snowed. And there, at Tamarack, he gathered a snow plant, packing it carefully to take home to the woman who would become his wife.

I mention all this because when we moved to Groveland, I began hearing familiar names (I had read my great-grandfather's journal of his trip to Yo-Semite) and so one summer I set out with notebook and camera to retrace his route to and around the park as closely as possible. Current reservoirs made it difficult in places, but the summer I embarked on this endeavor was a drought year, so New Melones and Don Pedro were unusually low, making it possible to gauge where ferry crossings had been.

In Yosemite, though places such as Hodgdon's, Gobin's, Hutchings', and Cosmopolitan House no longer existed, I had old pictures to go by and since the lay of the land doesn't change that much, I was able to figure out where these places had likely been. At the Hutchings site, for example, a tree still bore the scar from the roofline of the room that had been built around it.

I never knew my great-grandfather, but retracing the steps of his Yo-Semite journey, I could almost feel him with me. In the fall of 1991, I attended the ceremony where a time capsule was buried in the park containing memorabilia of the park's first one hundred years and was fortunate enough to write a short paragraph of my experiences in Yosemite, which was included in the capsule. I also signed a beautiful painting of some of the park's most famous sights done by a friend of mine from Oakhurst, which was included in the capsule as well—to be opened on the park's two-hundred-year anniversary.

I'm old (and lucky) enough now to have a Golden Age Passport to all national parks, and I make use of it as often as possible—especially to visit Yosemite. No matter how many times I've been there, I still marvel at its breathtaking beauty and grandeur.

"Mr. Hutchings knows how to explain that valley, and entertain tourists as no other man that has ever lived there can possibly do it, and that is what we want."

—L. R. Tulloch, speaking to Congress about
the state commissioners' management
of the Yosemite Grant, 1889

We Wouldn't Have Missed It!

Jeannie Tasker

THE YEAR WAS 1963. Our family vacation was a road trip to the Grand Canyon, with my parents, my young brother, and me towing our seventeen-foot Airstream travel trailer behind our red Chevy station wagon. On our return, my dad decided we should visit Tuolumne Meadows in Yosemite. Against all recommendations and posted signs at the time, my dad chose to pull our travel trailer up the old Tioga Pass road. Unlike today's two-lane thoroughfare, which brings many travelers to Yosemite from Los Angeles and Las Vegas, the old Tioga Pass road was steep, narrow, and treacherous.

This is an excerpt from my mother's diary of that trip:

Thursday, July 25, 1963

We went into Lee Vining for gas and groceries, then started up the famous Tioga road, route 120. Bill (dad) said the only problems were human. On a grade, the man in the car ahead stopped to talk to a down-coming car, completely blocking the narrow road. Bill honked, making the man start up, just in time, before we had to stop and lose our momentum. A convertible passed several cars, stopped at the "one-way only" part, just as we entered, but it pulled over. We went up, mostly in first gear. A few spots were almost too steep. As we entered that part of the road, the convertible pulled over in an area that was barely wide enough for two cars. We were in a section of road with a thousand-foot cliff on one side, straight down. It was generally paved, but the pavement was broken in places. At the top, we finally checked into Yosemite National Park, and took pictures to prove we were really there with the trailer.

After parking in a campsite at the Tuolumne Meadows Campground, my folks spied a bulletin posting a ranger-led overnight hike to Young

Lakes, beginning at 8:45 a.m. the next day. Although Mom and Dad were experienced backpackers, we had no equipment with us, and they had just spent the last of their vacation money on canned goods and other groceries in Lee Vining. The notice read, "No backpacking experience required; open to anyone over six years of age." Mom and Dad signed us up, saying we would make do with the food and equipment we had in the trailer.

Mom's diary tells the story:

Friday, July 26, 1963

We got up at seven-fifteen and frantically packed up, quilts and all. We had to carry canned food along, as that was all we had, even though it weighed quite a bit. . . . The "easy" hike turned out to be a moderately hard one rising to ten thousand feet, a climb of about fifteen hundred feet. Tommy had been sick the night before, worrying that we might meet bears, so he didn't make very good time. . . . The trail was a good one and fairly gradual, but long. . . . It was a pretty trail, through pleasant forest with many clear streams. Tom and Betty (mom) finally arrived last, at three-thirty, and found that Jeannie and Bill had the beds laid out. As soon as the ranger said there were no bears around, Tom felt okay. . . . We cooked supper over an open fire, a can of lasagna, Tang, and canned orange and grapefruit sections. The ranger, Glenn Coy, with his dried foods, special-ized dishes, folding grill, lightweight pack, looked us over and said we were breaking four rules of backpacking with our quilts, canned food, cot pads, and heavy sleeping bags, but we hadn't really planned on going on a trip like this, so just went with what we had, rather than not go at all. We did look like tenderfeet beside all the others, but we ate well, and slept warm. The night temperature dropped to forty-four degrees, a warm night for that altitude. Bill put the bacon in a tree, but all it collected were ants. We drank water out of the lake. The ranger explained that the water was so pure and clean because granite is like glass. . . . The mosquitoes were thick, a bad feature, because the scenery was so pretty with the lake nestled at the foot of granite peaks with snowy slopes. In fact, we were at snow level, 9850 feet, and mosquitoes are generally thick at snow level. . . . About 8:00 p.m., the ranger built a fire and we all sat around it. The sun set, the afterglow came on the peaks, then it began to get dark and chilly, so we all moved closer and closer to the fire. We all elected to go to bed at nine, and did so by the simple process of taking off our shoes and crawling in. The mosquitoes abated with the cold, and except for the hard ground, we had a good night's sleep.

Saturday, July 27, 1963

We woke at six, but got up with the mosquitoes at seven. We cooked a nice bacon-and-egg breakfast with cocoa and coffee. A fly flew into Betty's cocoa, fluttered and drowned, so she followed the ranger's recommendation, fished him out and drank the cocoa. . . . We packed up and left at 10:10 a.m., with the ranger and another family. We took the same trail back. It was amazing to see how much faster we went downhill!

Yosemite: A Learning Experience

Lucille Apcar

H ER VOICE CAME over the phone more a croak than its normal cheerful lilt. "Lucille, I'm sick," she said.

"Laurie, what's the matter?" I replied. The implication was unforgiving. Laurie, my regular tour guide for short, domestic groups was scheduled to depart soon with some thirty-four guests on a three-day motorcoach tour to Yosemite National Park.

"Been up all night," Laurie croaked again. "I think it's the flu, going to see the doctor at eleven o'clock but I know I'll never make it for the Yosemite tour."

The sinking feeling that started with my stomach spread upwards toward my head and down to my toes. Clara was away with her own group of seniors from the local senior center, Claudine had two day tours scheduled, Elsie was out of town. So that left me.

A worldwide traveler and escort for many complicated, lengthy tours mostly to Far Eastern countries, I was not exactly incapable of escorting a simple little trip to a very local destination, and no question I could spare a couple of days away from home and business.

One very daunting problem faced me; I had never visited or even seen Yosemite National Park. Just like so many procrastinators, I kept promising myself I would someday join one of our annual tours to the park to orient myself with California's great natural wonders. It never happened.

But to escort and narrate a tour for thirty-four people, most of whom were repeat visitors, already thoroughly familiar with every rock and stone, not to mention the waterfalls, the amenities, even the picnic grounds? I did not even know what the Lodge, our scheduled stay, looked like, the location of the restrooms, even worse, never traveled the route we were to take.

To add to my woes, Auntie Ruth, also a frequent visitor to Yosemite, planned to accompany us and was scheduled to stay at my home prior to joining the group. As usual I would be seeing the tour off at its starting point, bringing my big airline coffee container and lots of muffins for the midmorning restroom and refreshment break.

I called her up.

"Auntie Ruth," I said. "I'm going to have to escort the Yosemite tour. Laurie is sick, and there is nobody else to handle it. Don't you dare whisper even a word that this is my first sight of the Park."

Auntie Ruth was perfectly serene. "You can do it, Lou," she said, "and I'm glad you're coming."

Fortunately, with many annual tours to Yosemite in our history, the office files were well equipped with books, maps, routes, and amenities, as well as information on flora and fauna, names of the waterfalls, the hotels and campgrounds, even a fair number of historical events. I would be able to bone up, much as was my custom prior to taking any other tour groups. You never know what questions some people will throw at you.

It meant I had two days to study, so study I did.

Burning the midnight oil, I pored over maps of the route both going and returning, the entrance (Arch Rock) and its history, the names of the meadows (even the meadow where President Teddy Roosevelt signed Yosemite into the national park system), every trickle of water (in the month of May every crack and crevice is flowing with snowmelt), the names of the huge granite monoliths such as El Capitan, Cathedral Rock, the Three Brothers. I mistakenly said, "Three Sisters."

"Three Brothers," came a chorus from the back of the bus.

"Sorry," I said blithely, "never can remember whether it's sisters or brothers."

Intrigued, I even added a couple of touches of my own: I called the chamber of commerce in the small town of Mariposa to ask for the name of a recommended lunch stop and what we might visit on our way. The recommendations were excellent: a tiny coffee shop that laid out a bountiful buffet modestly priced, and a visit to the Mariposa Museum and History Center. The latter was a highlight—all our guests were enchanted with the presentation of the bespectacled guide who appeared well versed in Mariposa's place in the history of California.

My longtime love affair with nature served me well. The beautiful black oaks were easy to identify, as well as the majestic sugar pines, the dogwoods with their ephemeral white blossoms that seemed to appear unattached to their branches out of the gloom of shaded roadways, and the ever-present manzanita spreading their fingers over rocks and boulders. All this to add to my own awe over the statuesque sequoias, so different in their foliage from the coast redwood *sempervirens* to which we were familiar.

As we disembarked from our tour bus at our home destination, one of the guests paid me a compliment. "The best tour of Yosemite I have ever had the pleasure of joining," she said. I buttoned up my lip as I dared not tell her the truth. This was the first time I ever laid eyes on the Queen of our national parks.

Guess what? I retired to Mariposa, have lived here for the past twenty-five years, and since have served as pro bono tour guide to many friends and visitors.

Never have I tired of the pleasure of touring YOSEMITE.

The Yosemite Riot—A Happening

Pam Pederson

J ULY 4, 1970, in Yosemite Valley about four hundred hippie-type youth and a much smaller group of park rangers collided in a ruckus we can refer to as a *happening*.

A *happening* is an event that cannot be anticipated or expected and cannot be repeated exactly as it happened. The Yosemite Riot did not make headlines like Woodstock or Kent State, but the 1970 event occurred at the end of the hippie era and changed the course of national park history.

We were preparing for our wedding that day and totally unaware of a crowd gathering at Stoneman Meadow. Yosemite Valley is always packed with visitors on the Fourth of July, so we recruited a stranger to film our wedding using a Super 8 movie camera. It was to be a double wedding— two sisters and our husbands-to-be. We reserved wooden cabins near Yosemite Lodge so we could arrange our attire and have a couple of newlywed cottages for the night. Our apparel was fashioned after the popular movie *Butch Cassidy and the Sundance Kid* and the wedding was scheduled for 5:00 p.m. in the meadow across from the chapel. Nervousness and extra clothing made the afternoon feel like 110 degrees in the shade.

Friends and family made the trek to the national park to witness the wedding, and they brought lots of food as well as a thermos or two of mixed drinks. Rev. Davis from the Yosemite Chapel presided over the double wedding, and after he left we partied behind the chapel until after dark. A relative took black-and-white photos of the occasion.

Although our group of wedding spectators was a comfortable size, the group seemed to grow in number around sunset. Young people fleeing some sort of skirmish asked if they could join our gathering so they wouldn't appear to be drifters. There was plenty of fried chicken, potato

salad, and drinks to go around. We all felt quite safe and enjoyed ourselves despite whatever was happening in Stoneman Meadow about a
mile away.

We didn't realize the seriousness of the riot until we headed for our
lodging that night. The roads were blocked by rangers with nightsticks
in hand. They raised flashlights to shine into each car as they asked per-
tinent questions. Anyone without a reservation was turned back.

It was our turn to face the stern interrogators. My husband and I,
riding in a 1948 Chevy panel truck dressed like John Muir and Mother
Curry, showed the reluctant rangers proof of our reservations. We led
a caravan of cars that, one by one, were permitted to pass. Though we
were relieved, we had an uneasy feeling as we settled in for the night. It
was not a typical wedding night, as beds were shared with relatives too
tired to drive back home. My husband and I bedded down in the back of
the Chevy and whispered about what must have happened earlier that
day in the park until we fell asleep. We didn't realize we were part of an
event more memorable than just a wedding until we read about it in a
newspaper.

Every year on the Fourth of July we think about not only our wedding
anniversary, but of the special event known as a happening—the Yosemite Riot of 1970.

Memories of My Youth in Yosemite

Ralph Squire

For my twelfth birthday, my parents gave me a Baby Brownie camera, and took me to Yosemite Valley. Our first stop was near Sentinel Bridge. I noticed a fella that had a large camera set up on a tripod. He was under a cloth cover peering through his lens.

I went behind him to see what he was viewing. It was a great view of Half Dome with the Merced River in the foreground. I moved beside him and took a picture with my Baby Brownie. He came out from under the cloth and smiled at me.

All day long, we kept running into this same man, with his camera on a tripod, and I would again take pictures with my Baby Brownie and he would smile at me each time.

Years later, I read a copy of the biography of Ansel Adams. On the inside of the front cover was his picture. I said "Hey, that's the man that smiled at me." In chapter one, it said that as a small boy, Ansel's first camera was a Baby Brownie. No wonder he smiled, for he was seeing himself in me.

Three years later, my dad and I had what was my first camping experience in Tuolumne Meadows, with my uncle and my cousin, Hugh. We pitched a tent along the riverbank (where it now says "No Camping"). We had a great view of Lembert Dome.

I sat and stared at the sheer face of the dome and wondered if it could be climbed. Cousin Hugh, who was three years older, said, "Sure, let's do it in the morning."

The next morning, we walked along the far side of the dome, until we came to a crack. Hugh said, "This looks like a good place—let's see if we can climb it from here." We had no rope.

We started chimneying up the crack. Then we needed to jump and catch a small tree to hold. Soon we had passed the point of no return and could not go back down safely. We proceeded, with many death-defying experiences (at least I thought so at age fifteen).

Finally, we reached the summit. Hugh pointed out a steel box with a register book within and suggested we sign in. I wondered how the box got up there.

After enjoying the magnificent view of the meadows below, and the surrounding peaks, we were ready to descend. I hated the thought of going back the same route. Hugh said, "Let's go back down the trail."

I thought, "Trail! What trail?"

Hugh said, "I came up here with a ranger last year, so I know where the trail is." For a short second, I had a sudden urge to kill. I thought, "Hugh, you son of a gun, you knew there was a trail, and you led me up that life-threatening crack."

After another three years, Hugh suggested we climb Mount Lyell, the highest peak in the park. After arriving at Tuolumne Meadows, we went to the cabin of Carl Sharsmith, who was the ranger naturalist, for advice on route planning. Carl explained that there were three base camps to choose from. We could stop at lower base camp, where the meadow ended, leave our packs there and climb the mountain the next day; or we could go on to middle base camp, about halfway up to the third choice—upper base camp, where the route to the mountain left the trail. The higher we went, the less distance to climb the next day but the further we needed to carry our packs.

We arrived at lower base camp by noon and ate lunch. We were feeling great, so decided to go on and try to climb the mountain in the afternoon, leaving our packs at lower base camp. Big mistake—we were not yet properly acclimated!

When we left the trail beyond upper base camp, Carl had told us to watch for the ducks, because we would be above timberline, so there would be no trees to mark with blazes. We were young and ignorant; we didn't see any ducks—nor any geese either. But we did see these funny piles of rocks, which we followed.

We got about halfway up the mountain, when I got altitude sickness. I felt terrible, so we aborted the climb and returned to lower base camp.

A number of years later, my son and I joined a Sierra Club outing and climbed to the summit of Mount Lyell. The view was spectacular and brought closure to the earlier disappointments of my youth.

———————

"Conquer a peak?. . . as though one can conquer a peak by scrambling around on its top, as though that fly that alights on my table has conquered it!"

—Will Neely, Tuolumne ranger, 1957

The Measure of Success

Scott Stanley

THE HIKE TO the top of Half Dome is one of the most legendary day hikes in the entire national park system. They actually sell "I Made It to the Top of Half Dome" T-shirts so you can display your celebrated accomplishment.

In 1865, Josiah Whitney flatly declared, "Half Dome [is] perfectly inaccessible, being probably the only one of all the prominent points about Yosemite which has never been, and never will be, trodden by human foot." Is that so, Josiah?

Even though more than a million human feet have trodden the top of Half Dome since Mr. Whitney made his proclamation, it still seemed like he was issuing a personal challenge to me.

It's a very difficult hike, but something I really wanted to accomplish. I was two and a half years into a difficult midlife fitness struggle, and to go from sedentary and morbidly obese to the top of Half Dome would be the crowning achievement.

I wanted one of those T-shirts.

So my wife and I made our plans to visit Yosemite in June 2011. Our plan was to hike it on Tuesday, June 21. We arrived at the park late on Saturday and spent a couple of days getting to know the park and acclimating to the elevation.

No question we were ready.

After a fitful short night's sleep, we were at the trailhead at 6:15 a.m. on the twenty-first, ready to go. This was it!

The climb up the Mist Trail to the top of Vernal Fall was great fun. All of the waterfalls in the park were raging in late June of 2011 from all of the snow that winter. It was a torrent practically all the way to the top of Nevada Fall, as well. Amazing! Two waterfalls down, and things were looking good.

After that, the hike was pretty uneventful. Until we got to subdome.

I would guess we were somewhat past the halfway point up the grind of subdome when my wife asked me if we had to go back down the same way we were going up. Without thinking, I just said, "yes," and she made the crucial tactical error of looking back down from whence we came.

And that's where our uphill hike ended.

She had never had a paralyzing fear of heights before this, but trigger points are a funny thing. We sat down where we were and regrouped. Traffic on subdome was light that day, which was a major plus. After getting our bearings again, I insisted we go back down. As disappointing as it was to get this close, I knew that safety was the primary concern now. My wife wanted to see if she could press on, but in my mind, we had no choice. Anything less than 100 percent confidence on a climb like this could have very bad consequences. I just wasn't willing to take the risk.

Once down, we sat for quite a while at the base of subdome. I was trying to be as encouraging as possible about how great it was that we got as far as we did. There was no question we had the physical tools to make it to the top, which really was the main test anyway. Right? We hiked over eight miles and were less than one thousand feet short of the summit. That's 98.8 percent success. Right?

It was hard to start heading back down the trail. We knew we had another grueling eight miles ahead of us, and we weren't exactly feeling like the king and queen of the trail.

That first hour was pretty quiet. I spent a lot of time thinking about how we define success. I had been using this Half Dome hike as some sort of metaphor for life, so how should I look at it now?

Did we fail? I wouldn't accept that we failed. But did we then succeed? Well, no. Maybe it's not an either/or question.

It was a long hot afternoon and hiking down a steep trail is much more difficult than hiking up. It's way harder on your feet and knees, and it just takes longer. Gravity is not your friend; it's grueling.

Eventually we made it back to the trailhead. It was an exhausting day, both physically and mentally. Then we had to trudge nearly a mile back to where our car was parked.

Mr. Whitney won the challenge.

Two days later, we hiked to the top of Upper Yosemite Fall, another classic, beautiful Yosemite hike. Of course, when you get to the top of the rim and over to Yosemite Point, you're staring out over the Valley, right at Half Dome. I was still mad at that dumb piece of rock.

I stood there struggling with the nagging question of our success two days earlier. On the one hand, maybe it's not really all that important to look at it in terms of "success" vs. "failure." On the other hand, it's easy to say that if you didn't make it to the top.

Three years ago, I couldn't get around the mall without having to sit down and rest. That day, I had hiked more than forty miles in the mountains. In five days. Would eight hundred twenty more feet have made it more of a "success"?

That's an easy question intellectually. Emotionally, not so much. I still don't really have the answer. And I still don't have the T-shirt.

Roughing It in the Fifties

Betty Johnson

THE FLAMES OF our rock-encircled campfire were replaced by glowing embers, still hot and perfect for roasting marshmallows. However, that treat would have to wait. Right then, we were using long sticks to move chunks of burned wood away from foil-wrapped potatoes and corn on the cob buried in the ashes. The hot dogs were ready, and so were we. My older brother, Rich, returned from the river with a chilled watermelon he had faithfully guarded in shallow water for half an hour. It was dinnertime!

Mom, Rich, and I kept glancing at Half Dome while eating, waiting for the magical interval when the glow of sunlight on the face of the great granite landmark would be slowly darkened by a shadow creeping up toward the top. However, before the show was complete, clouds began drifting in, giving us cause to speculate on the possibility of rain later that night. Our sleeping bags were stretched out on the ground outside, but with plastic tarps covering them, we didn't have to decide right then whether or not to move them into our cramped umbrella tent.

Suddenly, distant shouts and the clanging of spoons on pots interrupted our conversation. We hurriedly shoveled our last few bites into our mouths, jumped up, and frantically ran to a neighbor's trailer with leftover watermelon, hot dogs, and marshmallows we had planned to toast. They grabbed the food and slammed the door before the bear arrived. This was long before bear-proof food storage boxes were provided. Unfortunately, we hadn't had time to clear paper plates, corncobs, and watermelon rinds off the table, and the approaching bear was eager to help. Mom and I transformed into fierce warriors armed with pots and big spoons, clanging and yelling at the bear, while Rich scurried away and hid from the hairy beast. The bear reluctantly ambled off in search of a less prepared campsite. As experienced Yosemite campers, we knew the bear would return later, hoping to find unguarded leftovers. So we cleaned up and took the tantalizing cobs and rinds to the trash can before retrieving the marshmallows to roast for dessert.

Later we left Camp 14 (now called Lower Pines) and walked into the meadow, where there was a clear view of Glacier Point. With time to spare before the 9:00 p.m. firefall, we continued toward Camp Curry. The area now called Curry Village was jammed full of people. Suddenly, silence fell across the crowd, as everyone listened for the first call slowly yelled through cupped hands. "Hel-lo, Gla-cier Point." Our eyes were trained on a spotlight three thousand feet up on Glacier Point, where a voice answered, "Hel-lo, Camp Cur-ry." The man below called back with the traditional words, "Let the fi-re fall!" And from above, "The fi-re falls!" We breathlessly awaited the first notes of the "Indian Love Call" that accompanied the firefall. "I am calling you-oo-oo-ooo-oo-oo-oooo." We sighed and smiled with upturned faces as the cascade of red-hot embers flowed down from Glacier Point and disappeared on a ledge far below.

Returning to camp, we joined neighbors around a campfire. After singing and telling our favorite bear stories, a group of us walked to the restroom both protecting each other and trying our best to make at least one scream in response to a good scare. Back in camp, we uncovered our sleeping bags and crawled in with flashlights handy in case of bear sightings in the night.

Much later, we were awakened by very loud thunder and flashes of lightning. It was scary! Before the rain could soak our sleeping bags and us, we dragged them into our claustrophobic tent.

The river rose several inches that night, but the storm passed, and there was a hint of sunshine in the morning. It was going to be another beautiful June day. Rich and I reluctantly waited till after lunch to take our old black inner tubes to the river, not far from our temporary homestead. The water was paralyzingly frigid, moving fast enough to deter most onlookers, but we had a tradition to uphold. Inching our way across slippery, submerged rocks till we were knee-deep in the water, we quickly settled into our tubes before the strong current could snatch them away. Thus seated, we were swept downstream to Stoneman Bridge by Camp Curry. It was exhilarating! It was also dangerous, and flotation is no longer permitted on that part of the river. The spot where we exited the river is now the entry point to a safer journey downstream.

Through the years we did all the traditional hikes, including Half Dome. However, as I got older and brought my children and grandchildren to this incredibly beautiful park, my activities changed a bit. Bicycling replaced hiking, and swimming in the river replaced tubing. Now, instead of trying to capture the beauty of the Valley with a Brownie Box camera, I use a digital camera, as well as a paintbrush. The beautiful mountains, waterfalls, trees, river, and meadows are incredibly challenging to capture in watercolor, but studying and experiencing the limitless essence of Yosemite is heavenly.

My young grandchildren love Yosemite as much as I always have. They continue our traditional plunges into the icy river, climb on big rocks and fallen tree trunks, look for deer in the meadows, and go on short hikes. They often start the evening calls for Elmer that echo around the campgrounds. Then they want to hear his story . . . again. I tell them about the lost little boy, whose parents frantically searched for him after dark in the campground long ago. Many people joined them in calling his name. One day my grandchildren will be the keepers of our family traditions, and I'm confident they will bring their children to this beloved place. They will play in the river, hike the trails, roast marshmallows, call Elmer, and gaze up at millions of stars before falling asleep in their cozy beds.

A Fall Day in the Meadows

Doug Quement

THERE ARE PEOPLE and places that, once experienced, redefine who you are. You may not know it at the time. You may not think about that person or place for years, only to have that memory seep back into the present. It can tug at your soul, settle in, and create an unmovable foundation for the rest of your life. But sometimes, on those very special times, you know it. You know how great the moment is. And the impact is immediate. A rock-climbing trip to Tuolumne Meadows was one of those times.

His name was Mark. I called him Abbo. He called himself MacGyver on a budget—frugal and pragmatic. I liked Mark because he was unique, unique in an effortless way that would be impossible for somebody that is trying to be unique to replicate. His dialogue was usually thought provoking, sometimes dreamy and idealistic but always adventurous and curious. When he talked about wanting to climb Cathedral Peak in the fall, I quickly volunteered as a willing partner.

The end of a good day usually starts with a good morning. This October morning was what you expect from a Yosemite October morning. Fall colors bleeding through the canyons backed by crystal clear skies . . . and not a breath of wind. Mark was boiling water and mumbling something about, "a backpacking stove I made last year out of a cat food can . . . ," clouds of frozen breath quickly rising. I was half listening, as I watched the changing light on Cathedral peak, just over Mark's left shoulder. Over Mark's other shoulder, I glanced at the small dome on the west end of Tuolumne Meadows. Dwarfed by all the neighboring and larger granite domes, it seemed friendly and inviting. The sun inched its way up the peak, a beautiful reminder of our late start. After packing up, we drove across the Tuolumne River, west toward the trailhead. Lembert Dome and Mount Dana faded away in my rearview mirror to the east.

By map, the approach to the southeast buttress of Cathedral Peak seems benign. And at three and a half miles long, the approach is relatively short compared to other Sierra backcountry climbs. As the trail snaked its way upstream of Budd Lake, toward its headwaters, I was surprised at how often I had to stop to catch my breath. It should have been no surprise though, as we have come from sea level to the current 9,800 feet (peak summit of 10,912 feet). Of the many things that stand clear in my memory from that day is the fleeting glimpse of Cathedral, through the old Jeffrey pines, that would tease you along the last half of the approach. Glowing with the morning sun on it and, even at this distance, the quality of the granite looked fantastic.

At the base of the climb, as we prepped our gear and flaked the rope, the true beauty and the incredible rock quality of this peak was undeniable. Looking upward at seven hundred feet of endless rock features, ledges, and unlimited protection options for gear, Cathedral was a dream come true for this trad novice.

Mark led the first pitch of incredibly fun and easy climbing. I have a framed picture at home that Mark took of me as I climbed up to meet him at the first belay ledge. An ear-to-ear smile and the facial expression of "there is no place I would rather be!" plastered all over it. I could not get over how good the rock felt in my hands and under my feet. We swapped leads and exchanged giddy laughs at every belay station. Pitch four is the highlight of the climb with a tight chimney that squeezes you through a couple of really fun moves and leads you to the last few hundred feet of the climb. As I was belaying Mark, I had my first good chance to absorb the surrounding scenery. Scanning from south to north, I took in the view of incredible peaks and was fired up to climb every one of them. In the years to follow, I did summit many of them: Mount Whitney, visible on this clear day; the long knife ridge of Matthes Crest; the fun spikes of Cockscomb; the barren openness of Mount Dana, the polished Pywiack, the proud and spectacular Mount Conness; Matterhorn and the Sawtooth range to the far north. Many of the peaks are still unchecked on my climb list but were within what seemed like arm's distance that day: Mount Lyell, Fairview Dome, and its buddy across the road, Daff Dome. A whole lifetime of climbing and hiking lay out before me on that belay ledge. And what a great life it will be, knowing that I am now a part of Tuolumne Meadows. And no one can ever take that away.

I think Mark summed it up like only he can, "Pretty cool huh?" Yes, Mark, pretty cool indeed!

Ode to Yosemite

Hannah Lucas Giarrusso (age eleven)

YOSEMITE, IT'S THE place I can roam.
Without a schedule, up to Half Dome.
To Yosemite Falls, to those roaring Cascades.
It's a kind of memory that never fades.
The hybrid shuttle, the forest floor,
Nature never shuts the door.
Out to dinner, the Yosemite Inn,
the experience of a lifetime with my kin.
Bridalveil! Vernal! Lower Fall!
I always answer to Yosemite's calls.
And at the end, as the adventure finishes,
the Spirit of Yosemite never diminishes.

Throw a Stick at It

Lauren Casey

I LIKE TO SAY that my dad has a repertoire of stories; a collection of memories from over the years. Among them is a top ten in the rotation which are regaled on shuffle mode at each and every family get-together . . . and they all pertain to time spent in the great outdoors.

One tale within this chosen lineup is set in Yosemite National Park.

My dad is a hiker. He has been hiking and backpacking for as long as I can remember. As youths, my brother, Ryan, and I were my dad's begrudging trail companions, though over miles blazed and years passed, we grew into willing participants, eager for the next opportunity to lace up the boots and head into the backcountry.

As my brother and I grew older, heartier, and able to carry a respectable amount of weight, planned backpacking excursions became an annual event; national parks of the West, the chosen destination.

After locale selection, there would be incessant discussion of trip details, reevaluations of last year's freeze-dried menu selection. . . . Did we like the "turkey tortellini"? Should we nix the "blueberry crumble"? And an itinerary meticulously constructed by father via Excel spreadsheet featuring flight information, gear assignments, and a down-to-the-GORP ingredient menu for each day.

We three loved talking about impending trips for months prior and retelling our tales from the trail for months and years after.

Yosemite National Park ignited our family hiking ritual, as it was the inaugural of our annual excursions. And the memory retold by my dad, to fresh ears and to ears that have listened dozens of times, involves rain, thunder, and a lot of lightning.

Our first day on the trail started off well, the breakfast was filling and the complaining, from the group's youngest trekkers, minimal. It had been raining, but only with an intensity that required a light slicker, as we hiked along the famed John Muir Trail. Tuolumne Meadows at our backs and nothing but breathtaking vistas in our views. After miles passed under-boot, we exited the protection of the coniferous canopy and hiked into a gorgeous valley of wide-open green expanse. With almost poetic timing, the first crack of thunder rang out.

My dad looked at Ryan and me reassuringly, at the same time encouraging a quickened pace. But within minutes, we were confronted by the trail adversary of a fierce thunderstorm. The flashes of lightning were nearer, and the claps of thunder louder than I had ever before experienced. And we ran, as fast as one can with an unwieldy pack strapped to one's back. My pack, in particular, threatened to inspire an experiment of Ben Franklin proportion. . . . I was donning an external, metal-framed pack.

We moved forward, motivated in equal parts by exhilaration and sheer terror. The torrential rain transformed the trail into mud and pitted down puddles, which served as inverted speed bumps on the path to shelter. At Sunrise Campground, shelter we did find; a cabin with four walls, a roof, and even a fireplace. We hurried in, drenched to the core, looked at one another with eyes wide and smiles even wider.

But Yosemite National Park isn't the scene of only one commemorated memory. Another such tale is so popular between my brother and myself that it inspired the formation of our own sibling story series. Its central characters: two baby bears.

Our second night, we established camp at a splendid backcountry site not too far from iconic Half Dome, under the tall pines, and near to a creek bed. Dusk settling in over the Sierra Nevada, and my dad retired to his tent to read a book. My brother and I sat and stoked the campfire, enjoying the warmth, the smell of the burning wood, and the visual display of the dancing flames . . . when two shadows in the near distance redirected our attention. With what seemed to be tandem recognition of the sight before us, Ryan and I turned and looked at one another. . . . The shadows were real, they were alive, they were bears.

I watched the young bears playfully explore the creek bed. Cute as they were, I knew Mama Bear must be nearby and Mama, I was quite sure, would not appear so cuddly. Physically motionless, my mind raced, repeating the bear safety tips my dad had instructed us upon in the weeks leading up to the trip, quizzed us on during the drive to Yosemite from San Francisco, and readdressed more than once on the trail. We called to my dad, in a sort of whispered yell, "Dad, Dad! What do we do if there's a bear in the camp?" The response from my Dad, advocate of rational reactions to bear interactions: "Throw a stick at it."

He thought we were joking, though he never emerged from his tent to be sure. We never encountered Mama Bear, though the next morning, we learned that our camp neighbors upwind had. A couple solicited aid from my father in retrieving the woman camper's medicine. It had been "misplaced" by a large black bear who the couple witnessed open and consume their supply of canned tuna during the night.

Since then, my dad has suspended his stick-throwing policy.

Though a trip into the great outdoors can present certain hazards, to my family, national parks like Yosemite serve as refuges where sights, sounds, and scenery create memories indelibly imprinted in our minds. And the experiences shared together from the laughs to the blisters to the dinnertime talks to the stinky socks . . . are so special to us that we revel in sharing our trail tales with others, even if they've heard the tale once or twice before. . . .

———•—•———

"This present season an female Bear with two cubs
has had a free pass throughout the valley and had
given ferocious chase to every Photo Artist who
has attempted to get a picture of the group."

—Galen Clark, first state-appointed
Guardian of Yosemite, 1907

What About Half Dome?

William Gartley

You can't camp on Half Dome anymore. You can't watch its shadow move across Glacier Point from your sleeping bag, as you shake off the cold at that 8,800-foot elevation. You can't look down on Glacier Point and see the firefall as it silently pours into Curry Village. Not anymore. But in 1962, you could.

Five of us met in Yosemite Valley to hike up Half Dome: Robert, Larry, Walter, and my best friend, Mike. I was seventeen and managed to challenge my friends to make the climb with me. I was the point man—I had done it twice before, and my exciting stories encouraged my friends to join me.

My first time up was with a group from Robert Louis Stevenson School for Boys in Monterey. I was fifteen. Our counselor convinced us there was an elevator to the top, but we would have to walk up because we were young and healthy. I remember struggling up the cables that first time and feeling so superior to the weaklings who had to use that elevator; then I remember the laughing as we all realized there was no elevator.

My second time up was with friends who joined me on an overnighter on top of Half Dome. We hiked up with our sleeping bags and dinner. Half Dome became the siren of my life, as it remains today, always beckoning, always a keystone.

But my third time up was a failure. The tent was mine, but my four friends shared it with me and, during the first two nights in Upper Pines campground, we were riotous and disgusting, as one would imagine a group of seventeen-year-old boys to be. We had watched the firefall each night, but mostly we watched the girls at Camp Curry. Considering how dorky we all were, the girl thing didn't pan out. But we were still focused on our endeavor.

Finally, we got organized and made our plans for the ascent. We would get up at 5:00 a.m. and have a quick breakfast, then hit the Happy Isles Trailhead before dawn. The cans of food and drink were pretty heavy, so we decided that Robert, Larry, and Walter would carry all the sleeping bags, while Mike and I would carry all the food and drinks. No problem. Except . . . I would swear our two packs were much heavier than theirs.

We were fine until we hit Little Yosemite Valley. By that time, Mike and I had started to fall behind and were ready for a smoke break. I had started smoking the previous fall when Mike told me how cool I looked with a cigarette. So, we sat by the trail many times and had many cigarette breaks. We needed to catch our breath anyway (at seventeen—go figure). We talked and laughed and told jokes. We drank a lot of our beverages. Then we would man up and hike another hundred yards or so—then stop for another cigarette. We had no idea why we were so winded. It was 1962—who knew?

Finally, we were so exhausted, we decided to call it quits and go back. Enough of this uphill stuff! We were probably two miles below the cables when we quit. Happy that we didn't have to hike uphill any longer, we were almost skipping down the trail, giddy with the thought of flirting with the girls at Curry that night. Which we did. We totally reinforced each other that there was nothing wrong with our decision—that our fellow hikers would understand why it was okay for us to turn back.

They didn't. At 3:00 a.m., I was awakened by a hard kick to my ribs, as was Mike. We were beaten and abused—called every foul name in the book, and kicked out of the tent for the rest of the night. Robert, Larry, and Walter had waited for us on top of Half Dome for hours, hoping we would show up with dinner. When they realized we weren't coming, the sun had already set. They started back down and managed to hike the eight miles by moonlight—a superhuman feat.

At first, I was defensive—my seventeen-year-old brain would not accept responsibility. I lost those friends. Mike and I drifted apart soon after. My failure to complete the hike, and more importantly, my failure to support my friends that day became an obstacle in my life, one that would follow me for years; it became a benchmark of my character for all of my future efforts.

But it made me a better person. As that failure grew in my conscience, I learned to face every challenge with the thought, "Don't let this be another Half Dome!" I learned how to not give up. I learned to support my friends. I gave up smoking a few years later. I pursued and married the girl of my dreams, and forty-four years later, I am still married to her, and she is still the girl of my dreams. In 1966, I got a job at the lowest entry level and told myself that this would be my career—no matter what. Last year, I retired from that same job, though at a much higher level. Along the way, I put myself through college, acquired a bachelor's and a master's degree—not allowing anything to back me down.

But what about Half Dome? I was determined to overcome that demon. At the age of forty-seven, I hiked to the top and finally put to rest that failure that haunted me all these years. And just to kick Half Dome in the butt, I hiked it again when I was fifty-nine. Both times, as I hiked, it warmed my heart to offer encouragement and kindness to the other hikers and to wish I could do more to make Half Dome as meaningful to them as it is to me.

The Sky Is Falling

William Gartley

WHEN I SEE those great piles of rocks at the base of Royal Arches, Half Dome, Glacier Point, I am in awe of the overwhelming force of nature that caused them to fall. And in my dreams, I see them cascading down with a mighty roar, resetting, restoring, repairing the Valley's feng shui, providing artists with new frontiers, children with new boulders to climb, and thrills in my heart at the grand march of time. The reality was that I nearly wet myself when my dream came to life.

On October 7 and 8 of 2008, I was camping with my wife, Sherry, and her sister, Lizanne, in Upper Pines, just a stone's throw (so to speak) from Camp Curry. My nephew, Billy, had joined us the day before. All of us had just finished hiking the Mirror Lake loop and were relaxing in camp. There was a distant rumbling.

"What is that?" I said.

"Thunder," Billy replied.

The rumbling grew louder, and it was punctuated with loud CRACKS that were the unmistakable sound of large rocks crashing against each other.

"Maybe it's not thunder," Billy added.

The sound was very much in the Valley—not from anywhere else. We looked toward Camp Curry and saw a giant plume of dust rising against the cliff, the lowering sun highlighting the growing apparition. We looked at each other with the same mounting awareness. In unison, we all turned our heads toward the cliff that was directly above our camp-site, and again in unison, we looked at each other and whispered, "Oh no!" and stood there in silence for a few minutes, listening, watching, waiting for more . . . more . . . what . . . ? This was new to us. What would happen next?

"Well, let's go over to Curry and see what's going on," I offered.

Jumping into the car, we started over, but by this time the area had been blocked off. We returned to our camp and started dinner. Billy was our star chef. After preparing a fine steak dinner, he leisurely stretched his arms out, sighed loudly, and said, "Well, I just remembered—I've got this big job going on and I don't think Al can handle it on his own. I think I'll pack up and head home now."

Sure, I thought. Leave us alone to be crushed by Glacier Point as it collapses in the middle of the night. We were kind though. "Have a nice trip home," we said. So Billy was gone. Sherry, Lizanne, and I sat around the campfire and rationalized that we were okay. I mean, sure, there are frequent rockfalls here. That's what Yosemite is all about. But look how rare it is—to happen in front of an audience. It would be years before it would happen again like this. And the odds of us being here when it did—astronomical! We might as well buy lottery tickets.

But I was cautious. "Now we know what it sounds like," I said. "So, if we hear that same rumbling tonight, run straight to the car and jump in. At least it may protect us if any rocks bounce into Upper Pines." Sherry and Lizanne assured me they were onboard and ready to save themselves.

It was an uneasy night for me. We were used to hearing an occasional rock bouncing down the cliff, and it was nothing to get excited about. But this night was different. Every sharp sound, no matter how soft, had me all puckered up and ready to sprint to the car. I made sure my shoes were next to my sleeping bag. I slept fully clothed. At this point, the women could take care of themselves. I knew I could beat them to the car.

I woke up to the usual cacophony of the jays and ravens as they were anxious for us to start breakfast. It was almost seven and I was congratulating myself for surviving the night. Then I heard a rock pinging down the cliff. No sweat, I told myself—somewhat weakly, it's only one rock. . . .

Then it let go. It seemed a hundred times louder than the day before. The only thing louder was the impossible, high-pitched shrieking in our tent.

"Another rockfall! Run for your lives," the voice screamed. I looked at Sherry and Lizanne. Still asleep. Who was screaming? . . . Oh . . . it was me.

"Wake up! Wake up," I yelled, "it's another rockfall! Run to the car!"

I whipped my shoes on, unzipped the tent, and started running, the shrieking screams following me the whole way. I jumped into the car, slammed the door, ducked down below the seat backs (hoping the crashing boulders wouldn't crush the entire car) and finally peeked over the top of the seat to see if Sherry and Lizanne were running to the car. No—they weren't. They were standing at the tent door, yawning and patting their sleep hair back into place—looking at the bug-eyed crazy man screaming in the car.

Great—now I'm the guy who would drive away in comfort while his family is being crushed to death by a collapsing Glacier Point.

The dust plume rose again from Camp Curry. Walking over there this time, we were amazed at the efforts of the NPS as their spokesperson stood in the parking lot, surrounded by campers and guests. He described what had happened and answered our many questions. We spent the day watching the helicopter swooping back and forth, as it surveyed the cliff above Curry. We watched the arriving news vans, as they congregated at Ahwahnee Meadow. Also, like everybody else that day, we were waiting for another rockfall.

After forty years of camping in Yosemite Valley, this was the most exciting year, and for me, of course, the most humiliating.

Just don't ask me who wears the big-boy pants in my family.

Falling Rocks

Ronald Smedberg

MY FIRST TRIP to Yosemite was in 1940. I was thirteen months old. Over the years I have fished in nearly every stream and creek in the park. My wife and I have been to the top of every dome (and waterfall) in the Valley, with the exception of El Capitan (which, of course, isn't a dome).

The story I wish to relate happened around 1950. We were showing some friends around the park and were in the Visitor Center showing them Smedberg Lake (not related to author) on the raised relief map. There was a lady who was clearly upset with a ranger at the main desk. It was getting pretty heated. When she finally left, my father just had to find out why the lady was so upset. Well, it seems that this lady, who had come all the way from somewhere in the Midwest, had taken in many of the waterfalls, seen the firefall, been to the garbage pit south of Camp Curry to watch the black bear forage through the garbage, and many of the other attractions of Yosemite. On her way back that afternoon from Glacier Point, she saw a sign that simply said WATCH FOR FALLING ROCKS. Well, this got her curiosity up, and she stopped her car. She spent over two hours sitting there and her complaint was not one rock fell during that time. She was upset about that! Everything else in Yosemite seemed to happen on time except the rocks; they didn't fall! We all, including the ranger, got a pretty big laugh out of that one.

3

A TRIBUTE

It's Our Park

Gaye O'Callahan

SHARE MEMORIES AND photos of Yosemite? It's impossible to choose! A photo of my grandparents' car driving through the Tunnel Tree in the thirties and then one of our family's car there when I was a kid in the late fifties? Photos of my first and subsequent High Sierra loop trips led by Ranger Carl Sharsmith, as a teen with my family? Or memories of my sons as kids and then teens by a rock at Olmsted Point? Stories of the loop trip with my son as a teen, sadly not led by Carl, but by a woman? But wait, she was fantastic, too, and mesmerized us with her flute in the high meadows. Or one of May Lake, the only place I could think to be for the moment of silence following 9/11.

In 1995 there was a memorial gathering for Carl, who had been the oldest ranger in the National Park Service. Set in Tuolumne Meadows, it was an appropriate celebration of his life. Even "John Muir" attended and spoke. But the most moving moment for me was the last speaker's lament at the loss of this park's notable steward. She went on to ask who could fill his shoes, who would carry on his work now? After a moment of quiet, someone in the crowd quietly stood and announced, "I will." And with that, one by one, the meadow slowly sprouted a mass of human volunteers. Carl's mark was on us all, and we would all carry on, cherishing and protecting this beloved park.

——◆——

"The hikers and naturalist had somewhat recovered
from the startling view of Tenaya lake over 2,500 feet
almost sheer beneath their feet, when, circling around
a shoulder of the mountainside among a chaotic mass
of huge granite blocks, they came upon the prize flower
discovery of the season . . . a garden of Sierra primrose,
which for size of area and number of plants surpassed
anything yet discovered for this rare plant in Yosemite."

–Carl W. Sharsmith, ranger naturalist, 1950

Persistence of Vision: A Tribute to My Friend, Ranger Dick Ewart

Beth Pratt

Our fingers touch a carving left by sheepherders over a hundred years ago. We try to puzzle out the date but the bark has transformed the numbers into an unrecognizable shape, like a drop of water blotting out letters in ink. The tree has made hieroglyphs of another time.

Around us, he points out the configuration of downed trees and wonders aloud if it might be the remnants of a sheep pen. I follow his gesturing hand and the scene comes alive for me: the corralled sheep, the men by the fire, sipping whiskey, perhaps singing a ballad to stave off the lonely sound of the wind. . . or carving a date in a tree, never imagining that one hundred years later a curious girl would stand trying to puzzle out the numbers.

We hike on, and I follow my guide, captivated by the sense of wonder he instills in me. I think myself lucky to have such a fine teacher. Further along he kneels and sifts soil in between his fingers. Ash from a volcano, the Mammoth eruption over seven hundred thousand years ago, he tells me. I bend down next to him and sift the soil as well, imagining the enormous volcanic cloud overhead and the chill wind that blew when the ash blotted out the sun.

This is what we see together while we hike. This is what he shows me.

The sentence of the lonely tracks of a mountain lion punctuated further along by its scat. An alpine meadow littered with the harvest of pikas, circles of cut alpine asters, their stems left to dry like bales of hay in a farmer's field. A stand of gnarled trees that becomes an image summed up perfectly in a word he conjures up: krummholz. The patterns of rockfall between the seam of the Granite Divide, the two formations blending in the middle: a sunset of rocks.

When we arrive at the top of the Granite Divide, it's quiet—the low quiet of the wind and of being above human noise. And I realize the landscape has changed for me. The patterns emerge from their obvious hiding places; it's like watching clouds and having them suddenly transform into a familiar shape. My eyes refocus and I see the interworking, the ice flow, the crack of the glacier, the mountain lion running over rocks, the sheepherder patiently carving his date into a tree. These things before had possessed a separateness now united by his way of seeing.

I am suddenly able to see his landscape.

And I realize the enormity of his gift: that I will never go back to seeing in quite the same way again.

Persistence of vision. Our eyes retain the memory of our vision longer than we focus on an object. Stare ahead at an object, then direct your eyes elsewhere. A ghostly image remains, still embedded in the retinas. What does this mean? That our eyes have memory also. We don't simply see what is—we see what was, layer upon layer of sight.

He has a talent for mechanics. He told me of tinkering with cars as a child, turning valves and gaskets and trying to discover how they work. And I think his rangering is no different a trait. He wants to know how things work in the natural world as well. Assembling a constellation from a diagram in a book. Handling a colored rock to puzzle out the geology. Sifting the dust from a long-ago volcano. Tracing the patterns of a glacier.

The park is a great natural machine for him, and as he did when he was a child, he overturns rocks and peers over cliffs in order to understand relationships.

On the hike down we try to find the remnants of a lumber pile abandoned by a miner. He tells me of discovering it when he first arrived in the park over twenty-five years ago. To cover more ground, we take different routes through the basin.

He walks on the ridge above me, and I hear the jangle of scree as he takes a step on the hillside. I want to find this wood, smoothed by hands over a hundred years ago. I want to return the gift he has given me in some way.

I continue my search. I scurry up and down the basin, energized by the exhilaration of such a limitless day. And when I find the wood, I know the reason is because of his gift of making me see differently.

We stand before the pile. I wonder what would make them abandon this wood. I press my hands on lumber hewn with the hands of a stranger in the last century. And then I think of his hands touching this wood twenty years ago, a chain of memory linked by happenstance.

It's these moments that count, I think, and the spaces in between are like lines connecting the dots to an unforeseen picture. Like the constellation in the sky that he is teaching me. Before he gave them shape, they lacked meaning. These moments now have meaning beyond themselves.

I smile, smile at the perfectness of the day, at discovering a direct connection to the past, and at his gift of new sight.

I want to tell him that these things will persist in my vision. That in twenty years, when I find the wood after seeking it on my own, his image will persist, along with the sharpness of an ax mark in a tree made a hundred years ago or the faint powdery scent of volcanic ash seven hundred thousand years old. I want to tell him that he will always be locked up in the contours of the park for me, inextricably linked to the landscape and to his teaching me a new way of seeing.

Bill Lowry

Robert H. Boyer

THE TELEPHONE WAS introduced to Yosemite
In the year nineteen-O-five;
Every scene of activity demanded one
For they knew it would make business thrive.
Stringing lines and hanging insulators was happening
All over the joint,
But the one job that stopped them cold
Was getting a line down from Glacier Point.
'Tis this one gutsy guy from Boot Jack,
Bill Lowry was his name,
Came up with a bold idea
That should put him in Yosemite fame.
He said, "Tie that line to my belt
And lower me away,
If my Irish luck holds
We'll ring that phone by the end of the day."
Down the face of that bluff Bill went
Over three thousand feet below,
And just as he had promised
From Glacier Point you could say "Hello."
The daring act of this lineman
Didn't win him fortune or fame,
A search through Yosemite history
Doesn't even reveal his name.
But the next time you walk on Glacier
And gaze on that chasm below,
Ask yourself if we've overlooked a hero
Who deserves a paragraph or so.

Dancing above the Valley

Collene Gaugh

H E FIRST SAW the motor home while peering over the fence into the neighbor's yard. It wasn't much, but to my dad it was just the thing our family needed. I was ten at the time and part of me was mortified watching my dad from the car as he knocked on a stranger's door and offered up five hundred dollars to take the thing off their hands. The other part of me, however, knew that this meant we were unstoppable vacationers and into the wild we were bound!

That summer was our first trip to Yosemite. I knew nothing about Yosemite except it meant an entire week of bike rides, hikes, and most importantly, s'mores! Mom loaded up the motor home full of snacks and treats only summer vacation camping trips could provide and dad piled the bikes on the homemade bike rack he had constructed just nights before. Before I knew it I was scouring the map and learning to navigate as we headed north, conquering the winding mountain roads at an awe-inspiring thirty miles per hour.

We spent the next week exploring trails, hiking waterfalls, rafting down the river, and simply admiring the sheer beauty that is Yosemite. I got my first camera that summer and spent every last picture of my first roll of film attempting to capture every last moment. From deer in the Valley and ice cream cones at Curry Village to watching the seasoned rock climbers return to camp in the dark of night, I finally began to understand my dad's vision while he had been peering over that neighbor's fence. On our last night in camp that trip, my dad and I sat staring up at the darkened face of Half Dome. He pointed out the lights from the hikers camped at the top and confided to his ten-year-old daughter that one day, that would be him up there, his light dancing above the Valley.

My parents continued their love affair with Yosemite, returning year after year to the Valley. However, I wouldn't return again for another fifteen years. It was my parents' twenty-fifth wedding anniversary, but instead of the grand celebration we had wanted for them, we found our family in a local restaurant humbled by our family's next challenge. Cancer. To know my dad is to know that cancer to him was exactly that, a challenge, and like any other challenge it was to be overcome with hard work and a whole lot of love and support. He immediately started treatment. That summer, six months into chemo, my parents made their annual trip to Yosemite where together they hiked Upper Yosemite Fall.

At twenty-six I had the opportunity to join my parents on their annual trip. My alarm went off at 6:00 a.m. and even though waking up at 6:00 a.m. on a Saturday morning was a little rougher than it had been when I was ten, I packed my bags all the same and loaded up the motor home. This time my dad and I both had our matching cameras in tow. Mom loaded the food, dad packed up the bikes, and I packed the s'mores. It was the second year of my dad's cancer, and though things were getting hard on him, there was never a question this little bump in the road was anything more than a bump.

Our trip was mellower than ones past. More time was spent lounging in our campsite, snapping silly photos under the shade of the pines, and walking around the Village. It was hard to ignore the pain my dad was in at the time. Elevation made breathing difficult and the shortest walks exhausted him. My dad ignored it all the same, even hopped on his bike and rode to Curry Village for their annual night out of pizza and beer— two things I'm sure his doctors would not have liked. It was a somber trip, but it didn't matter. We were together under the shade of Half Dome in a Valley we had all grown to love.

On August 4 we said good-bye to my father, less than six weeks after our last Yosemite trip together. He passed away in the comfort of his home, surrounded by family and friends. We buried my father in a cedar box picturing Half Dome and the chapel below it my parents had ridden their bikes to only weeks before. We celebrated my dad's life with over 250 of his closest friends and standing room only.

A year later, on the anniversary of my dad's last day on earth, my mom and I, along with a group of a few of our closest friends, woke up at 3:30 a.m., laced up our boots, and packed our backpacks with the fuel we would need for our fourteen-mile adventure. We set out to conquer Half Dome, the adventure my dad mentioned to me many years before. We weren't the seasoned rock climbers I had admired in the Village as a kid, but this journey wasn't for us, we were honoring him. As daylight broke and we passed Nevada Fall, it became increasing hard to ignore the white butterfly that seemed to follow us along the trail. Each time my heart skipped a beat, my stomach filled with the nervous sensations of doubt and worry, the white butterfly appeared. I can't remember the number of times I questioned myself that day, or even the conversations we had as we hiked. However, the memory that is impeccably clear is the image I have as I lay roses from my dad's service the previous year. Upon the farthest edge of the Diving Board was a little white butterfly dancing above the Valley.

A Legendary Encounter

Dave Todd

My BROTHER-IN-LAW, KLAUS Penning, taught me to cross-country ski. Klaus learned to ski in Germany in the 1930s. After service in World War II and release from captivity as a POW in the Soviet Union, he immigrated to the United States and got a job in Yosemite National Park in the 1950s doing various types of maintenance work. It was then that he first met Nic Fiore, who would become the legendary director of the Badger Pass Ski School. They became friends, and much later, in the 1990s, Nic invited Klaus to become a ski instructor at Badger Pass.

I met Klaus in 1969 after returning home from army service in Germany. Together we skied all of the trails that start from the Glacier Point Road at Badger Pass. The trails included Dewey Point, Ghost Forest Loop, Bridalveil Creek Campground, and Ostrander Lake. We also skied from Goat Meadow outside the park into the Mariposa Grove. Sometimes there was enough snow to make it to Wawona Point overlooking the Wawona Hotel and Golf Course. Thanks to climate change, the snow elevation is now seldom low enough to make those trips.

During the other seasons of the year, we would take backpacking trips into Yosemite's high country. The trails we hiked included Cathedral Lakes, Vogelsang, Glen Aulin, and Saddlebag Lake just outside the Tioga Pass Entrance to Yosemite.

For some reason, we had more misadventures going to Glen Aulin than on any of our other hikes. On our first hike in 1982, we camped in the lower campground at Glen Aulin. During the night a rainstorm hit and we were forced to pack up all our gear and evacuate to the upper campground when the stream rose. On our second hike in the late 1990s the weather was hot and dry when we started off on the eleven-and-a-half–mile trip. At around six miles, a torrential rain-and-lightning storm struck. I didn't bring a poncho or raincoat and was soon cold and drenched. Lightning hit all around us and there was no place to take shelter. We had no choice but to keep going.

The storm finally stopped and my clothes began to dry a little. We were about three miles from Glen Aulin when we saw someone emerge from the forest ahead of us. As he drew nearer, we recognized the familiar face of Nic Fiore! But Nic was not his usual jovial self. He was grimacing in pain. He was using his kerchief to mop at a stream of blood flowing from the top of his bald head.

When he reached us, we asked him where he had come from because he had not been on an established trail. Nic sat down on a large dead log and continued to mop at the blood on his forehead. He was sweating profusely. Nic said he always spent his summers managing the five camps in Yosemite's wilderness backcountry. When he had free time he would take off on an adventure hike just for fun.

Klaus asked Nic about the wound on his forehead. "Did you scratch yourself on a low-hanging tree branch?"

Nic said that it was nothing like that. He said that he was passing through an open meadow when suddenly he heard a goshawk screech and it began diving at him. He jumped out of the way, but the goshawk circled back and dove at his forehead. Nic used his cap to wave it off. The goshawk was relentless and continued its attack. Finally, Nic, alarmed, ran as fast as he could away from the goshawk. Nevertheless, the goshawk dived again and this time its talons raked Nic's forehead.

Klaus asked Nic if he had done anything to disturb the bird's territory. Nic said that he couldn't think of a single thing that he had done that could have upset the bird. Klaus looked at Nic. Then he looked at Nic's glistening bald head.

"I know why the bird attacked you," he said.

"Why?" Nic asked.

"She thought you were trying to steal her egg!"

After we all stopped laughing, we helped Nic bandage his forehead. Nic went on his way and we continued on our hike.

We finally arrived at Glen Aulin just before dusk. We set up our tents in the lower campground and went to sleep soon after dinner. A heavy rain began to fall. Once again, like our hike of nearly twenty years before, we were forced to evacuate to the upper campground. First we moved my tent to the upper campground. Then we returned for Klaus's tent. We returned with his tent to the upper campground. We spent most of the night trying to stay dry.

The next day the sun came out long enough to dry our gear. Our hike back to Tuolumne Meadows was much more enjoyable than the trip out. Every now and then we would think of Nic Fiore and the great egg theft and begin to laugh again.

Gulp Life

Hannah Hindley

THIS LAND HOLDS stories. Some are beautiful. Some are heartbreaking. And some will never be forgotten. Stand in Yosemite Valley and look up at sunrise: you can almost see Ansel Adams cresting one of those high granite faces in the first light, camera in hand. Look closely at the boulders as you hike. You'll find water collecting in the mortars where Ahwahneechee women once ground acorns as they watched their children from atop the rocks. Come across a black bear track in the dust, and with a little imagination, you might hear the crack of gunfire that killed the last grizzly, echoing through time from a century back for those who listen. Venture above the Valley to the little community of Foresta and, if you lived in the area or read the news in the 1990s, it will be disturbing to remember that this is where the decapitated body of Joie Armstrong was discovered: the fourth and final murder committed by the "Yosemite Killer."

As a memory, it is a horrific one. Yet as a story, Joie Armstrong's death was not a final chapter. She was twenty-six years old when she died—a vivacious adventurer and a dedicated educator with Yosemite Institute (now NatureBridge), an organization that brings students into national parks to learn and explore. She was lovely and beloved, and sight unseen she changed my life—and the life of Yosemite National Park—in the most breathtaking way possible.

When I was fifteen, I applied for the Armstrong Scholars Program: an opportunity for teenage girls to backpack for two weeks through Yosemite's backcountry. The scholarship was funded by the many people who had loved Joie Armstrong—and those who had never known her but wished to honor her memory. They hoped to keep her joy and courage alive by instilling it in other young women.

I had never backpacked before and didn't really know what to expect. When I arrived with eleven other girls, ready for adventure and equipped with untested backpacks, things got real. Our two leaders—vibrant, accomplished women themselves—opened up our packs and pulled out our change of shorts, our extra bras, our smuggled deodorant. "Dead weight," they told us. We just needed our bodies, the bare essentials, and open hearts.

Even without those confiscated toiletries in my bag, I'll never forget that first hill. Weighted down by forty-pound backpacks, with fierce summer sun on our necks and no slowing of pace, we pressed upward on hot, untried legs. This was no pine-shaded picnic. I was sticky and my hips were bruised and sore. Every few miles someone new would confess to a heel or a toe beginning to rub raw, and we would collectively dive on it, plaster it with moleskin, then rise and edge warily down the trail again, knowing that any of us could be the next casualty. I had to remind myself that we were here—as Joie Armstrong wrote in a poem once—to "gulp life." We'd come to celebrate the blisters alongside the beauty.

In this wildest of all classrooms, we learned together. We found that we were young women in the most powerful sense of that identity: strong, independent, and joyous. As we refilled our bottles from moving streams and took turns finding the route for the day, we saw that what we couldn't carry on our own backs, we didn't really need. What sustained us those two weeks were stars and stories, laughter and challenge, and a whole lot of dancing.

As I write this, thirteen courageous groups of Armstrong Scholars have trekked across Yosemite. Some will tell you that the trip was about the physical challenge. Others will say that the beauty of the experience lay in the friendships. But my biggest gift was that of the land itself.

In my journal, neatly folded and outlined in red, I kept a map of our route. It carried us nearly one hundred miles through country that most visitors to Yosemite never even suspect exists. Tracing the path with my finger, the places and the memories come back to life: wading with open arms through sprawling meadows still green with snowmelt; lying awake in our sleeping bags with no tents between us and the bright planets that spun above us; basking in snowfields at the tops of high passes; passing under the shade of trees monumentally older than ourselves; plunging uproariously into clear, cold lake water at the end of a dusty day.

The land came alive for me the most when, late in the journey, we separated from the group and each spent a solitary day and night in the wilderness. Alone with my thoughts, I watched the clouds bunch and unfurl in high, swift winds; watched the birds and chipmunks explore a little ice-melt pond nearby; and waited as the stars appeared one by one above the peaks that encircled my little patch of earth. I listened in the night to the sound of lapping tongues on nearby streamlets, to the soft patterings of tiny paws on the sand by my ears, and to the slow, muffled footsteps of my own heart against the walls of my sleeping bag. That night, my soul opened wide. Nestled against the living land, I felt that I had found a home.

At adventure's end, we hiked out Sonora Pass by the light of the constellations, climbed onto a bus, and scattered out into the waiting world. Each of us continued our journey in different directions. I still carry that landscape in my heart and in my imagination, and I like to think that Yosemite still carries us as well. As profoundly as places shape us, perhaps we shape them, too. Every story we weave in this vast granite cathedral endures in the curve of the rock, in the lift of the trees.

I later returned to work for Yosemite Institute—Joie's workplace. It was my hope to give back to the land I loved so much. Every day, I gulped life. Every day, I showed other young explorers to do the same. I added my own leaf to the story.

I never met Joie, but she changed me. She distilled my love for the earth beneath my feet and for the freedom of fearless exploration—and she changed the story of Yosemite, too. Ours is a story that buzzes now like hidden electricity through all of Yosemite's backcountry, and far beyond—into all the places where her Scholars have gone on to be deep lovers of the wilderness. Just as this light-filled Sierra Nevada range continues to push upward, one powerful inch at a time, Joie's story continues to expand in new hearts and in new corners of this boundless park.

—◆—

"Ah Yosemite! Thy heart holds the secret of the Universe. In spite of ourselves we are stilled by the spirit and grandeur and greatness, until the thrill of the pulse of the Universe is felt and appreciated."

—Cora A. Morse, 1896

Ben-Zee-Nees

Jeanne Antrim

My father-in-law told of his experience with Nic Fiore, from whom he once took a ski lesson. He never forgot the words Nic repeated over and over again, "Benzeenees, benzeenees," probably because it took the entire lesson for him to understand what Nic was saying, and how it related to his lack of ability. Nic, of course, was repeating the skier's mantra "Bend the knees."

When my children, now excellent skiers at twenty-eight and thirty, took their first lessons from Heidi, she reworded Nic's mantra to the now classic Antrim family cheer, "Tall as a tree—small as a bug!" which was yelled exuberantly as the toddlers maneuvered the learner's slope. I expected Heidi to be darling with my children (she was), I expected Heidi to teach my children expertly (she did), what I did not expect was for Heidi to promise to meet Christopher and Shea after lunch, at the chairlift, to take them on a special run, and their first chairlift ride ON HER OWN TIME! They never forgot it. It is the people like Nic and Heidi that continue to make Badger Pass at Yosemite National Park the best family-oriented ski resort in the country.

The Man with the Broken Hip

Jeannie Tasker

D AD WAS IN his forties when he had a bicycle accident and broke his hip. Recovering from his surgery, he discovered that screws, plates, and wires were now holding the hip together. That was March.

By June, Dad's normal restlessness required a camping getaway to Yosemite. Mom packed up the trailer, the three kids, two of our friends, and we headed out of the city for our favorite campsite in old Camp 11 (now Upper Pines). With camp set, chairs around the fire ring, table-cloth on the outdoor table, we decided to check out the rest of the campground.

Lo and behold, Dad's boss from work was also camping there with his wife. He quickly inquired of Dad as to the status of his healing hip. Dad told him that he was doing quite well, that we were planning to hike a couple of trails the next day, and perhaps he would like to join us. Dad's boss, though not an avid hiker, readily agreed.

The next morning, the group assembled (Mom, Dad, three kids, two friends, Dad's boss), and Dad announced that we were planning to hike up to Glacier Point via the historical, two-mile-long Ledge Trail. Once there, we would return via the regular Four Mile Trail. Round trip, six miles.

The two-mile Ledge Trail to Glacier Point closed shortly following our hike, because of its difficulty to maintain and hazard of loose granite on the talus slopes. One climbs swiftly up the canyon wall, easily acquiring breathtaking views across the Valley. Camp Curry, Ahwahnee Meadow, the meandering Merced River, campgrounds and roads, quickly become a real-life diorama.

Some places on the Ledge Trail you have to scramble on all fours, carefully staking out the next foothold. A couple of times, one of us kicked a rock and sent it tumbling, with a warning to those hiking below us. We felt like we were climbing up the route of the old firefall, straight to the top of Glacier Point, although in reality, we skirted the sides of the smooth granite wall over which those hot cinders were tossed.

Exhilaration, relief, and exhaustion overcame us as we reached the top. Moments to relax and relish the view while we enjoyed our packed lunch. Then Dad led us off on the Four Mile Trail of switchbacks back to the Valley floor. Two miles up, four miles down. Total: six miles.

Upon returning to our campsite, tired and dusty, Dad's boss made only one comment: "That's the last time I agree to go on a walk with a man with a broken hip."

A Memorable Summer Day

Leo F. Wurdinger

AT THAT PERIOD in my life when our children had not yet left the nest, we usually spent our leisure time each year visiting different national parks in the western part of the U.S.

Our favorite vacation spot was the fabulous Yosemite Valley, a storehouse of natural wonders, which must be seen to be appreciated. However, it is not the viewing of one of these natural treasures, awe inspiring as they may be, that remains paramount in my memory.

In 1962, we were camping in our most desired location, campsite number 11, where we frequently met other vacationers who came to the same area year after year.

One day, in mid-August, a park ranger car equipped with a loudspeaker, drove past the various campgrounds, announcing that a famous personality would arrive by helicopter late in the day, and we were all invited to welcome the distinguished visitor to the park.

At the designated time, hundreds of us lined the roadway to The Ahwahnee. The identity of the incoming visitor had yet not been disclosed and, as you can imagine, caused considerable speculation among us.

Eventually several automobiles could be seen, traveling very slowly toward us. As the entourage came closer, it could be seen that the leading car was a convertible with the top down. The passenger in the rear seat was finally recognized. It was President John F. Kennedy, smiling, very healthy looking, and extremely handsome.

As his car came closer, my wife raised her arm intending to wave as he passed by. Unexpectedly, he turned toward her, reached out as far as he could, grasped her hand, and gave it a brief, but definite shake.

Needless to say, she was ecstatic, and this incident became the centerpiece of many future conversations, and it became even more important to her after the president was assassinated in Dallas a short time later. In retrospect, all of this put into its proper place, is my recollection of a memorable summer day.

The Trail Builder
(in Honor of Jim Snyder)

Robert Pavlik

He builds his story in stone
where others are pathless,
he makes his own.
Through forests verdant
and meadows small
he shapes the rock
to build the wall.
Stone, sand, and wood
muscle, sweat, and steel
human desire and nature's goods
link the artificial world with the real.
So that others can find
their own place of peace
the Trail Builder leads
the way to release.

In Memory of My Dad

Rosanna Morris

"Climb the mountains and get their good tidings.
Nature's peace will flow into you as sunshine
flows into trees."
—John Muir, *Our National Parks*, 1901

My dad, James H. McMillin, as a teacher at the junior college level, instructing students in natural history, took a group of students each August to spend a week at Yosemite National Park in the seventies. His goal was to teach appreciation and respect for all that is wild in our natural world. I accompanied him, along with other family members to take part in the beauty Yosemite had to offer on these trips over forty years ago. My fondest memories as a child are of climbing into the alpine regions of Yosemite, pika, swimming in Tenaya Lake, our vehicle overheating on the climb up into the park, fifty-cent gasoline. Yosemite carved a place in my soul that will remain with me through eternity. Thank you, Dad!

The Naturalist, Indian Mary, and My Grandmother

Rosemary Dealey Woodlock

My mother was born in Yosemite Valley in a tent in the snow on Christmas Day, 1920—almost! Or so my grandmother Marie told me.

I'd say that's why love of Yosemite is in my genes. This story involves national park advocate and naturalist Enos Mills; Yosemite Valley celebrity Mary Johnson-Wilson, known as "Indian Mary"; my grandparents George and Marie Dealey; their daughter Martha Elizabeth, two years old; Marie's mother, M. E. "Mama" Drake, fifty-three, and sister Gladys, twenty-one.

My grandparents met Enos in 1917 in Estes Park, Colorado, while on their wedding trip. Enos was the driving force behind Rocky Mountain National Park and had just completed his guidebook, *Your National Parks*, where he described Yosemite as one of the great scenic wonders of the world, inspiring Marie to vow to visit someday.

In 1920, George and Marie, now with Martha Elizabeth, were living in Dallas, Texas. Gladys was finishing at the University of Kansas. An automobile trip would be her graduation present and an opportunity for Mama, Marie, and Martha Elizabeth to escape the summer heat in those days before air-conditioning.

The four ladies left immediately after graduation. With Marie and Gladys taking turns driving, they made good time, arriving from the eastern side of the park and catching their first breathtaking views of Yosemite Valley. They were soon settled in a tent cabin at Camp Curry in Yosemite Valley and ready to explore this enchanted place.

The spicy smell of Yosemite was invigorating. The sense of community among the campers was welcoming and fun. They enjoyed the camaraderie around the large campfires and watched the spectacular firefall off Glacier Point at night.

Enos was in the park, setting up the interpretive program with John Muir. Mama and Gladys, avid hikers, went on all the nature walks that were offered. One hike went from the Valley floor 3,200 feet up the steep cliff trail to Glacier Point.

Once there, Gladys wanted her picture taken on the spot where the coals were pushed over the edge to make the firefall at night. She posed on the ledge as shown in the impressive photo taken by Mama with her Kodak box camera. Years later, I asked Gladys if she had been scared. "Only when my boot slipped on the rock as I was going out!" she replied.

While Mama and Gladys sought out the natural wonders of Yosemite Park, Marie and Martha Elizabeth explored some of the interesting people who were visiting the park. They saw Leopold, former king of the Belgians. Marie met a couple who were great friends of Enos. This Mrs. Roberson fascinated Marie in that she wore the same practical khaki hiking skirt and blouse most of the other women wore, but with long strands of large natural pearls set off with a scattering of diamond broaches.

"Indian Mary," said to be a member of a Yosemite tribe, was also part of the scene, offering skillfully made baskets for sale. Marie bought several baskets and actively encouraged other visitors to buy the larger, more expensive ones. Their friendship developed over time, with Marie hugely enjoying her unofficial status as assistant salesperson and Mary profiting from the increased sales.

I have since learned that Mary lived next to the infirmary. She was Chukchansi Yokut on her mother's side, Spanish on her father's. The Yokut, Miwok, and Paiute tribes of California were renowned for their refined basketry. The baskets that Mary was selling were authentic American Indian art and are especially prized today.

Marie liked Mary and admired her enterprise. Marie especially envied Mary's convenient lack of English whenever she wanted to avoid answering questions because Marie too loved telling enhanced—but never untrue—stories herself. And this story turned out to be one of Marie's best.

As the end of summer and the closing of the park drew near, the Robersons told Marie that they were going to stay through the winter with Enos and asked if her family wanted to join them. The Mills party planned on staying in tents on the Valley floor. Marie, then six months pregnant, thought about how hot even Yosemite Valley was then and how much hotter and exhausting the drive back to Texas would be.

So Marie wrote to George, saying that they would stay over the winter in their warm tent in the snow. Indian Mary "at the infirmary" could deliver the baby, and Marie would see him in the spring as soon as the snow melted and they could get out.

Marie's story reveals odd discrepancies. First, in all the references to Indian Mary, not one said she was a midwife. Second, Marie hated snow: she hated it in Kansas where she grew up; she hated it in Dallas after she married. Finally, Marie stayed in a nursing home for a month after the birth of Martha Elizabeth and would for her six other children as a "vacation" from housekeeping. Having a child under pioneer conditions did not sound like the grandmother I knew.

But the letter she wrote had an immediate effect on George. If anyone kept records in those days of the fastest time to Yosemite from Dallas by train and Yosemite Transportation Company bus, George set it.

Once in Yosemite, he spent little time admiring the scenery, no time taking nature walks or photographs, and hardly any time singing around the campfire. He packed up Marie and the others so as to get out of Yosemite well before snow could close the roads into the Valley.

George drove the car lickety-split straight back to Dallas. So their first trip ended in plenty of time for my mother to be born on Christmas Day, but in a hospital in Dallas—just as Marie really intended when she wrote to George about her plans to spend the winter in Yosemite.

Raffi Bedayn: Rock Climber, Inventor, Advocate

Tom Gardner

YOSEMITE'S CLIMBING RANGERS have a unique method of interacting with their customers: they serve coffee, tea, and hot chocolate to rock climbers on Sunday mornings from May through September. In May, June, and September, it is served in Camp 4, the climber's camp, just west of the Yosemite Lodge. Not far from where the crowd assembles is a brass plaque that commemorates Camp 4's listing on the National Register of Historic Places in 2003. The beverages are dispensed next to the famous Columbia Boulder, and atop a granite slab memorial with the name and dates, "Raffi Bedayn 1915–1982" inscribed on it. Obviously, to be so honored in America's second oldest national park, that person must have been an extraordinary individual. I was privileged to have learned skiing, backpacking, and basic rock climbing from Raffi Bedayn on Boy Scout field trips in the early 1960s. His memorial in Yosemite Valley is a testament to just how highly admired he was. His life story is all-American.

Raffi's parents were lucky to have left Armenia when they did. His father came first and when enough money had been saved, he sent passage money for his bride. Raffi was born in California in 1915. His parents operated a grocery store in San Francisco, so it was easy for young Raffi to become interested in the Sierra Club social activities after he graduated from high school. These included skiing at Sugar Bowl, High Sierra camping trips, mountaineering expeditions all over the West, and a style of free rock climbing called bouldering. It was at one of these bouldering events at Cragmont Rock Park in Berkeley that he met the love of his life, Barbara.

In the mid-1930s, advanced rock-climbing techniques from the Alps were introduced to the U.S.A., and Raffi was an eager student. This involved more than just a rope; hardware such as wedge-shaped pitons and oval rings called carabiners allowed climbers to scale cliffs previously off-limits. Raffi was involved in several first ascents inside Yosemite Valley, and in 1939, participated in the first ascent of Shiprock in New Mexico. One of his partners was David Brower, who in later years served as president of the Sierra Club.

Like everyone else of his age, Pearl Harbor changed everything, and Raffi enlisted in February 1942. The army soon recognized his talents, and sent him to the newly forming Tenth Mountain Division, at Camp Hale, near Leadville, Colorado. He and Barbara were married on Christmas Day, 1942, and honeymooned near Aspen. By mid-1943, the army realized excellent training for the coming Italian campaign could be found in the headwaters of the Potomac River in West Virginia and established a large maneuver area that covered most of three counties surrounding the town of Elkins, West Virginia. Raffi was one of fifteen soldiers sent to form a rock-climbing school at a place called Seneca Rocks. His Shiprock climbing buddy, David Brower, was second in command; First Lieutenant Bedayn handled duties as supply officer. In the next year, thousands of GIs passed thru their camp for two weeks training in rock climbing, and about seventy-five thousand pitons were pounded into the surrounding Tucsarora Formation.

Two major events happened in the summer of 1944: a son, Richard, and D-day, which meant the end of training; soon all their mountaineering skills would be put to a more severe test. The Seneca Rocks School was closed, all but about one thousand pitons were recovered, and the instructors were dispersed to the three infantry regiments that formed the Tenth. By December of 1944, the division was in Italy, about to earn a combat record second to none, in some of the most difficult terrain in the entire European Theater. Its battles and distinguished veterans are well documented; Captain Bedayn came home with a Bronze Star, awarded for leading a week-long reconnaissance mission behind German lines.

The postwar years must have been thrilling for Barbara and Raffi. Returning to Barbara and baby Richard in early 1946, Raffi landed a job at University of California–Berkeley in maintenance and repair. Evenings, he studied toward obtaining a contractor's license. Raffi, now a family man, welcomed sons Rod, then Greg, and finally a daughter, Kathy. In 1950, he received his general contractor's license and began a very successful career in the San Francisco Bay Area.

The postwar years were exciting in the rock-climbing arena as well. New equipment, such as shoes, ropes, and other gear, was coming into use; Raffi made his contribution by first designing, and then manufacturing, carabiners made from aluminum alloy 7075-T6. This eliminated about five pounds from the usual climbing load, an important saving greatly appreciated by his customers. The Bedayn Carabiner became the standard for rock- and mountain-climbing enthusiasts around the world. They were used in the first ascent of Mount Everest in 1953, and by the first American Everest expedition in 1963, led by Jim Whittaker. Jim and Raffi were old friends, so it was a really big event when Jim gave a private slide show for Raffi, the Boy Scouts, and their dads.

Raffi retired from active climbing in 1966 and then phased out the contracting business. In the spring of 1972, the Yosemite Lodge wanted to expand and set their sights on bulldozing Camp 4, plus there were rumblings about an outright ban on rock climbing in the Valley. Raffi, on behalf of the American Alpine Club, spearheaded the fight for the preservation of Camp 4, continued Valley climbing, and getting the National Park Service more involved with the climbing community. He was successful on all three counts, and the Camp 4 memorial recognizes his efforts in leading that fight. Raffi continued skiing until shortly before his death in February of 1982. His funeral was attended by over three hundred people. David Brower sent a eulogy via videotape. Following the service, the family was astonished by the dozens of former Boy Scouts in attendance, many of whom reported that Raffi was a great role model for them, second only to their own fathers. Son Greg, now deceased, began the drive to erect the Camp 4 memorial in 1983 and saw it installed a few years later. Barbara passed away in 1997.

Camp 4's preservation has been guaranteed by its listing on the National Register of Historic Places, something that would please Raffi. That his memorial is used for Climber Coffee would please him even more.

Merced River Dad

Carol Eve Ford

I HIKE THE MIST TRAIL.
Everywhere I look, my father is here:
in the strength, the steadfastness of the massive granite places,
each carved with exquisite detail, delicious variety,
each named and remembered in awe and in fondness;
he is here in the intricacy of the lichens on the rocks
and the flashing mica gold in the white-sandy pools,
the rich emerald green of the mighty Merced
as she sweeps and dives over the polished granite,
plunges down the glacial cuts and slides.
He is here in the humble, dusty trails,
in the sweet smell of vanilla in the deep cracks of the
        Jeffrey pine bark.
He is here,
in the wonder of the falls,
in the breathtaking majesty of their roaring foam,
their silent mists.
He is here,
in his fishing hat and vest,
corduroy jeans and high-topped boots,
carrying a pack I can't even pick up empty,
full of everything we need—
carrying it as if it were nothing, up the rugged rocky trails,
always a quiet voice, a gentle presence on the path.
Steady, powerful, and boyish, he casts his fly into the clear pools,
happy, intense, and sure like the quick bright brook trout
        themselves.

This is where we have him to ourselves—where we see who he
    really is—
where we are of one piece—with him, with each other,
with the water, with the granite.

Gus

David Worton

I'LL CALL HIM "GUS." When we met he was setting up camp where the Clark Fork of the Illilouette crosses the Merced Pass Trail. My friends and I had stopped for a late lunch on our first day out, ready to leave the trail for the next eight days heading cross-country for Thousand Island Lake. Gus explained that he was on the penultimate hike to meet his goal of walking all of Yosemite's trails. Having never backpacked before his fifties, he was a dozen years into this quest, and had only one additional section of trail left that he hoped to finish later that summer. Gus had no friends who backpacked and had logged all those trail miles on his own.

We were impressed, but so was he as we traced our intended route on the map across the trail-less landscape to the east. In fact, there were two parallel trails in our way that we intended to cross, but not follow, in the upper Merced drainage. Gus was heading over Red Peak Pass on one of them. As we shouldered our packs to set out into a partially burned but trackless meadow, I said, "Well, maybe we'll see you out there." Just the kind of thing that backcountry travelers say to one another.

We saw only one other party a week later before returning to the trail, in the beautiful wilds of the North Fork of the San Joaquin after leaving the park by crossing over Electra Peak. The first few days we traveled at a leisurely pace crossing Gray Peak Pass, heading the upper Gray Peak Fork and then over to and down the Red Peak Fork of the Merced.

I love to hike off-trail in Yosemite and have done so, often alone, especially in the northwest corner. By some odd chance I had managed to put a party of eight together for this adventure in the southeast. Since we hadn't yet begun the inevitable discussion about what we were going to eat when we got out, Gus came up in conversation. Here he was, on his own, close to completing his mission that sent him literally into the grooves of the trail system, and here we were a large group whose goal was to avoid the trail altogether.

The morning of day five started with crossing the Merced and hopping over the River Trail into the Lyell Fork of the Merced. Though steep, it was easily passable. We stopped for a swim in a deep round pool below one of the many beautiful falls the Merced drainage seems to have in abundance. We continued climbing and as it got close to noon we approached our "step-over" of the High Trail. And there he was coming down the trail—"Gus! I told you we'd see you out there."

Memories of a Summer Trip to Yosemite in 1917

Marilyn Tower Oliver

IN 1917 MY MOTHER, Ruth Scott Tower, age sixteen, and her family took a vacation from their goat farm in Coulterville to visit Yosemite National Park. She recorded her experiences in her diary she called "Diary of a Country Jake." The follow are excerpts from the diary.

August 2

Here we are in Camp 7—the grandest place. We have two tents and are about seven feet from the Merced River, and everything looks painfully messy and campy. People are camping in all sides of us and are very friendly, too. Camp Curry is a little way across the river.

Right in front of us is big Glacier Point. It is so painfully high and every night they drop fire from the top. I bet we have the grandest vacation.

August 3

The next morning I'm sitting on a box in front of our little camp stove. The river is about three feet from me. It rained last night and our "duds" all got damp.

Last night we went to the entertainment in Camp Curry and saw the firefall from Glacier Point about four thousand feet high. It was beautiful. Afterward we went to the dance. My! Such a love of a floor. It is maple.

Just as we entered the door, someone grabbed my arm and said, "I know those girls." It was John Dupolly. He is nice and wore the swellest outfit. He is a wonderful dancer and gave me several new one-step tips and said I was a dandy little dancer.

August 4 at four-thirty in the afternoon.

Oh, Lord! My feet. We only walked eleven miles this morning. Went over to Happy Isles and started up the trail to Vernal Fall. We never dreamed it was so far. And after we started we wouldn't turn back. The trail was almost straight up and nothing but ledges to walk on. It was three and a half miles up and the same way back.

The fall was beautiful. It falls about eight hundred feet. There is about a half mile called the Mist Trail. The water falls on the trail all the time.

August 6

Almost breakfast time.

Yesterday I met a good-looking ranger. We talked about half an hour. Then I came back to camp and made fudge. We went bathing in the river. I borrowed the perfect love of a bathing suit. It was white-and-green jersey and had a bright orange cap. I met an awfully cute fellow from across the river. I think he took my picture. The folks are going to Bridalveil Fall, but I'm going over to my new friend's camp. She invited me over for dinner.

August 7

I'm all in after a hike to Glacier Point. My heel is blistered and I'm sunburned. I feel like the last rose of summer. We met the nicest young fellow today—tall, good looking, from San Francisco. He walked a ways with me and helped me over the bad rocks. He carved this on my walking stick. "R.S. (my initials)/LWW (his initials), 1917." He dances and maybe we will see him tonight. I wonder if I can dance with a blistered heel. I'm going to take a nap 'cause I can hardly keep my eyes open.

August 8

I had a dandy time last night at the Camp Curry dance. I danced the first and last dance with Ed and most of the other ones, too. He didn't give the others a chance. He treated me to an ice cream twice. He sure is nice—real citified and has a college education. He's just a little too mushy. He just keeps squeezing my hand. If I had the least bit of nerve I would tell him to stop it. He asked me to "drop him a line when we get home," but I won't. If he wants to he can write to me, but I doubt that Mom will let me answer it. Another guy talked to me for half an hour. He's from San Francisco, too. I think he must be past twenty. I would really like to ask him how old he is. He asked me if I would go to Bridalveil Fall with him. He said he would bring over his "Overland" car. I never dreamed that I could go, but I said "Yes" without thinking. When I told the folks, they threw a purple fit. Said I couldn't go and to tell him any old thing to get out of it. They said they didn't know a thing about him. Now I'm in a real pickle of a fix. I'm going to tell him the truth. I wonder if he'll write to me. He is awfully nice and tall and good looking.

Later I told him the truth, and he was just as nice as can be. Said he understood. He has a sister and said his mother never allowed her to go out with strange fellows. He said "I'll drop you a card once in a while." Mom says I shan't answer any of them. I wonder if he really will write.

August 9

We're on our way back to Coulterville. We're stuck on the road about fourteen miles from Yosemite. Dad's cleaning the spark plugs. I've walked up most of the hill around here. Gee! How I hated to leave Yosemite. It was so much fun. I'm so sad I almost bawled. I'm glad I've got you, Mr. Diary. Even if you are only old wood pulp, it helps to tell my troubles to someone.

"I have spent the happiest months of
my life in this glorious valley."

--Hon. Therese Yelverton, Lady Avonmore, 1869

Walking from San Francisco to Yosemite in the Footsteps of John Muir

Peter and Donna Thomas

In the summer of 2005 Donna was backpacking the John Muir Trail, a 212-mile hiking route that travels along the crest of California's Sierra Nevada mountain range from Yosemite Valley to Mount Whitney. Donna was hiking with a bunch of veteran backpackers. They would hike and talk for hours, telling stories and making plans for future hikes. One day, just on the way out of Evolution Basin toward Muir Pass, talk turned to backpacking gear and food. One of them said, "You know, John Muir would just grab a loaf of bread, put some tea in his pocket, throw a coat over his shoulder and walk to Yosemite. . . ." It's the story Donna had heard before, but this time she heard something more in it, maybe it was a call from Muir in the wind whispering down the pass, and she said to everyone, "I want to do that. I want to step out my door and walk to Yosemite."

When Donna got home she told me what she decided to do. I surprised her by saying that I wanted to go, too. I say *surprised*, because even though we had enjoyed camping and backpacking together, I preferred surfing to hiking and had rarely shown interest in long-distance walking or walking for pleasure. But this idea: to walk across California, to walk in John Muir's footsteps, it intrigued me. It intrigued us both. Would it still be possible to get to Yosemite on foot? Donna felt sure it was and vowed to find someone who had already done it and mapped out the route. We could then leave on the trip the next spring.

But we could not find anyone who had ever retraced Muir's 1868 trek to Yosemite. We wondered if it could still be done, and decided to find out. We had often driven to Yosemite, and knew what the trip was like in a car. We wondered what it would be like to walk: what we would see and experience as we took the trip at a human pace.

In six months we had gathered enough information to determine Muir's actual route. What we found was a bit discouraging: the little dirt roads Muir had followed in 1868 were now mostly paved roads, busy city streets, or highways. But by this time we were committed to walking in Muir's footsteps. Donna wanted to just go ahead, even if it meant walking on asphalt. She thought to take our time, go slowly, look closely, use "John Muir's eyes" to see California and appreciate nature the way he did.

We started studying more maps trying to find some other option. A map from the San Francisco Bay Trail Project revealed the existence of a public walking/cycling path along the edge of the bay just a few miles to the west of Muir's actual route. We then noticed similar trail systems running along the Guadalupe River and the Coyote Creek through Santa Clara County. It seemed that with minor detours on city streets we would be able to get all the way from Oakland to Morgan Hill on trails.

In that instant the whole thing fell together. Just as Muir did not follow the expected route to Yosemite, we would not follow his exact footsteps. We would walk to Yosemite parallel to Muir's route, not on roads, but on public pathways, bike trails, nature trails, through city, county, state, and national parks and open spaces, so that we could experience a natural California. If we had to we would use sidewalks or little streets, or even busy roads, but we would walk in the spirit of his trip rather than in his exact footsteps, always trying to find the places that still looked and felt like the California Muir experienced in 1868. Our goal would be to always stay within a few physical miles of his route but we would stray to visit wild places. We would make it a walk through history, reading other travel accounts from California in the late 1800s to better understand what Muir would have seen and experienced. We would make it a "scouting party" to find an "urban backpacking" route that would give nature-loving Bay Area residents a way to walk where they usually drove in cars. We were so excited we could already imagine a future with little hostels and cafes springing up along our new route to house and feed travelers on the trek to Yosemite.

We left San Francisco on April 2, 2006, the same day Muir had left, but 138 years later. We then spent the next month walking to Yosemite following the three-hundred-mile "Muir Ramble Route" we had mapped out. Just like Muir, we began our trip by taking the ferry to Oakland. We followed the Bay Trail's intermittent bike paths south through Alameda County, then passed through the Santa Clara Valley following the Coyote Creek and Guadalupe River corridors. We backpacked over the Diablo range on hiking trails through Henry Coe State Park, crossed the San Joaquin Valley beside irrigation ditches, and climbed the Sierra Nevada foothills on a combination of small rural roads and busy highways. From Coulterville we backpacked on dirt and gravel roads through national forest land, and finally descended into the Yosemite Valley via Crane Flat and Tamarack Flat on wilderness hiking trails.

The trip was about three hundred miles and took about thirty days. With Muir as our guide we saw how much California has changed. In 1868 California had few people, few buildings, and very few roads. The roads helped travelers on foot, horseback, or stage to cross the mostly undeveloped landscape. Now there are many more roads but much less open space. The irony is that today it's actually harder to walk across California than it was a hundred years ago. Freeways, private property, and lack of accommodations in rural areas make it tough for the self-powered traveler. Our 2006 trip convinced us we had to do something to help the public reclaim the right and routes to walk across California. What we did was write *The Muir Ramble Route*, which is a guidebook for walking from San Francisco to Yosemite in the footsteps of John Muir.

John Muir

Lucas Lynch

To log for the timber was their horrible ploy,
to break, to take, and eventually destroy
But a man stood in their path, he stood in their way,
he would not give up, not even a day.
They fought and fought but defeat they could not,
this man would not budge, nor would he be bought.
Because this land of such natural splendor and beauty,
was in need of protection and he felt it his duty.
He pleaded and pleaded and wrote many a letter,
to the people who could change things for the better.
He brought people with vision and power to see,
what the wonderful peaceful place could be.
One of the men to which he pleaded,
stood before Congress and could not be defeated.
On this great country this man left his mark,
when Yosemite became a national park.

4

OUR
SECOND
HOME

Is This My Forest?

Michael Frye

IT SEEMS SO obvious now. Yes, of course we should set aside special places and preserve them for future generations. What else would we do with them?

But until Congress and President Lincoln gave Yosemite to the State of California for just that purpose in 1864, it had never been done before. In Europe, all land was privately owned except for a few city parks. In America, the government held land only temporarily until it could be homesteaded, ranched, or mined. Preserving natural landscapes for public enjoyment was a new and radical idea.

My son, Kevin, grew up in Yosemite Valley, that tract of land that Lincoln, Congress, and visionaries like Galen Clark and John Conness had the foresight to preserve. I worked as a freelance photographer, and my wife, Claudia, managed The Ansel Adams Gallery. We lived in a small house attached to the back of the gallery, where Ansel and Virginia Adams once lived. Kevin attended the small elementary school in the Valley.

Kevin grew up right underneath Yosemite Falls, the tallest waterfall in North America. He could see the park's most famous icon, Half Dome, every day if he cared to look. Of course he didn't notice the scenery— he'd grown up with it, and the cliffs and waterfalls were the everyday backdrop to his life. But Kevin could roam freely in this publicly owned landscape. He loved to play in the woods and along the river. He learned to swim in the chilly waters of the Merced River, underneath the three-thousand-foot granite face of El Capitan.

As a teenager he and his friends walked and rode their bikes throughout Yosemite Valley, and went swimming in the wild Merced River nearly every summer day. They were joined by thousands of visitors, all walking through the woods, swimming in that cold river, hiking, climbing, and lying in the meadows gazing up at the waterfalls. No fences or Keep Out signs hindered their movements or enjoyment of this beautiful Valley.

When Kevin was little we often made long road trips to wildlife refuges or other national parks. Coming home, usually late at night, we would ascend into the mountains from the farmlands of California's Central Valley with Kevin asleep in the backseat. But then he would wake up, smell the pine-scented air, look out at the tall conifers lit by the headlights, and, sensing he was close to home, ask, "Is this my forest?" And we would answer, yes, Kevin, this is your forest. We're almost home.

And even though Kevin no longer lives in Yosemite, it's still his forest, his river, his mountains. And mine, and yours, too.

———◆———

"I will state to the Senate that this bill proposes to make
a grant of certain premises located in the Sierra Nevada
mountains, in the State of California, that are
for all public purposes worthless, but which constitute,
perhaps, some of the greatest wonders of the world."

—Senator John Conness on the proposed
Yosemite Grant, 1864

How to Win Friends and Impress Anybody

Michelle Stone

I IMPATIENTLY ENVIED HANG GLIDER pilots launching from Glacier Point one early Sunday morning on my first visit to Yosemite. Imagine soaring above the Valley strapped to gossamer butterfly wings. Eagerly inspired, I found a group of interested flyers and immediately learned how to hang glide. Hang gliding gave me an unmatched sense of scale. Winging the crisp morning air at seven thousand feet, suspended under a slight framework of aluminum tubes and brightly colored nylon showed just how small the world could be. You catch a bit of this thrill by walking out to Glacier Point and peeking down the sheer cliff into the Valley. Sadly, the park suspended hang gliding from the point in the late eighties after a pilot broke his leg in a clumsy landing.

So, unlike most other rambunctious pilots who moved on, I became an amateur astronomer and relocated to the Yosemite area to pursue my new interest with a different type of adventure seekers. We have some of the finest dark skies here in the country. In the anxious pursuit of galaxy hunting, I acquired a telescope.

The normal human brain can't fully appreciate or comprehend the complete scale of the park's natural wonders. All one can do is stare up . . . way up, and gawk. Yes. That's what we do. Sadly, gawking only provides a partial experience. Getting a closer peek gives you a delightful sense of scale for our colossal spectacles.

My brother and his teenage son had come to visit and we were planning some short backpacking trips in the backcountry. It was the first time I took a telescope out to Glacier Point. I set up the tripod and carefully inserted a quality eyepiece. Before I had finished putting the gear together, twenty people stood in line for a peek. I trained the scope on the top of Half Dome where eager hikers walked about, exploring a part of Yosemite that few get to see. My brother patiently waited, the last in line, to look through the eyepiece. He was shocked to see people on top of the dome, invisible to our naked eyes. The rock now showed its true scale with people on it. They were natural yardsticks we could comprehend.

"You can go up there?" he asked anxiously.

"Of course," I answered. "If you'd like, we can do it easily in a couple of days. We can get a backpacking permit to stay in Little Yosemite Valley. Or, if you want a killer workout, we can do it all in one." I'd been backpacking with anyone who'd go with me for years and was anxious to take him there.

My brother, aged forty, exclaimed, "Wow I want to go there. Mom would never let us go up there!" I laughed so hard I started to cough.

So, without mother's permission, we secured a reservation and made the trip. The climb to the top of Half Dome is a favorite topic of conversation with my nephew to this day, some seventeen years later. He never realized just how big Half Dome was until he hiked to the top.

As I grew older and was forced to give up backpacking, I renewed my old interest in photography. I knew I'd never be an Ansel Adams, but that wasn't the point. It gave me an excuse to engage with new friends, organize expeditions, and get back to the park more often. I acquired a better telescope and started taking it with me on every excursion. I still set up on Glacier Point from time to time, but I discovered people were much more interested in watching climbers on the vertical face of El Capitan.

Visitors stand out in the Valley's grassland anytime of every day straining and squinting to pick out climbers on the cliff's face. Yes, they are a captive audience and don't even know. It sometimes takes me two or three trips to carry the equipment out to the Valley floor from the parking space. I promise first peek to the first honest-looking family I find, if they'll watch the equipment. Oftentimes they offer to help carry equipment from the car. The big refractor, the real investment, is of course the last package to make its way out into the grassy area. I never need to ask help to take the equipment back.

For the two hours or so I have the scope set up, scores of people watch the climbers scale the sheer cliffs, shimmy up the cracks, or set up their slings to cocoon themselves in for the night. You can't beat that kind of entertainment. And . . . there are no commercials.

I can't tell you how many hundreds of people have looked through my telescopes. I can tell you these visitors represent every part of the world. I practice my Spanish with some and get by with Portuguese and Italian. The difficulties with other languages are easily overcome with smiles of appreciation and warm handshakes of human gratitude.

I've discovered over the years that it wasn't my ever-increasing number of hobbies that kept me coming back to the park. No. . . . hang gliding, back packing, photography, astronomy, and even botany were only inventions and excuses to return and share with humanity the love I have for this nature. My hobbies change, but the love I have for Yosemite's wonders remains eternal. I stay in touch via email with many of my acquaintances. I have new friends from around the globe. They always remember the lady with the hang glider, backpack, camera, dichotomous plant guide, or telescope who challenged them to truly expand their perception of the best granite on the planet.

Generations

Alyson White

My story of Yosemite starts decades before I was even born. My grandma's family grew up in San Francisco, and Yosemite was a favorite destination. The number one story of my grandma's is about her brother doing a handstand on Glacier Point. I've been told there's proof via a photo but I am still searching for this picture.

The tradition of Yosemite continued with my mom, who introduced all of its glories to my dad.

My first trip to Yosemite was at six months old. There is slightly unnerving photographic proof of me in a shady harness on my dad's back as he climbs the Mist Trail. I just can't imagine being confident with a child in such a contraption.

I like to reflect more on the pictures of me and my sisters year after year at Tunnel View, where the only parts of the picture that changes each year are me, my sisters, and our clothes.

But really, any picture of me at a young age in Yosemite gives me a sense of pride. I don't know what the reason is exactly—but the fact that I have been going to Yosemite every couple of years, sometimes less often, sometimes more often, makes me proud.

For the first dozen or so trips, my family was able to get Cabins 26A and 26B in Camp Curry. We would paint watercolor pictures of Half Dome and waterfalls and feed the squirrels. . . . Back then we didn't know any better—I swear!

I recall the flooding in 1997, which was also the first year we decided to try out Housekeeping Camp because we couldn't get our typical cabin in Curry. When we arrived, we found out that Housekeeping Camp was flooded but LUCKILY they had room for us at the tent cabins in Curry. We were lucky for two reasons: 1) We were able to continue our vacation; 2) We didn't have to stay in Housekeeping Camp.

I also recall a time when getting cabins got harder and harder, and then there was the big rockslide that closed even more precious cabins. To this day my family wishes we could sign a waiver to stay in those abandoned cabins.

My fondest memories of Yosemite are visiting The Ahwahnee at dusk, floating down the ice-cold Merced in inner tubes, barbequing at Cathedral, and simply gazing up at the best part of Yosemite—Half Dome!

So what is it about Yosemite that has brought my family back so many times for almost a century? For me it's the sheer awe of the momentous granite mountains, the tranquility of the many waterfalls, the unchanging landscape, and the feeling that my family owns a part of the Valley. We have our trips down to a tee with very little variation. Yosemite is our second home.

Several years ago boyfriends, then fiancés, and now husbands joined us on our travels and this past year we started the next generation's Yosemite story. My sister's three month old came to the park for the first time, and even though she probably couldn't see it, we visited Glacier Point, and just like always, my stomach sunk when I imagined my great uncle doing a handstand on that steep ledge!

Where Are You From?

Katie Wallace

It's inevitable, right? Every time you travel to a place that sees a lot of visitors, you're bound to get that question.

I should know—I live in Yosemite.

So, when the question is posed in my direction, I should see it coming, should have an answer at the ready. Somehow, it trips me up every time. I stammer a bit, mind reeling.

"California." "Central California." "The foothills." "East of Merced." If pressed, I might come up with, "A small town up in the mountains."

It's not that I am ashamed. No, quite the contrary—I am proud to call Yosemite my home.

However, you drop the Y-bomb, and suddenly the pleasant vapidity of get-to-know-you banter veers down an ever-predictable, and utterly confounding path.

"Wow." (The first word of response is always "wow.") "Wow, Yosemite, huh? What's that like?"

"Amazing, drop-dead amazing. Watching the seasons change is my favorite part. Winters of ice and soft, dark light, less visitors but more community, all comes to rest. Spring full of energy and greenery and fuzzy things frolicking and sunshine and skirts and water, water everywhere. Summer brings the hordes back to the Valley and the land sighs a little, but the high country sirens call for talus hopping and sky pilots, and the mountains truly feel like mountains. Fall breathes of cool and warm, leaves falling into place, the mountain makes its "last call" for high adventures before the white blanket returns.

"And I could go on and on about the beauty, but I would be remiss if I didn't mention the people. I came because of the beauty, but I stay because of the community. People have each others' backs—it's small enough where everyone sort of knows everyone, but not quite. It's a degree or two of separation, but not much more. Dogs and children run feral in the street because it's safe. Every two weeks, the taco truck comes into town and that's the biggest social event around for miles. There are probably more down coats and plaid shirts per capita than any other rural area in the state. My neighbors are talented and kind—want to learn a song on the ukulele or practice your Spanish or obtain a killer sourdough starter or figure out how to knit the heel on a sock or make the perfect piecrust? It won't take long to find the perfect person to teach you how. They're also educated and well traveled—run into your neighbor in the street, and you could end up talking for an hour or more about the pros and cons of eating sugar or their eminent bike journey across some landmass.

"And the adventures are never ending. I have a bucket list as long as my arm, of places I want to go, that I couldn't hope to ever complete, and there are always things to add. While living in Yosemite, I've been inspired to push myself to new limits—solo hiking the entire length of the Merced River, running my first fifty miler, and skiing across the Sierra Nevada. The people and serenity of Yosemite cultivate an adventurous spirit, and the potential for personal growth is unlimited.

"And sure, I get fed up with the traffic and crazy driving in the summer, but I try to remember what one of my co-workers once told me: 'What other place in the world do people forget everything they've ever learned about driving because something so beautiful and captivating made them stop in the middle of the road?' And when there are so many visitors that I am late for work behind a string of cars at the entrance station, I fume for a few minutes until I remember how beautiful it is that people are taking advantage of the wonderful American gift of our national parks. If that's not enough to calm my temper, all I have to do is listen to the Merced River flow or catch the late light on Sentinel Rock or wander through a meadow, and I remember why I live here, and all is good again.

"You asked me, 'What's it like?' I have this saying that I use: 'Never a bad day in Yosemite,' and though that's not exactly 100 percent true (because life happens), it comes pretty close."

But I don't say all that.

Their eyes would glaze over and their feet would start tapping in anxious desire of departure, and their husbands and wives would be pulling at their elbows, erstwhile thinking, "Sheesh, it was just a polite small-talk question."

Even if they listened intently to my long-winded soliloquy, I would undoubtedly fall short of all that life in Yosemite means to me. I can't begin to write it all here in an essay, much less share it with a stranger on a thirty-second ride in an elevator in San Francisco.

So, if pressed for my take on what life is like in Yosemite, I give my stock answer with a smirk and a twinkle in my eye:

"What's it like? It's a rough life, but somebody's got to do it. Where are you from?"

I Bleed Granite Gray

Cherie Stephens

MY CONNECTION WITH Yosemite goes back multiple generations, as many visitors might also say. Both my parents vacationed as children in the park with their families during the 1940s and 1950s. In the late 1950s, my dad, Jim Avenell, spent his college summers working as a guide at the High Sierra Camps. He took affluent families to the high camps by mule, enjoying the individuality of each camp and its location. He would tell stories of hiding turkey bones from the previous night's dinner and "finding" them the next day to show the guest and relay some story about the fossil he discovered. He often told me that his favorite camp was Merced Lake. Upon marrying, in 1958, my parents chose Yosemite as a honeymoon destination, staying at the Yosemite Lodge. I spent many summers as a child riding my bike around the Valley, climbing over rocks, camping at Lower Pines campground, Housekeeping Camp, or Curry Village. I remember the firefall, hikes from the Valley to the top of Yosemite, Vernal, and Nevada Falls, and saying good night to Elmer from the campgrounds.

As a history major at University of California–Davis, I focused on U.S. history with an emphasis on California. This gave me the perfect opportunity to work as a "Volunteer-in-Park" at the Pioneer Yosemite History Center during the summers of '81 and '82. I played the real-life character of Elizabeth Hodgdon who, along with her family, brought their cattle from Knights Ferry to Hodgdon Meadow for summer grazing during the 1880s. My job was to engage in conversation with park visitors so that they left with the understanding that not all people were in favor of this proposed national preserve. Visitors would learn that sacrifices were made by a few, in order for future generations to enjoy the park as we know it today. Hodgdon Meadow, located on the northwest side of the park, was included as part of the watershed area that would protect and provide water for the Yosemite Valley waterfalls.

In 1983, my family was fortunate enough to win one of the coveted lottery drawings for the Bracebridge Dinner. We were entertained by the Oakland Symphony and never had I heard before or since a more beautiful rendition of "Oh Holy Night." In 1983, a ticket was eighty dollars per person and was quite an extravagance for our family but completely worth it. The first course of the ten-course meal was foie gras. My brother and I were young and without sophisticated palates. Due to the lavish cost, my mother told us to eat every bite of our dinners. My brother leaned over and said, "This tastes like cat food." We did not know it was an appetizer and that a little would go a long way. . . . My mother had told us to eat every bite.

I have ice skated at Curry Village Ice Rink with my children, attended weddings at the Yosemite Chapel, performed a wedding at Glacier Point, dined on Thanksgiving dinner at The Ahwahnee, rafted the Merced River, skied Badger Pass, skinny-dipped in Ostrander Lake, trekked the High Sierra Camps three times, hiked Half Dome seven times (before permits), been to the top of Clouds Rest, and seen parts of Yosemite that only 2 percent of visitors will ever get to witness.

I organized a group of women to hike Half Dome in September of 2001. It just so happened we were scheduled to hike two weeks after the 9/11 tragedy. We were a flag-carrying, patriotic, bound-together group that challenged itself to be better national anthem–singing hikers. I will never forget holding my old flag, and the entire dome singing "Oh, say, can you see . . ." From this moment the Hiker Chicks were born, and we have been hiking the U.S. national parks ever since.

Upon the passing of my dad in 2007, my mom, Joyce Avenell, at the age of seventy-two, seventy-three, and seventy-four, volunteered during the summer with the Yosemite Association (now Yosemite Conservancy). She lived in a tent, showered at Curry Village, guided and informed guests on the wonders of the Yosemite Valley. We always felt my dad's heart was in the park. So in 2008, my mom, my daughter, and I took a framed vintage photo of him on his mule with a guest and placed it in The Ahwahnee Great Room on a highboy against the wall. It was our little secret, and each time we visited we would round the corner and peer into the room to check to see if "Gramps" was still there. Each time we saw the picture had not been removed, our hearts were filled with joy. His picture remained for eighteen months until the Great Room was redecorated in 2010. My father's name, F. James Avenell, now resides permanently on the wall at the Visitor Center.

Today, my connection is stronger than ever, I am now a vendor in the park. In 2009, I saw an opportunity for a niche I thought I could fill. My husband and I are farmers in Northern California. I make and sell uniquely packaged jam, honey, and gourmet products to the Delaware North Company, who is the concessionaire for Yosemite National Park. Currently my products are at the Village Store, Wawona General Store, the Lodge gift shop, and Curry Village. Not only do I get to play in the park, but I also get to visit many times a year on business. Life is good.

My life's story cannot be told without Yosemite as an integral part. Yosemite has always felt like home, a place to let out a sigh of contentment, a place to share with others, and the place for them to discover its beauty and many wonders as well. Yosemite is magical, I am blessed to have known its glory.

The Jeffrey Pine

Kathy Dubnicka Schneider

IN THE 1950s, wall murals in homes were a design feature. My mom and dad chose a six-by-four-foot mural of a tree growing out of some granite. They worked really hard to mount it carefully and surround it with wooden molding. It was on the wall behind our couch and took up a good portion of that wall. The tree was in every photograph taken if you happened to be sitting on the couch. With a family of seven, that was often. Many years later, my children in tow, we hiked to the top of Sentinel Dome to see the tree in person. I had a catch in my breath when I saw and touched "The Tree." I would call it a spiritual event. On every trip to Yosemite we would hike again to see the tree. When I received the news that it was down, I wept. We still visit Yosemite but I won't hike that dome again.

My memories of that precious Jeffrey pine started when I was four years old and will remain in my mind and heart until I take my final breath. Then I will ask God if the reason Yosemite feels so spiritual is because he really is there all the time. On every trail, in every rock, in the blue sky, in the water, in the air, and in the trees.

Yosemite, My Home

Nina Gassoway

I AM HERE TONIGHT to speak about my home. Now I'm sure you're all going, that's great—your home—what's so special about that? But I promise I will leave you tonight with not even a shadow of a doubt of why this place that I call home is so spectacular, but first we must start at the beginning. What is my home?

Throughout my life I have moved around a lot. I have lived in thirteen different houses in six different states, so it is difficult to name one particular building home. But I can tell you the place I have grown up. A place that has seen me grow, and that I have seen change.

Some people say that "Home is where the heart is." If so, then this place is definitely my home because my heart and soul will always and forever belong there. My home is Yosemite National Park. Right now, I'm sure you are saying, "A park? What kind of weird girl is this?" But please, let me explain.

Yosemite is a national park the size of Rhode Island and is located in the High Sierra of Northern California. It is sprayed by thousand-foot waterfalls and framed by monumental granite formations, including El Capitan, which is the world's largest exposed piece of granite, and Half Dome. It is the most famous glacially carved landscape in the world. And that's just the Valley.

There is the peak-ringed and wildflower-studded Tuolumne Meadows and the giant sequoia redwoods with trunks so large cars could drive through them. There is natural wonder in every corner of Yosemite.

When I was younger and living on the West Coast, we went there practically every summer. Summer without Yosemite is like cookies without milk; incomplete and less desirable. So many of my memories growing up were made in those campgrounds, on those hiking trails, driving around the park listening to John Denver, or floating down the Merced River.

I have hiked to the top of two of the three highest peaks, rode to Half Dome on horseback, bicycled all around the Valley, rafted down the river, and still find new things to do every time I go back for a visit.

It is said that you could hike one trail in Yosemite every day for the rest of your life and never have to hike the same trail twice. The moment I set foot in the park it's as if my soul is instantly set free. Free to gallop through the meadows with the wild mule deer or fly high through the skies with the hawks.

The formations and surroundings of Yosemite are some of God's great work and could never be duplicated by man.

One hundred fifty years ago, a man wrote in his journal about his first sighting of Yosemite, "None but those who have visited this most wonderful Valley can even imagine the awe with which I behold it. As I looked a peculiar exalted sensation seemed to fill my whole being, and I found my eyes in tears and emotion."

I agree. There is some mystical feeling about Yosemite that words or pictures cannot explain. A feeling that lingers with me, always reminding me, that no matter where my house is, THIS is my home.

I Got to Live in Yosemite!

Jane Magee Lundin

WHEN THE CALIFORNIA Teachers Association instituted a pension program, my grandmother, Jane Wilder, started looking for a one-room school where her skills from forty years earlier would be appreciated. This was 1941 and she was sixty-five, but she planned to teach long enough to earn a pension. For three summers I kept her company while she visited possible schools, and we finished each trip with the midweek special at Camp Curry.

It took that long because she wasn't going to take the first school that wanted to hire her. She wouldn't consider a school with outhouses or a stove she'd have to stoke herself. But in 1943 she gladly took the job as principal and upper-grades teacher in the two-room school in Yosemite. I went with her and started sixth grade that fall.

Living in Yosemite was so different from being an only child in San Francisco. It was a small, close community where the same group of kids went to school and Sunday school. Everyone played together and we were all allowed to ride our bikes and hike the trails unsupervised. There were all kinds of firsts for me—from snow to piano lessons.

And then there was Ansel Adams, my classmates' dad. Unforgettable in black lace on Halloween, playing Chopin. Rolling the oranges that had filled out the top of the dress over the piano keys with his left hand. It truly was an enchanted childhood.

Blending Memories

Kelsie Nelson

MORE OFTEN THAN not, people who live near special landmarks have never actually gone to them. How many native New Yorkers have actually been to the Statue of Liberty? How many people of Seattle have been in the Space Needle? I am lucky to be able to say that is not the case for me. I have lived in the Sierra Nevada all my life and I have been to Yosemite countless times. I have always felt blessed to live so close to a place like Yosemite. Every visit to the park has helped me grow closer to my family, and gain a deeper wonder and appreciation for nature.

I have always held a sort of personal ownership over Yosemite. It is my park, my place to show off, to play tour guide. Much of my family would never have had a chance to go if I had not lived close by. When they come to visit, we spend a whole day in the park among the trees, the rivers, the granite, walking the trails, and exploring the sights we want to see.

The beauty of Yosemite is evident before we even step foot in the park. There is a turnout along the road that looks out on the Valley. From there, Half Dome stands tall, dominating the skyline. Its gray body and smooth face rise out over the green of the trees, its presence capturing attention from every wandering eye that looks in its direction. Many times I have posed in front of the wondrous sight, with family that has come from far and wide to share this experience with me. There is just something about Yosemite that makes us leave with a smile and unforgettable memories, and a desire to return.

My memories of the park have blended into one beautiful experience, spanning through all four seasons and natural attractions. One of my favorites is the Mist Trail. I love walking the aged path, winding through the dark trunks of tall trees, squirrels and chipmunks darting this way and that, and climbing up to the base of the great waterfall. I would stand there, eyes gazing up, soaking in the beauty and power as my clothes became drenched in the mist. It is an experience I have had many times, and one I hope to have again.

It is not just the sight of the park that is so moving. It is the feeling I get when I am there. Yosemite is teeming with history and life, a feeling that surrounds me as I travel through. I remember having lunch with my family there. Sitting around a table, resting our legs from a long day of walking, and replenishing the energy lost. We sat there, arguing about what a person from Yosemite would be called. Yosemitian? Yose-mite? Yosematarian? It was a simple, funny little conversation, and yet I remember it so clearly. Yosemite has strengthened my family and brought us closer together. The memories are not only just those of the park, but of the people who were there with me.

The park has a way of blending memories of beauty and love, family and nature, to create something that lives not in the mind but in the heart. A memory to call up in a dark time, a memory to make you laugh, to smile. A treasure to hold close and never forget.

—————

"One of the things I think we witness when we go to the parks is the immensity and the intimacy of time. On the one hand, we experience the immensity of time which is the creation itself. It is the universe unfolding before us. And yet it is also time shared with the people that we visit these places with."

—William Cronon, historian, 2009

Moment of a Lifetime

Julia Easterling

I GREW UP GOING to Yosemite, as my family had a house near Grove-land. I had been in the park many times and had seen the beauty and felt the majesty of the park. I always loved the area and call it "my mountains." I have to return periodically to recharge and breathe the air, which is mixed with the special smell of pine and sage.

One year I went up at Thanksgiving and it snowed. We all had four-wheel drive so we went into the park and bought sleds in the Valley store. We brought the kids to a place where they could play and have fun. We had the whole place to ourselves! The kids were throwing snowballs and sledding down the hill. After a few minutes I noticed that I was alone at the top of the hill. It was SO QUIET AND LOVELY! It is the most beautiful silence I have ever heard. The light was making the snow and ice crystals glimmer and sparkle. . . . It was amazing. The trees had a nice white flocking of snow and the views were magical. I have never forgotten this moment in the park, in my mountains. It is a highlight of my life! Whenever I think of that time I am at immediate peace and my breathing slows a little. What a gift. Thank you, Yosemite! You make me feel the presence of God when I'm with you!

Yosemitebear

Paul Vasquez

I came to Yosemite with my parents when I was a young teen. It had a powerful impact on me, and when I was in my early twenties with a car and money, I came by myself and stayed a week at Camp 4. I was in love and I decided I had to live in this magical Valley. At age twenty-two, I landed a great job with the concessionaire as a firefighter and EMT. After a few months of living in Yosemite I decided I never wanted to leave.

I met a Yosemite Indian woman, an Ahwahneechee who was a direct descendent of Chief Tenaya. We married and had two children. We raised our children in the Yosemite Indian culture with its powerful ceremonies based in the park. In 1988, I purchased land just outside Yosemite and turned it into a farm, and rainbows started coming all the time. I filmed them and put them on YouTube; one of them, of a double rainbow, went viral.

Both of our kids have lived and worked in Yosemite, and with the Indian ceremonies the park is a big part of our lives. My daughter's picture is in the Valley Visitor Center, not too far from Abraham Lincoln and John Muir's photos, as one of today's protectors of Yosemite. She educated herself and is working to preserve the park for the future.

We all love Yosemite. It is a park of our culture, our ceremonies, it is where we live, work, and play. We are fighting to protect and preserve it for the future of humanity. Ah Ho. All my relations.

El Portal Hotel, California
(Yosemite Institute Residence, early 1980s)

Robert Pavlik

It is a small kitchen with two stoves and one sink with a new Formica counter. The sink's drains are filled with bits of lettuce, mushrooms, soup mix, dough, and thin oily soap bubbles, the strainers tilted to release the water from their bloated contents. The counter is virtually unseen, covered with clean and dirty dishes, cups, knives, plates, cast-iron skillets, battered aluminum pots. Two or three people are crowded at the small basin, with water running and splashing on their pants and on the floor, the green streaked linoleum looking like a melting forest floor.

A portable radio perched on one of the kitchen chairs (red vinyl with chrome legs, the seat suspended in air by the chrome bars that sweep from the floor up and under the seat and behind the back) plays a mockingbird variety of music—jazz, rock, soul, funk, reggae, Glenn Miller's "In the Mood." People move to the sounds, their synapses clicking to guitars and saxes and clarinets. Seven, ten people are busily engaged in food production for their Yosemite Institute housemates, the occupants of this old two-story building that sits alongside Highway 140 and the Merced River, on the western boundary of Yosemite National Park. Knives are chopping scented garlic, can openers are chewing the tops off tomato cans, sandy-colored dough is rising under coarse-grained cloth, cheese and lettuce and mushrooms and onions dabble their muted colors with carrots and beets and broccoli. Bowls filled and half filled with assorted ingredients are scattered on the small wooden tables and counters. The human inhabitants, clothed in blue cotton denim and gray wool and tan cotton and plaid long tails, carry on conversations about the food, the music, their students, wine, pipe fittings, car repairs, backcountry skiing, books to read, movies seen, and methods of baking, wildlife sightings, their words as colorful and diverse as the food and the music. Conversations rise and fall and pause, as people drift in and out of the room like memories on a Saturday afternoon, leaving remnants of their presence but no solid evidence of their being there.

The human tide wells out into the dining room, which is attached to the kitchen by a small dark hallway where bathroom and pantry rooms stand off from one another. The bathroom is well lit, airy, with a large porcelain tub and five or six different kinds of shampoo, hair conditioner, loofahs, soaps, and lotions arranged asymmetrically around its perimeter. The toilet does not stand alone, the sink nearby embraced by a counter along the same wall. The opposite wall is lined with more counters and drawers to hold who-knows-what the cabinetmaker had intended; now it is just dust. On the opposite side of the hall, the pantry harbors mops and brooms and dustpans, along with fifteen shelved and doored cubbyholes, cramped with and concealing a variety of grains, cereals, nuts, noodles, flour, cans, each cubby labeled with a separate number in shiny metallic in order to distinguish one from another among the three horizontal rows five doors deep.

In the dining room, two heavy wood picnic tables sit end to end colored a rusty brown and decorated with dark rings from various hot pots and burning dishes left on the varnished surface without protection. The tables run perpendicular to the wall where the hallway door to the kitchen intersects. Around the perimeter of the room hum six refrigerators of various vintages, crammed with perishables (some of which have already perished). Next to the door is a blackboard, dusky gray from its accumulation of chalked messages forever lost to the sweep of fingers and felt erasers. What words had this board held? Whose eyes were meant for these forgotten notes? What news, events, commands, pleas, questions, directives, sketches, phone numbers, names did this message mirror blaze to the gazers?

A series of windows laced with cobwebs, and vertically interrupted by a chained and bolted door, keeps vigil to the east, upstream and toward Yosemite Valley, bringing the first light of morning and the last head-lights of night to this room of tables and refrigerators and the meeting place of friends.

"Nature is the teacher; the classroom is outdoors;
the textbooks are the very things you see."

–Freeman Tilden, 1970

Yosemite's Stunned Light of Memory

John Lemons

"AT TIMES IT RETURNS, IN THE MOTIONLESS CALM OF THE DAY,
THAT MEMORY OF LIVING IMMERSED, ABSORBED,
IN THE STUNNED LIGHT."
—CESARE PAVESE, "THE NIGHT," 1943

WHILE A RANGER–NATURALIST for the National Park Service in Yosemite, I often was asked what I most liked about place. "Light," I said. The American Indians who named a large part of what is now Yosemite "Pywiack," meaning "Land of the Shining Rocks," knew the permanent essence of this incomparable place is light.

In *Reason in Religion*, George Santayana struggled with the problem of how things and experiences of our witness might be made less fleeting and more enduring. In a sense, Santayana thought the ephemeral, which all things are, could be made immortal—not literally but at least lasting until our own mortal demise—by the endowment of memory. In *Memoir from Antproof Case*, Mark Helprin said that the ephemeral can be made to last through devotion to that which has been loved, and that this requires the obstinacy of memory.

Yosemite is an ephemeral place. Part of it is ephemeral like the Greeks meant—"lasting for a day," but other parts are ephemeral because one's forgetting makes the forgotten, that might still otherwise exist, no longer exist for the forgetter. Horsetail Fall in golden hibernal sunlight is seen in early winter sunsets when snowmelt and cloud cover are just right, and then disappears with no certainty about when it will return. Mayflies unpredictably swarm one day for several hours above Mildred Lake, and then their short adult life is spent. A fleeting glimpse of an early-morning shaft of sunlight on a yellow monkey flower in a dark forest becomes golden splotch of beauty, only to disappear because the sun changes its angle slightly. A Sierra wave forms after an early-evening rain shower, layers of pink and orange and red and magenta spread in an enormous cloud along the Sierra crest, slowly giving way to darkening ripples by the approaching night. Riparian vegetation changes by a seasonal flood. The soft touch of skin of a woman I fell in love with while lying with her beside a small stream near Medlicott Dome is remembered, albeit barely. And while I remember the smell of Carl Sharsmith's baked beans, which he cooked for dinner every night in his tent, I have not remembered all of the many stories he told me while puffing on his old German pipe. Half Dome and the rest of Yosemite Valley formed over a geologic speck of time, and they will last until they become eroded away by the flow of time's rivers. Against the measure of immortality, all things are ephemeral or "last for only a day," whether mayflies or the base of Half Dome plunging deep down into the beating heart of the earth.

* * *

This is my last day as a ranger–naturalist. It is a day to be lazy and reflective. No one else is in this high lake basin, and I find a soft spot to sit and eat my lunch: cheese and crackers, lemonade, and an apple. Light washes onto this day. Will it be remembered or forgotten? The surrounding peaks, the lake's surface shimmering from a gentle breeze, the small insects roving the ground's detritus—all are awash in light. I drink the light because my thirst cannot be quenched—the thirst being memory's constraint that can help make things in Yosemite (and everywhere) ephemeral. I want Santayana and Helprin to belay me against the inevitability of ephemerality, a plunge into forgetting things I have witnessed in this incomparable place. I want this day along with all days in the Sierra to be fixed on the emulsion sheet of my mind.

* * *

Years later I sit at a table at the Principe di Metternich in Trieste, Italy, and watch the enormous ripe blood-orange sun plunge into the Adriatic. To the south a purple hue is cast on the coasts of Slovenia and Croatia, and to the north there is a pinkish tint on the snow-covered Dolomites. Small fishing boats circle on the water in the bay, with one or two men in each boat straining to pull in the nets with the day's catch.

Glimmers of sunlight dance to and fro on the azure smooth-as-glass sea—a sensuousness like the afternoon light in the Sierra reflected from an aspen's lovely smooth white bark. Or, like that of the owner of the Principe di Metternich who flits about, talking to her staff, the people eating at tables covered with quaint red-and-white-checkered table-cloths. Wine bottles are on every table, baskets of bread, fried calamari. She is classically beautiful, her long black hair extending to that soft spot in her curved lower back, where her lovers' kisses lingered. Her daughter meets her and they walk intertwined arm in arm like stalks of swaying Delphinium on the lower slope of Mount Dana one breezy golden sunlit afternoon. I love being in this moment. Who wouldn't? And yet . . . a CD of Bruce Springsteen plays in the background: "You've gone a million miles, how far have you come?"

What orchestrates this symphony of poetic light dancing and linger-ing in this exotic ambience like Puccini's music resonating in my ears long after his last played note? The light of this evening is a provoker of memory and propels me into a simultaneous witness of the past and present of my life, allowing escape of the confines of forgotten time. I see the sun setting into the Adriatic, and it is like seeing through a lens to the past, to memories of where I lived and whom I loved in that place where light was essence. I once thought Yosemite was comprised of things ephemeral and ultimately perhaps no longer remembered. But after nights like this, I know that Pavese's stunned, returned light makes that incomparable place immortal as places can be. No matter where I am.

———•———

"Sitting by our camp fire, the next evening a mass of
rocks fell from the cliff near us, loosened, probably,
by the previous rain. Starting like a crash of thunder,
it came like the tread of an earthquake, while rocks
and trees dashed into the valley, whose twilight solemn
stillness was broken by the uproar, prolonged by
innumerable reverberations. We retired with feelings
fully impressed by the awful manifestations of Nature."

—Thomas Ayres, artist, 1856

5

RESPECTING NATURE

The Bear Canister

Tom Arfsten

ON NOVEMBER 13, 2009, I was helping at the Valley Visitor Center sales counter during employee lunch breaks. A man approached me carrying a bear canister, and I greeted him, asking if he was returning it. He said yes, and this conversation ensued:

"I may owe some money on this. It's a bit overdue," he said.

"Don't worry. The rental is for the duration of the trip, even if it extends a bit over the due date."

"It's got some scratches on it. I will gladly pay for it if you want."

"Oh, these get scratched up all the time. Don't worry. Just as long as it still closes, it'll be okay." (I hadn't closely looked at the canister at that point.)

While the man waited for me to log in the canister return, I opened it to ensure it was clean and that it still closed okay, and placed it on the table behind me. I then returned his white rental agreement, with his personal information on it.

I then asked: "Did you have a good trip?"

"I just left the clinic. It was a long trip. . . . I got lost. Search and Rescue had to come get me."

"Oh wow. What happened?"

"I was lost in the snow for fourteen days. I've been out since the end of October. I woke up and found snow was waist deep and couldn't move. I only had two days' worth of food in my canister, and I ate most of that early on, before I started rationing. I made my way out into a meadow and tried to carve out an SOS with my boots. I lost a lot of weight." (He stepped back to show his pants ballooning out a few inches.)

"How did you survive? Did you build a snow cave?"

"After a while I did. After a while, I didn't think I was gonna make it. I even was scratching my will into the bear canister."

It was then that I realized the significance of the canister. I picked it up and started examining it. He pointed out a few things to me. Sure enough, his last will and testament were carved in the plastic. He also scratched out debt forgiveness to friends, expressions of love and regret, along with pleas for forgiveness from family and friends. It was so beautiful and moving.

"How did they find you?"

"Well, they didn't start looking for me for a few days. Not until I didn't make it back to work (in Georgia), and it was then that they found out I missed my flight." He hadn't told any colleagues where he was going or when he was expected back.

"That is an amazing story. I am glad you made it. Thanks for telling me about it."

Word quickly spread among Yosemite employees who stood in line to see the canister . . . to touch it. It soon became a powerful symbol of the dynamics of the power of nature, the endurance of man, and the compassion of brotherhood.

It is a precautionary tale of respect for the wilderness, the importance of planning, and the limitations of self-reliance.

The returned canister is now in the Yosemite Archives for posterity.

The Dome

Paul Winckel

IN 1991 MY good friend Leigh-bro and I celebrated turning forty with an epic ten-day backpack trip in some classic Yosemite high country, ending with a side trip to . . . Half Dome.

A couple of days ago Leigh and I crossed paths with a young man hiking solo. After brief introductions we traded tall mountain stories until our yarns were spent.

"You're doing The Dome, aren't you?" he asked. "I've done The Dome ten times!"

"Is it worth it?" I returned.

"Oh yeah," he bellowed. "You haven't done Yosemite until you've done The Dome."

Leigh and I looked at each other, reading our collective mind. Half Dome, that mighty granite monolith, was on the way. Should we try it?

So this morning, Leigh says, "If we make good time we might possibly do The Dome this afternoon," and like a man obsessed, Leigh is gone. I lope along, shooting photos, delaying.

Half Dome has made its presence felt to us almost every day. Since the Indian Steppes it has loomed in the distance as a beacon toward home. Even as I rest here in a meadow beneath its shadow, it welcomes, it invites. So, to the Little Yosemite Valley camp we go, joining the hordes, the families of other campers. Our backcountry experience has almost turned urban. We were only five short miles from the Valley and its three million–plus annual visitors, and our inclusion in this throng seems to diminish the intimate roles Leigh and I have played in our wilderness drama. So, after a brief rest, we pack our cameras, a couple cans of fish, some water, and off we go on a three-and-a-half-mile jaunt, to ascend the 2,700 feet, to do The Dome. We trek up Sunrise Creek and the Clouds

Rest Trail. Up, up, and up, through ponderosa and cedar and white fir, passing throngs of hikers returning in a steady stream. Some returnees seem elated, and others defeated, though all of them exclaim, "Yeah, sure, I did The Dome. . . . Totally worth it. Are you staying the night?"

After over an hour of tiresome, sweaty climbing, we bump into a sign, "Half Dome . . . 2 mi." Then a father and his two teenage sons come by, stumbling and grumbling. "That's the longest two miles I've ever walked. We left The Dome two hours ago! More like three, maybe four miles!"

Undaunted, onwards we hike toward a dome that was nowhere in sight. Then we spy another sign, one written in three languages and warning: "Danger! If clouds appear anywhere on the horizon . . . stop hiking! Half Dome gets struck by lightning every month of the year!"

Clouds, billowing and expansive, loom everywhere to the east. Still, on and up we go. Up the side of this granite peak, ascending giant steps, which are carved into the rock face, switching back and forth. My knees creak. I rest after every ten steps. Leigh disappears ahead. Breathing in pants, I continue on, anxious to clear the top until, cresting a granite rise, I spy Leigh talking to a hiker. A hiker who has quit, given up, and as I lean into my staff to propel me, I see why.

"Hey Rip," Leigh said. "We haven't even hiked the 'quarter dome.'. . . THAT'S HALF DOME!"

Before me looms the largest, most ominous, sheer, steep, precipitous monolith of polished granite I've ever seen. It blocks out half of the sky, framing its lonely route to the top. My eyes follow what from a distance appears to be two thin strands of wire disappearing above over an endless horizon of granite. Two steel cables are propped by steel bars, which are injected perpendicularly into the rock-face cliff. I'm supposed to pull myself, hand over hand, up these cables to a top I can't even see. I watch an ant-like person disappear out of sight.

"I don't know," Leigh says, "I've got a wife and two beautiful girls . . . and this is crazy!"

"I'm going up," I said. My childhood infatuation with tree climbing, my stupid yearning to clamber, to explore, to go to the top spurs me on. Reason and sanity, I deserted them almost two weeks ago when I left home, and this was no time to consider the exhausted, malnourished state of my physique. I feel great, I think. Besides, this was The Big Yo! I have to do The Dome!

While Leigh and I rest, we watch eight teenaged girls on a day hike begin their ascent, their pull up the precipice. They were followed by a young married couple, the husband toting a daypack. . . . No, it wasn't. . . . It was a papoose! A baby pack!!! Inside was their one-year-old, cackling and howling . . . with glee!!!

Suddenly, with the entire party not twenty yards up the sheer cliff, the leading teenage girl comes to frantic grips with her folly and begins a horrific wail. . . .

"I CAN'T DO IT. . . . I DON'T WANT TO DIE. . . . I'M TOO SCARED. . . ." She's standing on one of the protruding steel bars, clinging with white knuckled tautness to the cable. I turn to Leigh, "I can't handle an accident, man, I can't watch."

Everyone below the frantic girl shifts precariously to one side of the cable route, the baby wails in ecstasy, the girl screams in terror. Slowly, she and a girlfriend inch their way back down toward horizontal ground. Finally, able to stand, they hug and laugh, having fun again, safely alive. Leigh and I watch as the remainder of her troupe continues on, slowly disappearing beyond the granite horizon.

"I guess I gotta do it," Leigh said. Now it was our turn. At the base of the cable route lay a pile of used gloves. Wear a pair and you'll better grip the metal strands. And grip you do. No gentle slope, this. Immediately, The Dome spurts up nearly perpendicular. I try first. Pulling hard on the cables, pushing my boots against the rock face, hand over hand, foot over foot, my heart races, my breathing quickens, my sunshades steam, until I rest and stand upright on one of the metal bars protruding from the cliff. I look down. I have gone barely thirty feet and already I have to rest my middle-aged ticker. Poor old heart. The altitude shock of the last nine days wasn't enough. Nor the many mountain passes, nor the adrenalin overdoses of the Bear-wars. No. I have to abuse myself further through this anaerobic lunacy of scaling a rock face by pulling myself up these precariously limp steel cables. If nerves and altitude aren't enough, surely this blood-gushing exercise might cause a fatigue-prone error. One slip . . . and I'm done . . . rock fodder.

I look down . . . past my feet . . . at Leigh.

"Come on, man," he implored, "Let's go!"

I'm rested, I'm psyched. . . . Pull, pull, step, step, PULL, PULL, STEP, STEP . . . thump-THUMP, thump-THUMP, goes my heart. Blood is pounding in my forehead, loosening drops of sweat that want to hang forever from my nose.

Below me the two girls yell, "C'mon. . . . You can do it!"

Up, up I push, maybe another thirty feet. I stop. I'm exhausted. I cling to the cable, wrap my leg around a steel bar and bounce off of the rock face.

Leigh passes me, huffing, and disappears above, beyond the endless horizon of rock. Adrenalin pins my eyes open, yet I see only granite and cable. No clue as to my surroundings, to the endless drop, just me and my grip on the rock.

Again I psyche myself. The girls below cheer. I don't need that. Up I go, racing, anaerobic tugs and pushes, another thirty feet, another rest, I'm dangling from the cable, gasping to breathe; this old fart will not be denied . . . not yet. On and up again, just like this, thirty feet at a time, on this precipitous, eternal journey, dangling and gasping and grasping and sweating . . . until, finally, The Dome rounds and I can almost . . . I can . . . I can walk! I can't see the top, or Leigh, but my weight is on my legs! I sit and gaze down the dizzying sight of the cable route disappearing over the side. Winded, I begin to amble toward the top with a cool comportment, while my knees shake.

Before me is the top of Half Dome, an expansive flat of rock larger than a football field. And beyond this Dome all about me are waves and waves of valleys and mountains and rivers and trees and clouds. . . . Thunderclouds!!! I almost collapse in joy as I capture each panorama through my camera.

Leigh and I joke and walk and watch and point. Somebody takes our picture. "Old farts on The Dome" they thought . . . but we belong . . . we do. . . . We did Yosemite. . . . We did The Dome!!! . . . Give me five, bro'. . . .

Congratulations, though in order, perhaps should've waited. For as death defying as was our ascent, this descent is interminably endless. Hands gripping the cable white-knuckled taut. I go down feet first, looking down between my knees at each step and not one inch beyond. Leigh comes down the cable as if walking down stairs, exposing himself to the panorama of his doom, and mine, were he to slip. Watching my feet, feeling my grip, hearing my gasps, smelling my fear, the inconsequence of what we were doing was made great because the cliff demands perfection.

Finally we touch ground. Thank God, we're down! One of the craziest things I've ever done but . . . I did The Dome!

A young man, pack on his back, passes us en route to the top. He turns and asks, "Is it worth it?"

"Oh yeah," Leigh and I chime, "you bet! Just take your time. . . . You'll do The Dome." The three-and-a-half-mile walk back to camp seems to fly by and as the sun sets in a pale sky we turn and look in awe and respect up at The Dome . . . Half Dome.

———✦———

"Half Dome rears its ice-scarred head fully five thousand feet above the level floor of Yosemite Valley. In the name itself of this great rock lies an accurate and complete description. Nothing more nor less it is than a cyclopean, rounded dome, split in half as cleanly as an apple that is divided by a knife."

—Jack London, 1900

Bounded Chains; Boundless Freedom

Jack Rich

HALF DOME
Full steam ahead,
Bounded by chains,
Yet boundless desire,
Thirsty, struggling,
Grappling for links.
Summit freedom!

Search and Rescue Brought Me Down

Robin Martinez Rice

Rıck woke early and slipped his feet into his boots as he rolled off the cot in the Yosemite Valley Housekeeping Camp unit. The group set to climb Half Dome had agreed to leave at 4:00 a.m. Thank goodness he was old enough to go this year. The makeup of the group—three doctors and a couple of nurses—convinced Mom and Dad he would be safe.

Rick had come to Yosemite Valley every summer of his life. At fourteen he had been on lots of hikes—Yosemite Falls, Vernal Fall, Nevada Fall, and Glacier Point—but he had never done the greatest hike of all.

Half Dome.

"You up?" Dr. Graham whispered, peering into the Larsons' camp.

"Yep. Just getting my lunch out of the bear locker."

"Be sure to eat some breakfast. Here are some extra power bars."

Rick tried to open the heavy iron latch quietly, which was nearly impossible. No clunk, but the metal hinge protested with a grumbling squeal. He grabbed a bag of chips and two candy bars, stuffed them into his day pack, along with his water bottle and the power bars.

"I wonder if anyone ever jumped from up there." Danny picked up a rock and threw it toward the river.

"You mean like with a parachute or suicide?" Rick glanced back at the group of grownups. These doctor guys hiked fast. They all had those little ski-pole things and seemed to get into a rhythm. They only talked to each other when the group stopped for a break or to take pictures. And they made announcements: fifteen-minute water break, one hour on the top, meet at the bottom of the cables at eleven o'clock.

Danny and Rick had been the first up the cables, pushing ahead and skittering up quickly. It was great to get here so early, before the long stretch of wire and granite was crowded with hikers.

But when the boys had climbed back down, Rick felt a headache come on. He used to get them when he was younger and drank a lot of red punch. His mom gave him medication for the headaches, but he didn't have any pills with him.

Danny took a slurp of water and nodded down the trail. "Race you?"

Rick pointed up the cable. "What about them?"

"We know the way back. My dad won't care." Dr. Graham was Danny's father.

Rick licked his dry lips. He had finished his water a long time ago. He had looked around for a place to fill his bottle but didn't see anything. He stuffed his mouth full of chips and nodded to Danny. "Let me finish eating first."

Three minutes later the two boys raced down the trail, hopping from edge to edge, bouncing off the smooth granite boulders as if they were on their skateboards. Danny executed a jump, and Rick had to one-up him, jumping off a huge boulder and scissoring his legs rapidly in the air before landing. They whooped and hollered down the mountain.

* * *

Laura glanced at her watch, yet again, and turned to Callie. "They should be back by now. I hope everything's all right."

"It's only five. They took a lot of kids this time." Callie reached for the clam dip. "If something was wrong they would have sent someone back to tell us."

Laura turned pale and pointed. A ranger car had slowed to a stop in front of the unit.

Callie felt her chest tighten. She walked toward the road, keeping her pace casual. The ranger got out of his patrol car and walked toward her.

Callie forced a smile. "You're not looking for the Larsons or the Grahams are you?"

The ranger didn't smile back. "What's your name?"

"Callie Larson."

"Oh." The ranger frowned. "You're the mother."

Callie sank to the ground as all the gravity in the world took ahold of her heart and ripped it out.

The ranger grabbed her as she fell. "He's okay, he's okay."

Dave raced across the campground. "What happened?"

The ranger turned to Dave. "Your son is fine. He couldn't finish the hike. He's being carried out and you can meet them at the clinic."

The ranger couldn't tell them much more. Rick had collapsed and had to be carried out by the volunteer Search and Rescue team. Dave and Callie raced to the car and took off for the clinic.

The tight fist around Callie's heart finally released its deadly grasp when she saw Rick sitting up in the bed in the clinic. Smiling.

The doctor leaned down and whispered something to Rick. He turned and smiled at Callie and Dave, then motioned them out to the hallway.

"Seems he didn't have the right food with him, and very little water. He was running a lot today. An entire bag of chips, followed by dehydration will extend the bowel. Very painful." The doctor smiled. "I left him alone with instructions to pass gas."

Callie slipped through the curtain. Rick was hunched in the bed and his face reddened when he saw her.

"Can't I go in the bathroom or something?" Rick looked at the IV in his arm. "Will you get them to take this thing out?"

Callie kissed Rick's head and sighed, thankful for the team who had saved her son. She thought about the T-shirt she had bought for him earlier that day—I Made It to the Top, with a picture of Half Dome.

Maybe they could add a little something with a laundry pen.

I Made It to the Top—But Search and Rescue Brought Me Down.

Yosemite Valley's Apple Orchards

Tom Gardner

I'M FAIRLY CERTAIN that I first heard about apple orchards in Yosemite Valley from Ansel Adams himself. The year was 1974 or 1975, and I was serving in the navy based in San Diego; he was on a nationwide lecture tour with slide show to sold-out audiences. It seemed half the presentation was about Yosemite Valley, and the specific photo was titled "Half Dome, Apple Orchard, winter 1935." On the right side of this image, one can see a freshly plowed road up against a substantial snowbank, plus several inches of fresh powder clinging to old fruit trees against a cloudless sky. It was probably taken right after a fast-moving Sierra blizzard, which happens frequently almost every winter.

Some of those apple trees were already seventy to seventy-five years old when Ansel Adams recorded the image. Two of the first English-speaking inhabitants of Yosemite, James Lamon and James Mason Hutchings, planted those trees during the 1860s in the "Johnny Appleseed" tradition. Moreover, these early residents tended vegetable gardens and kept dairy cattle. The simple economic reasoning was Yankee self-reliance: if they were going to operate tourist hotels, they had to get as many visitors as possible, while minimizing excess freight and baggage, all delivered over rough trails on horseback. Apples were used in a wide variety of baked goods, preserves, juice, and hard cider. Lamon planted two orchards of about five hundred trees each; today they are known as the Curry Orchard (shuttle bus stop number fourteen) and the Lamon Orchard (shuttle bus stop number eighteen). Hutchings planted one hundred fifty trees near today's Yosemite Elementary School.

Those two men were seen as pioneers to some and squatters to others. Lamon was already living there when President Lincoln gave control of Yosemite Valley to the State of California in 1864. Hutchings moved there in 1864. Both men cited the existence of their orchards as proof of the legitimacy of their claims, even though the Valley had never been surveyed. Their cases dragged on until 1873, when they were bought out by a U.S. Supreme Court decision. Lamon left the Valley and died in San Francisco a few years later. Hutchings continued to promote Yosemite, writing a detailed travel guide in 1888. In it, he describes his orchard: "The spring succeeding the completion of the cabin, called for the cultivation and fencing of a garden-ground, and the planting of an orchard. Many of the trees for the latter were grown from seeds of choice apples that had been sent us, the plants from which were afterward budded or grafted. In this way a thrifty orchard, of about one hundred and fifty trees, came into being, and now bears many tons, annually, of assorted fruit."

The opening of toll roads into the Valley in the mid-1870s allowed stagecoaches and freight wagons to reach the park. Maintenance of the orchards passed to the various leaseholders for the rest of the nineteenth century. When sustainable agriculture inside the Valley was no longer important, the vegetable gardens disappeared, but the orchards continued to be maintained. During the Depression, National Park Service employees and the concessionaires held collective harvests, preserving what could not be consumed in a month or two. The orchards fell into disuse during World War II and the postwar era. In 1976, a tree "census" was conducted, and in the Curry Orchard there were still 178 trees producing apples. In the Lamon Orchard, 252 apple trees and 1 pear tree were still bearing fruit. The Hutchings Orchard held 68 apple trees, 2 cherry trees, and 2 pear trees.

Today, the Curry Orchard serves as a parking lot and is possibly one of the least charming spots in Yosemite Valley. When the ground is not muddy, it's dusty. The trees themselves are downright ugly, as decades have passed since they were given a proper pruning. Yellow pines inside Curry Village have grown up so tall that it is almost impossible to find the spot where Ansel Adams took his famous photograph. The trees in the Lamon Orchard are just as ugly, and despite the pines and cedars which have reestablished themselves, one can see how these apple trees were planted in rows. One of Hutchings' apple trees can be seen at the bottom-right on Yosemite Conservancy's webcam of Yosemite Falls. The tree is most visible when it is covered in white blossoms in April and May, or in November when the leaves turn color.

As the twentieth century progressed, the objectives of the National Park Service shifted from development goals to one of conservation, and nonnative plant species were to be eliminated. However, the orchards presented a difficult challenge to the NPS, as the trees were older than the park itself. Plus, over the decades, other apple trees have sprouted, singly or in small clusters, in different parts of the Valley. Further complicating the situation is since people are no longer consuming the fruit, the local bears will, thereby creating a headache that Yosemite's park rangers do not need. Their website clearly states the issue: "Help Keep Yosemite's Bears Wild. The historic, ripe apples attract bears to developed areas and alter their natural diets. By removing the apples, bears will return to their natural food sources found throughout the park and not become exposed to humans and their food."

Apples have been picked for more than a dozen years in a coordinated effort by NPS employees and volunteers, usually sometime in mid-August. For example, in 2009 the green fruit harvest yielded over six thousand pounds, gathered by twenty-five NPS employees and one hundred eleven volunteers. That averaged out to roughly fourteen-plus pounds of apples per tree, a remarkable output for something untended and about 150 years old. Furthermore, everybody can keep all the green apples they want. I participated in 2011 and had a fine time. With luck, I'll be able to participate again.

Skiing the Trans-Sierra

Dave Todd

Don Pitts, then the chief federal magistrate at Yosemite National Park, and Chief Ranger Don Winton founded the Yosemite Winter Club Cross Country Section (YWCCC) in 1978. I started cross-country skiing in 1978 and skied to Dewey Point, Ostrander Ski Hut, and many other areas with my brother-in-law Klaus Penning. I joined the ski club in 1993 because it offered multiday trips with stays in cabins at Glacier Point, Ostrander Lake, and, my favorite, the Trans-Sierra.

The first Trans-Sierra ski trip I participated in was in 1996. It was especially memorable. We flew across the Sierra to the east side and landed at the town of Lee Vining near Mono Lake. Then we hitched a ride to the Tioga Pass Road (State Highway 120) gate. The resort was still open during the winter then, and they would send down the snowcat to pick up our packs. We hiked up to the snow line and skied from there over Tioga Pass (9,943 feet, 3,031 meters) to the Tioga Pass Resort. The road is very steep. Skiing with a full pack at that altitude leaves you gasping for a breath of the thin air.

On this trip there was a substitute to replace a club member who had to cancel at the last minute. He was a young architect named Dave from Chicago who said he had been cross-country skiing for twenty years. As I skied alongside him up the road, I noticed he was having trouble keeping up. He looked pale and was gasping for breath. I asked him if he was feeling okay. He said that he had a severe headache, and it was hard for him to breathe the air. I recognized the symptoms of altitude sickness because I had it on my first trip to Ostrander Lake. Altitude sickness, or acute mountain sickness, is caused by exposure to the lower volume of oxygen usually at altitudes above eight thousand feet.

I told Dave that he should keep going since we would soon be at Tioga Pass Resort. I said that he could decide after a full night's sleep whether he felt well enough to continue. I continued to ski alongside of him and he made it to the resort before dark. In the morning, Dave decided to quit the trip. Before he left, I asked him where he had acquired his cross-country ski experience. He told me that all of his skiing had been done in Minnesota. Minnesota is very flat compared to the Sierra Nevada.

On another Trans-Sierra trip, we were skiing on the last day. I had been skiing with my friend Phil when I realized that a woman I'll call "Mary" was no longer with our group. Mary was a National Park Service ranger. She was scheduled to retire at the end of the month and wanted to ski the Trans-Sierra with us before she left the National Park Service. I told Phil that we needed to turn around and look for Mary. We skied back the way we had come for about thirty minutes when I saw her. Mary was hanging upside down by the tips of her skies from a tree well. A tree well is a hole or depression under a tree that is sometimes filled with loose snow. Her backpack was hanging down below her head. If a skier falls into a tree well headfirst it can be difficult or impossible to escape. If the well is filled with snow, the skier can suffocate quickly. Luckily for Mary, this well was not filled with snow. However, it was clear that because she was hanging upside down, she would soon lose consciousness if we didn't pull her out. At this point I was faced with a choice. I could take a picture of her hanging upside down and then rescue her or forget about the picture and get her down as quickly as possible. I knew that the photo would be printed around the world, but I wasn't going to leave Mary hanging there while I set up my camera. We helped Mary get out of her skies. Then she was able to get out of the tree well.

Several years later I was faced with another dilemma involving a photograph. Again, it was the last day of the Trans-Sierra trip. I was skiing with my friend "Donald." We had finally reached the switchback trail that leads from the north rim of Yosemite Valley down nearly four thousand feet to the floor and ends behind Mirror Lake. We put on the hiking boots we had carried for this purpose. Then we began the long, slow, careful descent down the trail. Donald loves to talk and kept up a steady conversation until we were about a third of the way down the trail. Suddenly, he disappeared. He was no longer in front of me. I looked ahead but didn't see him. Then I heard a faint voice calling "Help, help me!" I looked over the edge of the trail and saw that Donald had fallen on his back into a seasonal creek that had formed because it was a wet year. Fortunately his backpack cushioned his fall. He was lucky. If he had slipped off the edge of the trail a few feet further, he would have landed in Yosemite Valley. Once again, I had to make a decision. I could take a picture of Donald before I helped him out of the icy cold water. I knew the picture would be published everywhere. But I couldn't leave him lying there while I took a picture. Somehow I always miss out on the best photos I never shot when I ski the Trans-Sierra.

Celebrating and Mourning

John Lemons

One afternoon I was sitting outside my tent with Carl Sharsmith, the renowned ranger–naturalist in Tuolumne Meadows in Yosemite where, ultimately, he spent over sixty summers of his life. I was young and just beginning my career as a ranger–naturalist, and Carl was sort of my mentor. I was listening to Carl muse about the changes he had seen in Yosemite during the decades that he had worked there. He spoke softly and gazed into the distance. "Will it all remain?" he asked.

Carl was not speaking about Yosemite remaining in any literal or practical sense, but rather: would it remain untrammeled? Carl's concern was how Yosemite had changed over the years due to its greater popularity with more and more people and, later, with the existential threat of global climate change arising primarily from humans' use of fossil fuels (and historically and per capita–wise, disproportionately from the United States).

This book is part of the celebration of the 150th anniversary of the original Yosemite Grant that led to the establishment of what we now know and love as Yosemite National Park. Celebrating Yosemite is a way to pay homage to a place not only worth remembering but keeping in trust for the future. But in so doing, we must not forget that our celebrating should give us pause to consider how we are faring in fulfilling our trust responsibilities.

After visiting Yosemite in the early part of the twentieth century shortly after automobiles had made their first entry into the park, Lord Bryce Everhart (*University and Historical Addresses*, 1913) wrote:

"If Adam had known what harm the serpent was going to work, he would have tried to prevent him from finding lodgment in Eden; and if you were to realize what the result of the automobile will be in that wonderful, that incomparable Valley, you will keep it out."

Lord Bryce Everhart was prescient about how the onslaught of auto-mobiles and over three million visitors annually, and the developments they desired, would conflict, for the most part, with an untrammeled Yosemite. For about thirty-five years the NPS has been grappling with promulgating an approved park management plan, but so far none has been approved.

Unfortunately, Yosemite already experiences wounds beyond what Lord Bryce Everhart called to our attention. Warming conditions from human-induced climate change are pushing populations of the high-altitude pika upward, wherein, as the trends continue, pikas will be faced with extinction because their existing habitat, ever high on the slopes of Yosemite's highest peaks, will be too warm for them. Alpine chipmunks likewise are being pushed into higher elevations as tem-peratures increase, and their genetic makeup is changing as a response, perhaps to be followed by extinction. When I worked in Tuolumne Meadows I saw yellow-legged frogs in every lake and pond; I haven't seen one for decades. Finally, large swaths of Yosemite's forests are brown and parched from a drought lasting over a decade. The decline of frogs and browning of the forests might not be due completely to climate change, but no doubt such change is a significant factor.

The pioneering ecologist Aldo Leopold wrote that to have an ecolog-ical conscience is to "live alone in a world of wounds." The great conser-vationists of our time—Edward Abbey, David Brower, Rachael Carson, Aldo Leopold, and John Muir, to name a few—all spoke of the value of places like Yosemite to foster celebration of natural beauty and its impor-tance to our lives. But a fundamental part of their celebration also was mourning, as paradoxical as this might seem.

It is well documented that Muir mourned the loss of Hetch Hetchy until he died. In addition to knowing Carl Sharsmith, I was fortunate to know and work with David Brower, head of the Sierra Club for so many years. Both celebrated the joy of being in Yosemite every day they were blessed with being there. At the same time, they mourned the losses of

Yosemite. First, because of development and overcrowding, and then because of climate change rearing its head.

But how or why should mourning accompany celebration? Each of the people I have mentioned mourned losses to Yosemite's natural and aesthetic wonders, but the mourning was not confined in relation to the self and, importantly, it was lifelong. This extended mourning stemmed from losses they were seeing to a place they loved deeply—it was a practice many centuries old. And the mourning provided them, and those who knew them, with an alterity that changed ethical views about our relationships with the land.

We need to celebrate Yosemite for what it is and for what it does to us, especially for what it does to us when we venture into its beauty and solitude and when we listen to its voice. We need to celebrate, but in a manner that allows mourning for the wounds we have caused to this great place, and in so doing let our mourning enable us to think deeply about an ethics, a different way of living, that allows us to transcend overcrowding and overdevelopment, and the greater and more existential problem of global climate change that threatens to cast the imprint of humans on Yosemite more than anything imagined.

"What should Yosemite Valley be? It should be what it once was: the kind of place where a person would know himself lucky to make one pilgrimage there in his lifetime. A holy place. Keep it like it was."

—Edward Abbey, 1977

The Postpile

Charles F. Nelsen

THE POSTPILE HOLDS a unique part of Yosemite's impressive history. Most people today don't know that the Postpile and surrounding area was once part of Yosemite National Park.

In 1905, part of what was then Yosemite National Park was reduced in acreage. The Mount Ritter region and Devils Postpile were both eliminated from the park boundary. The reason for the severance was a gold mine. Many wealthy landowners used political connections to remove this land from the park so they could operate the gold mine.

Unfortunately for the investors, the mine was salted; there was no gold there and never will be.

To salt a mine a person may empty the shot from a shotgun shell and replace the shot with gold dust. Then fire at the face of the proposed mine. This fooled investors, but after close inspection gunpowder was found mixed with the gold.

The investors lost all of their money; many lost everything they owned. Fortunately, both regions were returned to public land but not returned to Yosemite.

A Giant Sequoia in the Mariposa Grove

Esther R. Makower

YOU STAND, A silent sentinel
guarding the secrets of the millennium.
You bear the scars of countless
fiery holocausts and the arrogance of
humankind who, in their ignorance,
disrupt the web of life that sustains you.
Yet you endure and like a saintly martyr,
twisted branches reaching to heaven,
you bless those who stand in your
presence with peace and awe.

Don't Look Down!

Mary Gross Davis

My husband, Tony Gross, had gotten a job far away from Sequoia (where we lived) and Yosemite (which he had been exploring since his boyhood). Before we moved away, we had to take the boys to the top of Half Dome. The kids were eight and ten and just about a year old. So the little one went onto Dad's back in the carrier, while the other two ran ahead.

Six hours later, after much beautiful scenery and more breaks than most hikers would care to take, we were at the base of the granite monolith. The defining rock of Yosemite. Since there was a baby involved (big enough to unbalance a climber), we opted not to take him to the top, so I was elected to watch him at the base.

The views were breathtaking. The kids were exuberant. They had ALMOST made it! Up went Tony. Up went both of the boys, climbing boldly . . . until the bigger one said to the smaller one, "DON'T LOOK DOWWWN!"

Of course, he did. So did his big brother. And the enormity of the rock, the immensity of the drop, and the very smallness of themselves stopped them cold. There they were, halfway up the ladder, frozen in place. I watched as they slowly, carefully, very safely, inched themselves backward until they had reached the grassy place. Ambling. Sheepish. We'd come all this way (and would be walking a lot longer to get back) . . . but they had broken the cardinal rule of climbing: don't look down until you're at the top!

They're grown men today. And I hope they still have a hankering to go back someday and go all the way to the top of Half Dome WITHOUT looking down!

We Climb Anyway

Audrey Camp

THE BALD FOREHEAD of Stately Pleasure Dome offers no relief from the July sun. I crawl all over the top before finding the single, squat yellow pine jutting from the rock. Its trunk curves toward the sky; its base is ringed with colorful cordelettes, left behind by climbers on descent.

I crouch at the precipice, my raw palm resting on the rough bark of the tree. The golden-gray slabs of granite roll down and away like a waterfall, hundreds of vertical feet, striped with sparkling mineral deposits.

Suddenly, my shoe loses traction on the rock. My foot kicks forward a few inches. With a gasp, I catch hold of the tree. Tiny bits of granite and dirt roll helplessly over the edge into the wind.

I cling to the rappel tree in a cold sweat. I crab walk back from the edge to a secure spot. I close my eyes and wonder why anyone would choose to climb.

Many visitors to Yosemite National Park go to gape at the yawning granite cliffs and domes, the park's signature, remnants of an ice age. Some go to scale those cliffs and domes with their bare hands.

That July Saturday, my group had begun at the base of Stately Pleasure Dome, a wide-open rock face at the eastern end of the park which boasts a dozen bolted climbing routes. There were seven of us: three experienced climbers, three beginners, and me, somewhere in the middle.

Our mission was Hermaphrodite Flake, four pitches of granite slab and jagged cracks. I felt confident, having completed the route once before with my husband, Jonathan. While he, Brian, and Jeff, the strongest climbers in the group, sorted the gear, I braided my friend Cindy's fine, curling hair. Cindy, her boyfriend, Brad, and Jeff's fiancée, Amy, had never climbed a multipitch route before. When they spoke, a tremor ran through their voices, triggered by the towering run of rock beside us.

Jonathan and I scrambled up the two hundred unprotected feet to the first belay station. The rock felt familiar under the sticky soles of my climbing shoes, but I worried about my friends. The beginners walked up slowly, holding onto a rope Brian had lowered. It wasn't protection, but it made them feel safer. Jeff dug his toes into the granite and ascended in strong, fearless bounds. Only air cushioned the space between him and the dark ribbon of the road to Tuolumne below.

With each of Jonathan's movements, a blur of rope followed him up the wall, winding through my belay device; the friction warmed my palms. On routes like Hermaphrodite Flake, permanent bolted belay stations are located every fifty to one hundred feet, the length of a single pitch. Over the years I've become more comfortable being clipped into those bolts by only my two daisy chains.

At the third belay station, I peered down the rock. Brad stood atop the big flake above the second pitch and had Cindy on belay. She wore a pink drawstring pack with nylon straps, completely inappropriate for the excursion, but it was all she had to haul their lunch and water. Her gray-green eyes searched the rock for her next move. She seemed suddenly and overwhelmingly vulnerable to me. What if her harness wasn't secure? What if she had tied the wrong knot?

Some climbers do it for the strength training. Others for the love of solving puzzles. Many climb solely for the rush of adrenaline.

The morning before our group took on Hermaphrodite Flake, Jonathan and I had climbed Zee Tree, a six-pitch slab route on Pywiack Dome. After two hours of smearing our toes and scraping for invisible holds on the sparkling rock, we topped out. Black thunderclouds tumbled in from the west, losing stability in the thin air of the high country. Blue sky continued to sparkle above us, but thunder pounded in the canyons. To the southeast, the storm swarmed toward Cathedral Peak, and Eichorn Pinnacle, sharp in a land of domes, stuck out like a lightning rod. I pulled off my helmet and let my brown hair whip in the wind.

On that July Friday in 2010, as I sat on the warm stone watching the storm arrive, another young woman was falling.

Christina Chan, a thirty-one-year-old doctoral candidate at Stanford, and a very experienced climber, had completed her free solo attempt on Eichorn Pinnacle. No gear, no ropes. Chan and her climbing partner, Jim Castelaz, had begun their descent.

Then a piece of rotted rock crumbled under her fingers. Or the wind caught her lithe torso and blew her from the face. Fate or a mistake. Castelaz heard a sound and, from his helpless vantage point above, watched his friend fall out of sight.

Back at the base of Stately Pleasure Dome, having conquered Hermaphrodite Flake, my friends and I wade into Tenaya Lake. For the beginners, it has been the scariest, strongest feat they've ever accomplished. For the experts, there's been the added stress of taking newbies to the top. For me, the hardest part of the climb will come later, when we hear the report of Christina Chan's death at the campground. A recovery team found her body almost four hundred feet below Eichorn Pinnacle.

The seven of us will walk from the campground into the glow and hum of Tuolumne Meadows at dusk. The translucent wings of a recent hatch will flutter around us.

We will be unable to stop ourselves from thinking, Climbing is dangerous.

But in the early afternoon, as we plunge our sore feet into the lake, we think nothing like that. Far above, other climbers inch up the granite in colorful tandems. Amy wipes a smear of blood from her ankle. Cindy's braids have unraveled. We pull beers from coolers, blow whistles across bottle tops. I hold Jonathan's hand.

We are victorious. We are alive. And this feeling is why we climb anyway.

Caught in a Lightning Storm

Victoria Peet

MY FATHER AND I went to Yosemite for a nice vacation. On the third day, we went fishing on Lyell Creek, a tributary of the Tuolumne River. It was a beautiful, sunny, and hot day. So we drove up to Lyell Creek, an hour and a half drive, and set up to fish. We could already see threatening clouds, but we thought they'd just pass. So we kept fishing. It started to sprinkle a bit, but we didn't care. We caught a fish and were happy. My dad pointed to the red circles lining its sides and told me it's a brook trout.

We heard thunder in the distance. We didn't think it'd come too close to us. Then it started POURING. We could hear more thunder that sounded a little closer. My father told me to put my rod down and I followed him under a boulder hanging over the river. My father thought it would be one of those mountain storms that only lasts about thirty minutes and then clears up. So we sat under the rock for about ten minutes until it started hailing. The thunder sounded even louder, shaking us as though we were toothpicks in a bag of bowling balls. I was terrified, but my father told me to calm down. I was getting extremely cold, and the hair on my arms was popping up so high because of fear and cold. I shivered wildly. I begged him to let us leave, but he said it's more dangerous to be walking out in the open with fishing poles during a lightning storm. The thunder came even CLOSER, and we saw the lightning flashes ripping the sky and sizzling earthward. I was freaking out and begged him to just leave the demonic poles and get the heck out of that place. He said no and told me the chances of getting hit in a lightning storm would be three million to one. I was still terrified. We'd been under the rock for about twenty minutes, we were soaking wet, my wet hair and clothes clung to me, and the storm hadn't passed. Mucous poured from my nose and mixed with the pure rainwater coating my face.

Then we actually saw a lightning streak about A QUARTER MILE AWAY. And right after that, the thunder was TREMENDOUSLY LOUD, crackling, booming, then crackling again. I covered my ears with my hands. I started crying and my dad told me to take a deep breath, and he repeated that it's nearly impossible to get struck by lightning. I was so afraid that I'd die. So afraid.

But the storm just wouldn't pass. I REALLY wanted to go, so my dad said, "Okay, we'll pack everything up and make a run for it." Our Mini Cooper was about one and a half miles away, in the Tuolumne Meadows Lodge parking lot. It was a long sprint back. By now, there were big puddles everywhere, and the once-clear-cut trails were flooded. I dragged my socks over my sopping feet and stuffed them into my green Converse. I was afraid to carry fishing poles through a lightning storm.

My father picked up our fishing bag and his fly-fishing rod, and I carried my pole. We jogged, except when leaping over newly formed rivers. We slogged through muddy puddles and we were soaking as if we had jumped into a dirty pool. I could feel the water and mud in my shoes, giving me blisters. The sky was so dark, and the lightning was terrifying. And the thunder was so loud! I felt as though we were running through the end of the world.

Once on our run back to the car, I counted the seconds between the lightning I saw and thunder I heard, and I got to two. I was pretty scared. We climbed slippery rocks, battled the stinging hail falling hard on our arms and face and head, and it was freezing. I was shaking so violently and covered with goose bumps. And though the rain would wash the trail away, my dad knew where to go. I licked the delicious rainwater from my lips on the way to our car.

But finally, after about forty minutes of crackling thunder and terrifying lightning, stinging hail, and freezing winds, we made it to the car. The parking lot was flooded, so we had to wade to shelter. I could barely even move, I felt so cold and my muscles were frozen in place! And we could see more lightning streaks in the sky. It was like we were facing the apocalypse.

My dad and I started laughing, we were so happy. My father turned on the hot-air blast and I got much warmer in that car. But as we were talking about how we were going to take nice hot showers when we got back to our campsite, we saw that the Tioga Pass Highway was blocked by Forestry Service barriers. There had been several landslides and water was just pouring off the side of the road like a waterfall. So we had to turn around and find refuge in the little store at Tuolumne Meadows Lodge. My father and I went straight to the fireplace and sat in front of it and ate some cookies. Many people were in there and didn't look too scared. I wondered how they could possibly be so calm when there was this huge storm going on and the thunder was almost unbearable. After about an hour and a half of boredom, my dad asked if the road was cleared.

The clerk said yes. We were so happy we could go.

It was quite some storm. I can still see the white lightning streaks in my head. I was so afraid I'd die. So afraid.

Spirit Renewal through the Forest

Nastaran Rahnama

WALKING THROUGH THE Mariposa Grove of Giant Sequoias feels like a slip in time. Some of the trees have been around for two thousand years, digging their roots into the soil of the earth and stretching upward toward the sun. A spectacular sight from above or below.

As symbols of longevity and strength, the sequoias need no words or movement to demand your attention. With silent admiration, I took in their presence. I felt small and protected; like floating in plasma . . . back in the womb.

Holding a sequoia cone in the palm of my hand I thought about how given time, it will outlive me . . . for centuries. Given time, it will no longer fit in my hand. And given time, I will only be dust in the bare mineral soil where its new seeds will take root.

Even if these trees fall, they retain their beauty and power . . . so majestically.

They will still outlast us, in their death.

Just as they should.

———✦———

"There, blocking the way as a light-house might,
rose the mighty bulk of a tawny-barked tree over
thirty feet in diameter. . . standing apart. . . and contrasted by
smiling young firs, they were overwhelmingly grand.
The impression was absolutely new and
without comparison."

—Jessie Benton Frémont on visiting
the Mariposa Grove, 1890

6

YOSEMITE LOVE CALL

The Lucky Ring

Sheryl Senser

I HAVE TWO VERY special memories of Yosemite. One is when my fiancé, John, proposed to me on top of Sentinel Dome, and the other took place about five months after we were married.

For our wedding, we designed, and had a custom jeweler create, two highly unique wedding rings. John's ring sported a gold nugget in the middle flanked by small gold embossments of two bald eagles that John and I had photographed together during our dating years. The embossments were, amazingly, created directly from John's actual photographs, which a very talented jeweler was able to digitize and transfer into the ring via the lost-wax process. The gold nugget was large and handsome and the finest one we found after weeks of searching Sierra rock shops. To say the least, the ring was one of a kind.

My husband, John, is a landscape and wildlife photographer. Every year he instructs (and I assist) a winter landscape photography workshop based in Yosemite Valley for Yosemite Conservancy. In January 2010, we were about to begin another workshop. It was a memorable winter of heavy snows, and as we drove into Yosemite Valley we were delighted to see over two feet of fresh snow on the Valley floor.

John was to instruct the winter landscape photography course over a three-day period, which would take our group all over the Valley floor. On day two of the photography workshop, our group hiked up to Mirror Lake and made several stops along the way on Tenaya Creek to photograph the snow-laden landscape. All along the way, the group had to maneuver through deep snow, tripods sank and lenses fogged in the cold air of the deep canyon, but it was a fantastic morning photographically.

In the late afternoon, John guided his workshop group out into the snow-covered Ahwahnee Meadow to photograph the evening light on

Half Dome. Later in the evening we moved the group to Sentinel Bridge to photograph the last evening light on Half Dome. As night closed around the rosy top of Half Dome, the class folded their tripods and seemed very pleased with the day's work.

In the evening we grabbed a quick bite of dinner and then we were off to the Yosemite Library to meet the group for one of the evening critique sessions, where the day's work is downloaded and projected.

After this intense second day, late in the evening as John and I were in our room preparing for another busy third day, John noticed his wedding ring was missing. We looked all over our room and in our photography gear packs and luggage hoping to find the ring. No luck. Although we were tired from the day's activities, we spent a sleepless night, upset about the loss of the ring. I assured John that even though it would be expensive and not exactly the same, we could have another ring made. John said, not so fast. He was convinced he could find the ring.

The next day we met the group for the day's photography outing. Although the photography was wonderful, John was more than a bit upset by the loss of his very special ring. After the workshop ended, we went to the Valley Lost and Found office and filed a report with the ranger. We felt it was a long shot that we would ever recover the ring.

John and I also retraced the areas we had worked with the group at the Ahwahnee Meadow and Sentinel Bridge. There was still two feet of snow on the ground and the prospect of finding the wedding ring was growing slim. A ring of gold, one of the heaviest metals, we realized, if dropped would sink very deep into the fresh snow . . . and he had no idea where he had even lost it. We had covered miles that day and his gloves had been pulled off dozens of times to work the small buttons and focus rings of cameras. Sadly, we had to return home without the precious ring.

John had a Horsetail Fall workshop to instruct about a month later in February 2010. We planned to arrive in Yosemite early and hike along Tenaya Creek up to Mirror Lake to search those areas we had not time for during our previous visit. More than a month had passed and I knew it would be a long shot to find it. The only positive thing we had going for us is that the two feet of snow that had previously been there during the January winter workshop had melted due to a warm spell. The ground was mostly free of snow, at least for a while.

We started our search day by retracing every place we had remembered stopping the previous month. The morning was cold, frosty and overcast. About a half mile from Mirror Lake, John remembered he had led the group off the main trail and down along Tenaya Creek to photograph the rushing waters swirling around some snow-covered boulders.

John and I keenly scoured the boulder-scattered shoreline looking for any signs of the golden ring. We searched under rocks and scanned the extensive sands and gravels. Suddenly, the sun came out for a brief moment and we both saw something small and shiny sparkle under a large rock. Dropping to my knees, I scooped from the course gravels (not two feet from the rushing water's edge) my husband's wedding ring! Needless to say, we were both ecstatic. It was a miracle!

The sky once again returned to overcast for the rest of the day. John instructed the Horsetail Fall workshop that evening. Although the water of Horsetail Fall did not glow that particular evening, we sported our own glow.

In 2011 our first child was born. We named her Tenaya. A reminder of our lucky find on the banks of Tenaya Creek.

Yosemite Secrets

Cathie Wlaschin

THERE WERE STARS in our eyes as we awaited the stars in the skies the first time we visited Yosemite Park as a newly engaged couple. It was late summer, 1965, and we were on an adventure, driving together in Dave's 1958 Ford Fairlane 500 from California to Minnesota, which was home for both of us.

After a chilly night watching the spectacular firefall show from sleeping bags under the stars on the Yosemite Valley floor ("Let the fire fall!"), we enjoyed a walk in Tuolumne Meadows and were heading toward Tioga Pass to exit the park when we stopped at a large but gradual granite incline on the north side of Tioga Road. "One last hike," he said. About seven hundred feet upslope from the car, we stopped by a small character pine, and we sat down. While we enjoyed the magnificent view, Dave related with animation the story of his climb up Half Dome on his way to California six weeks earlier, long before I had joined him for the trip home. When we finally stood to leave, he said, "Stay right here a minute!" as he ran to the car. He returned with a pen and a piece of paper, and together we composed a short paragraph about the moment . . . the date, the time, the amazing view, plus a declaration that we would be back one day as man and wife to find this record of our visit. He then found a Pepsi can that had been littered nearby, and we dropped our note into the can and buried it a few inches under the soil, about one foot from the base of the lonely pine. (In 1965, we were sadly, but blissfully, unaware of ecological concerns!) I snapped a Kodacolor photo of him by the pine with my Instamatic camera; and returning to the car, we marked our well-studied Yosemite map with an X to record the location for our future revisit. Though the photo is now faded beyond recovery, the map is still a treasure; and for two awestruck visitors, the memory of that special day nearly fifty years ago is vivid still!

Fast forward: The vehicle is a 1977 Dodge Aspen station wagon, the year is 1979, and there are now four passengers; we're eager to show Yosemite National Park to our two children, ages eleven and nine. It's been fourteen years since we "planted" our love note. Would we recognize the location . . . especially since we were now heading westbound instead of eastbound? Yes, there it was. . . . We both recognized the granite expanse at the same moment. The kids excitedly jumped out of the car, with the two of us following closely behind. But, wow, how the landscape had changed. The trees—no longer small character pines—had maintained their foothold in the hard rock and had grown mightily; and try as we might, we were unable to find a spot under any of the possible trees that could even hide a Pepsi can in a few inches of loose soil. Even if our treasure had remained undiscovered over the years, the steel can had likely rusted and deteriorated by now; aluminum beverage cans didn't emerge until the late sixties.

Undaunted by our failed effort, we piled back into the car to show the kids where their dad had climbed Half Dome so many years before and to experience both the Valley and the vistas; and we enjoyed the beloved park no less than if we had reread our words of so long ago. Yet the kids enjoyed the romance of the unrecovered note so much that, before we left, they begged to do the same. Today, ten feet up a pine-canopied slope along Tioga Road, across from an asphalt turnout overlooking the South Fork of the Tuolumne River that serves as a marker, is the residue of a handwritten note with four signatures, buried at the base of a mature tree. Reflecting the beginning of a more eco-sensitive era, our note was planted unprotected and is now part of the ecosystem. While there is no photo to record the event, a second X on the well-worn map remains; and now, for four awestruck visitors, the memory of that day over thirty years ago in fabulous Yosemite National Park will never fade.

The Birthday Party

Brian Byrne

YOSEMITE VALLEY, EL Niño, the Yosemite Park and Curry Company, and the Yosemite Institute. An unlikely blend that changed the life of an Australian teenager in 1982.

The University of Queensland arranged summer jobs in the U.S.A. Being a struggling student from the tropics with no winter wardrobe, I asked the placement agency if I could go somewhere warm. They obliged by sending me to clean cabins in California, in Yosemite Valley, in January, in the middle of one of the worst El Niño winters in many years. But the incredible quiet and beauty of a snow-covered Yosemite Valley is something not to be missed and it far outweighed the inconvenience of the cold. There was also an amazing camaraderie among the brown-clad soldiers of the Curry Company as we trudged through knee-deep snow from Curry Village (where they hide the staff in winter) up to Yosemite Village. We were due at work at 9:00 a.m. and the first shuttle was at 10:00 a.m. so a brisk walk started every day.

The snow got worse, closing access to the Valley and crashing trees down onto the Curry Village WOBs (rooms WithOut Bath). We were quickly relocated to the empty cabins in Yosemite Village, where we got to mingle with the real people. My nineteenth birthday came around, and the guys I worked with invited any eligible female to join the party. That evening there must have been thirty of us crammed into a four-bed cabin. At one point the door was open, letting a twenty-degree breeze enter a ninety-degree room. Three very cute girls were standing outside while one of my Curry Co. workmates tried to convince them to join us. After a few minutes I looked up and my first words to my future wife were, "Either come in or stay out, but shut the bloody door!" Luckily they decided to take the risk and join our disreputable group.

At the time, my wife-to-be was a seventeen-year-old high school student on a decidedly underchaperoned Yosemite Institute (now Nature-Bridge) trip with her high school. They should have left days ago but the same blizzard that moved me to Yosemite Village had kept them trapped in the Valley. She asked about the reason for the party and was directed over to the skinny Aussie sitting on the end of the bed nearest the door. We clicked straight away. We both had so much in common. The fifth child from big Catholic families, Catholic schools, and a love of the same music, movies, and books. All of this stuff in common except for the small point that we lived seven thousand miles apart. I walked her back to her cabin and after a lot of good-night kisses, said good night.

We had one more day together before the storm abated and her Yosemite Institute bus headed back down Highway 140 toward Merced and then on to San Francisco. We made all sorts of plans to stay in touch, none of which I thought would come to fruition. But I guess there's something special about a relationship formed in the middle of Yosemite winter. For three years we stayed friends, relying on the prehistoric medium of letters in the mail. We complained about our respective boyfriends and girlfriends, and got to know each other in a way that only written communication can support. Then she came to Australia for a vacation and we got engaged. She had a year to go at Cal so I agreed to move to California until she got her degree. Twenty-eight years later and we are still together, living in San Francisco.

My wife's parents were avid campers and their favorite destination was lake Tenaya (back in the days when you could still camp by the lake). Like most Australians, I love the water and on my first trip I dove into the lake, thinking that if I just swam long enough I would warm up. Rookie mistake. I reached one of those flat rocks in the middle and eventually my circulation started up again. Took me quite a while, lying there looking at the granite domes mirrored in the water, to raise the courage for the swim back to shore. I really loved those trips to Tenaya. My father-in-law was a pretty gruff character but when he got to the lake, the tranquility mellowed him, and I think he even smiled a few times.

Of course we have been back to Yosemite many times over the years, but last April we took our two children back to stay in Curry Village. It was a little daunting to think that my daughter was now the same age as I was when I stayed in WOB 282 and got up to all sorts of questionable and occasionally illegal activities. I shared a sanitized version of the past with my kids.

That April there was still a lot of snow on the ground and it really took me back to that incredible winter thirty-one years ago that changed my future. Yosemite will always have a special place in my life.

How I Found a Diamond Tennis Bracelet and Marital Bliss

Bruce Klein

M Y WIFE AND I married in Yosemite in the small Yosemite Chapel. Unbeknownst to me, my wife wore her sister's husband's mother's heirloom diamond-studded tennis bracelet as something borrowed. It was beautiful. "Have you seen the bracelet?" my wife said. No, I hadn't, but I soon discovered my wife's sister hadn't asked permission of her husband to borrow the heirloom. It was priceless, loaded with family history, and irreplaceable. Panicked, we started searching.

Imagine, in the darkness, 3:00 a.m. in our jammies, flashlight in hand, searching the trunk of my wife's Jetta, the ground around the Wawona, and our room.

"Great," my wife said. "Great, just seven hours married and already the marriage is ruined."

I still remember my wife sobbing as she threw herself on the bed. I remember crawling around our Wawona room saying, "We'll find it. I'm sure we'll find it."

Of course I wasn't sure. Who knew where it was. After the wedding, we'd explored the Valley, gone sightseeing, and had dinner out. If we didn't find it, until the day we died, at every family gathering, Thanksgiving, Christmas, anniversaries, casual Friday dinner, the gossip of how the lost bracelet had ruined the wedding would haunt us.

I could envision my mother whispering at the Thanksgiving table, talking to my auntie who would lean forward, pat my hand, and say, "You poor boy." Pity was the look I got. I could hear the whispering for years, and feel the guilt.

Guilty until we die.

Of course I hated all this. Who cared? It was a bracelet, for God's sake. Of course we'd replace the bracelet. Even if we were paying it off into our nineties. It was the difference between the East Coast and the West. Between Berkeley and Yale. Between status, tradition, freedom. Getting married was the important thing. Our love.

Over breakfast the next day, the consensus was our wedding was ruined. Or at least on life support. My closest friend excused himself and sped from Wawona down to the Valley floor to start searching. My wife and I followed. Everything was to be kept quiet. While wedding joy blessed our families, fear terrorized my wife, her sister, and me.

NASCAR had nothing on me driving down from Wawona to the church. The minister opened the church for my wife and her sister. I watched them crawl away from me on their hands and knees up the chapel aisle searching. In shock, I stepped outside. Looking across the road at Yosemite Falls, I wondered why this had happened to us?

For reasons I will never quite understand, I thought: my wife must have walked up the pathway leading to the church. In my bridegroom suit, I got up, and on my hands and knees began crawling along the pathway. I really didn't know what I was doing. But I found myself, blade by blade, searching the moist muddy grass leading to the church.

I must have looked pathetic. My best friend later said seeing me frantically crawling in and across the grass, he found himself filled with a great pity. I knew nothing of this. I just knew everything was hopeless, and I must do something.

Then it happened.

A young couple with two kids came walking up the pathway toward the church. For some reason, I saw his clod-hopping feet moving in slow motion. The sole of his right foot was as big as the universe. It filled my entire visual field, like the Hindenburg dirigible collapsing on that doomed person scampering to escape its collapse.

And just then, I saw a faint glimmer, a sparkle in the wet grass.

That's it, I thought. That's it.

I must have exceeded the speed of light because my fingers were digging the tennis bracelet out of the muddy wet grass before the young boy's foot touched the ground. He screamed. I screamed. He ran to his mother's side. I held the bracelet in my hands like a demented prospector discovering gold; laughing uncontrollably, all smiles and wide-toothed grins. When I turned to his parents to explain, they turned away walking as fast as they could to their car.

What did I care? I had saved the day. Later, if and when the park rangers came to arrest me, I could explain everything. We would all have a good laugh, and they would congratulate us on getting married.

When I put the bracelet into my wife's hands, the color came back to her face. Sunshine shown again. The wedding was saved and I found marital bliss.

At least for that night.

Yosemite Couple

Dale E. Claes

W<small>E ARE A</small> Yosemite couple. We met while I was a winter employee for Yosemite Park and Curry Company working in the food line at Yosemite Lodge. She was what was called a weekend warrior, people who came into work on the weekends relieving regular workers. We met in February of 1965, when I saw her as I was coming through the food line. My thoughts were, "She's kind of cute." When she saw me, she accidentally put coffee in a guest's teapot! That guest said that he liked coffee in his tea. We went on walks to the falls, along the river, and to the Indian Flat Bar and Grill for dancing.

That summer she took a job in a settlement camp in Washington, DC. I left my job in Yosemite to follow her. Back in California, I moved to Fresno, where she lived. I asked her to marry me many times with the response of "we'll see." She eventually said YES! We were married in the Yosemite Chapel on March 18, 1967. Our reception was prepared with the help of John Curry at The Ahwahnee in the Solarium. We enjoyed a light dusting of snow during the church service and during the reception. The granite cliffs were spectacular, but my new wife outshone all of them. We honeymooned at Yosemite Lodge under a pseudonym because many Yosemite work friends were still in the park. Our wedding day dinner was in the Cliff Room. We commented to one another about a rowdy crowd in the bar section, only to find out later that they were friends from our wedding. The following year we came back to work on weekends in the Valley and were then asked to manage a High Sierra Camp. That summer of 1968, we managed the Sunrise High Sierra Camp.

Our visits to Yosemite are still many times a year. Initially we traveled to the park on a motorcycle at night, shared camping sites with others, and cooked on a curb (when this was acceptable). Or we just drove up for a day visit to the Valley or Tuolumne Meadows and beyond. We have celebrated many of our anniversaries in the suite we spent our honeymoon in at Yosemite Lodge. After forty-five years of marriage, we still view Yosemite National Park as love.

———

"That night we made the acquaintance of
Mr. and Mrs. Curry. We felt as we still do, that we had
met two people chosen by God to be the genial hosts to
mountain lovers who came to enjoy the wonders of Yosemite.
We were made to feel we were their dearest friends
because we loved Nature, the mountains, God's great
outdoors. I'm sure they made everyone feel the same."

—Mae B. NattHemper, describing her
honeymoon trip in Yosemite, 1912

The Ring

Glenn Birkemeier

Don't drop the ring. Seriously. Don't drop the ring. That's all I could think. We were on a rock in front of Vernal Fall, maybe 250 feet above the Merced River. It felt like ten times that. I could clearly envision one little fumble that would send the ring tumbling in slow motion into the rocks, only to be found years later by an amazed hiker. But I was not letting go. I had it in my pack the whole time, every minute of that trip so far. I don't know if she got suspicious that I was always wearing my backpack wherever we went in Yosemite. I've done trips with a week's worth of food and supplies on my back and they never felt as heavy as the ring. Thirty-one diamonds and three big emeralds on yellow gold. Green and gold are the colors of her beloved Green Bay Packers. She thought we were going to pose for a picture out on the rock. Our buddy on the hike was a professional photographer. He knew what I was really up to.

I almost proposed the day before in the Mariposa Grove. We were never in what felt like the right spot and it got dark earlier than I expected. So I waited a day. We were hiking up the Mist Trail. Some dark gray clouds were forming overhead. The 30 percent chance of rain from that morning's forecast was ticking upward by the minute. It was now or never. Well, not "never" but definitely later. Hey, this spot looks nice. "Dan, can you take our picture out on this rock?" WINK, WINK.

We walked out there and—oh great, she wanted to stand behind me in the picture. That won't do. She didn't like the way her legs looked in her hiking pants. She was wrong, of course. She looked beautiful, as always. But more to the point, I needed to be in front so I could kneel on the rock safely. She wasn't cooperating. No kneeling for me, then. I pulled out the ring's box and opened it. Even though my mind was locked on holding onto that ring, I somehow said, "Anessa, you are my favorite person in the world and I don't think we'll ever be in a prettier spot. I love you now and I'll always love you. Will you marry me?"

A year and a few weeks later, we were back in the Mariposa Grove. I found what felt like the right spot this time. We had our wedding ceremony in front of a giant sequoia, surrounded by our own grove of friends and family. The ring took on a different meaning for us. Like the rings that grow each year inside a sequoia, it now symbolizes our ever-growing love.

The Myth of Stoneman Bridge

Jason Burita

"THE DARKEST SCRIPTURES OF THE MOUNTAINS ARE ILLUMINED
WITH BRIGHT PASSAGES OF LOVE . . . ."
—JOHN MUIR, *The Mountains of California*, 1864

THIS IS THE love story of both my parents and Yosemite—a romance of nature and a romance of two minds. By all rights, the story, if told by my parents, would begin in Yosemite, but for me, the story begins in the bleak streets of Chicago where my father was born. As a youngster, my father escaped the dreary existence of skyscrapers and dirty streets by looking at pictures of Yosemite through a View-Master. I always imagined my father as boy prostrate on the cool basement floor, both eyes pressed against the plastic, boxy eye pieces of the View-Master, peering at the projected majestic slides of Yosemite—dreaming, dreaming of a better place and a better life. The lure and pull of Yosemite (and California) cast a romantic spell on my father even as a youngster. It is this romanticism that eventually drew him to California, where he met my mother after a tour in Vietnam. In some ways, I owe my existence to Yosemite, and to some extent a View-Master, and, more directly, I owe my own romanticism with nature to my father.

My parents' love affair was a May–June romance—they met in May and fell in love by June. The stories about their love and the catalyst of their love—Yosemite—has been told many times in our household, so much so that it has taken on a mythology of its own. Not in the sense that these stories have become exaggerated or fictitious, but in the sense that Yosemite and their love became a culture in our household. This intertwining of Yosemite and their love has left a lasting impression on me; it has shown me the importance and fidelity of love and the importance and fidelity to the love of nature; thus love and nature became a sort of religion. So the mythology goes that my father returned from Vietnam with Denny, an army buddy, to San Jose, California, where by a stroke of chance, he had a sister. Once they met, my mother and father became inseparable. I like to think that my father saw the same incomprehensible beauty in my mother that he saw as a child as he peered at Yosemite through his View-Master. At eighteen, my mother, by any standards, was a blonde, foxy, California girl, and by all rights, my father, albeit tall, dark, and handsome, looked scrawny, hungry, and a bit lost, but she saw some magic in him, something intangible, much like the nature of Yosemite itself. Nevertheless, the brief courting commenced, and from all accounts from my parents, it seems to me that my mother did most of the courting, and my father, delighted, gallantly denied fried artichokes, burritos, and other California cuisine that my mother attempted to fatten him up with.

At this point, like most romances, their kindred spirits were still not unionized, and like some romances, it is likely that, if not for some event transpired, it could have dissipated like many other romances before theirs. However, in June of 1968, they drove a Volkswagen bus not only into Yosemite Valley to camp for a week, but, unbeknownst to them, toward their own destiny. This was an eye-opening experience for my mother and father in many ways, as their love basked in the transcendent harmony that is Yosemite Valley. On a fateful day, they reached Stoneman Bridge in perfect light. The Merced River surged underneath them, and as they held hands and gazed into each other's eyes, they simultaneously experienced a powerful charge. It was as if the spirit of Stoneman Bridge conducted the power of the Merced through their bodies and allowed them to experience the grandeur of nature and their own love. However the charge occurred, they were "zapped," as my father later put it.

Thus, the comingling of nature and love became one in our family, and some of my early memories of childhood lie on the Yosemite Valley floor. By 1969, I was born, and, by 1970, introduced to Yosemite, and, though in just Kodachrome memories, I remember myself snuggled to my father's back as he trekked up a mountainside. At four, I remember hiking Lower Yosemite Fall with my parents—my father leading the way, long dark hair, shirt off, with dark lean skin, and slightly impatient, while my mom, blonde and fair skinned, cajoled me up what seemed like a grand sheer rock path. They both encouraged me to continue, even though I was tired. At the top, there was no wise speech, just the spray of the fall on my hot face, and the grandness of the fall descending . . . the grandness of it all, familial love and nature.

I have been lucky enough in my life thus far to share this familial love and the love of nature with my own children; they have been carried, strolled, and walked to the base of Yosemite Falls to hear the deafening collapse onto the rocks below. My parents' love for each other and nature has transcended itself to my own children, and my wife and I feel closer to God, and each other, nowhere else but in the embrace of Nature.

And even now, as my father struggles with cancer and my mother tries to fatten him up again, there is a certain tranquil love that comes over both their faces when they retell the mythology of their love and Yosemite; it is a union that has been extended to myself and a culture and religion passed down to my children. This "sense of wonder" with nature and love is the greatest gift that my parents and Yosemite ever gave me; it is this gift that will be passed for generations to come.

My-Semite

Joan Cunningham Gorsuch

WHEN I WAS about eight years old in Virginia, for Christmas I received a Tru-Vue with black-and-white film strips, with Yosemite National Park being my favorite. I vowed then that I would go there someday. Twenty years passed with schooling, home, and work, and then in 1964 I was given an opportunity to live in Sacramento and work for Aerojet Corporation. I made plans to drive across the country in my '61 Comet with my mother and a friend, with Yosemite as a major stop in two weeks of touring.

After driving through Arch Rock Entrance into Yosemite, we set up our Camp Curry tent cabin as home base for a few days. The park was everything I expected to see and more. Not wanting to miss anything, we saw Yosemite and Bridalveil Falls, Inspiration Point, Mariposa Grove of Giant Sequoias (including a drive through the famous Tunnel Tree), Half Dome from Glacier Point, etc. One night we gathered with hundreds of other people to see the firefall from Glacier to a rock ledge above Camp Curry. The air was still and a call went out from Curry, "Hello, Glacier." A voice answered far above, "Hello, Curry." Then the voice from Curry rang out, "Let the fire falllllll. . . ." The glowing embers were slowly raked over the edge of the precipice, giving the rock the look of a live waterfall. Sadly, the next day we left for Sacramento.

My roommate Dollye worked at Aerojet with seventeen thousand others, and it felt daunting to be there with so many people; however, I met new and interesting people, including a young editor named Lee Gorsuch. About nine months later I was caught in a large layoff and decided to return to Virginia. Before leaving, I decided to drive to Fairfield to say good-bye to friends. While there, a newspaper caught my eye with an advertisement from Yosemite Park and Curry Company. My lightbulb moment said this would be an opportunity to see more of Yosemite before heading back east, so I made arrangements for an interview in San Francisco. When the time came to leave Sacramento, I loaded up the Comet again and felt sad at leaving my new friends. When I arrived in Yosemite, it was snowing on blooming dogwood trees and my sadness lifted immediately.

My job was working for Yosemite Park and Curry in the commercial office in Yosemite Village, and I lived in the women's dormitory close by. At lunchtime I often ate while sitting on a rock gazing up at the falls.

Every chance I got I explored the Valley and beyond with friends from the dorm. We hiked to Vogelsang High Sierra Camp. Once we photographed the rising moon from the porch of the Glacier Point Hotel and saw the top of the firefall. There was a pay telephone on the porch of the dorm and when I used it, a family of roly-poly raccoons would come out to entertain me. One night about 11:00 p.m. when I returned to the Valley, the moon was so brilliant that I turned off my headlights while driving for about a mile.

One special event that I will always remember was, while at work I received a long-distance telephone call from Lee with a proposal of marriage since he was coming to visit in a week's time. Needless to say, I didn't do much work for the rest of the afternoon. By Labor Day weekend I realized that absence did make the heart grow fonder (Lee, of course) and decided that it was time to give notice.

Forwarding many years ahead, we married, had a son, Glenn, and a daughter, Pamela, and live in Tuolumne County. The proximity to Yosemite has enabled many visits to the park. When our son was small he asked, "When are we going to my-semite?" They loved being drenched by the spray of the falls and climbing on the rocks.

It is now fifty years since I first visited Yosemite, and I have wonderful memories of each trip. Some of the people I met there include Mary Curry Tresidder, Nic Fiore, author Shirley Sargent, and Huell Howser while he was filming Yosemite for his television series. Indeed, Yosemite is "my-semite," which has brought me a lifetime of joy and pleasure. I still enjoy tour guiding family and friends when they come for a visit.

Surprise Engagement

Robert Bimbi

MY GIRLFRIEND AND I have hiked to the top of Yosemite Falls many times. We use it as a gauge in our relationship. First major hike as a couple, first early-morning hike, first hike after I quit smoking. When I decided to propose, I wanted it to be in a place special to us. So on the day of my proposal, we could not find a quiet spot on top of that huge mountain! Everyone seemed to be there! So I talked her into hiking to Yosemite Point. There, after she told me this was the most perfect place she had been, she turned around and saw me on one knee, ring in hand, asking for her hand in marriage. To this day we still love reliving that moment!

How We Got Engaged at 8,835 Feet

Sarah Bohr

W<small>HEN WE WERE</small> planning our Yosemite trip, I had no idea Kevin was going to propose. Then again, neither did he. One thing we both knew was that we wanted to hike to the top of Half Dome. Everything fell into place, we got our wilderness permit, and were able to reserve a campsite . . . barely.

Our permit was for June 6 and 7. We started out early (for us) on the sixth and hiked the very steep but beautiful four miles to Little Yosemite Valley backpacker's camp. After a quiet night there, we set out to hike the even steeper and more beautiful three and a half miles to Half Dome. The first three-ish miles isn't too bad but then you get to sub dome.

Subdome is basically Half Dome's butt. It's a smaller granite formation on the "back" of Half Dome, and to get to the base of the cables you have to climb it first. It's about five hundred feet of vicious tiny switchbacks, which are themselves made up of stairs hacked out of the rocks. Most of the stairs are twice as tall as stairs should be. I can honestly say that subdome was the hardest and least fun part of the hike.

Finally, at the top of subdome and the base of the cables, we decided to take a long break before the final ascent. We watched other people slowly pulling themselves up the cables while we ate lunch and wondered why the hell we were doing this to ourselves. "There's no way they're as steep as they look from down here!" I remember thinking (spoiler: they were steeper!).

Finally working up the energy and pulling on our gloves, we started up the cables. There are no words to describe how steep the cables are— pictures don't do it justice. It took us a solid half an hour of hauling ourselves up, but we finally made it.

The top of Half Dome is deceptively large—about the size of two football fields. The views are absolutely breathtaking. We started exploring and finally made our way over to Ansel Adams's famous Diving Board—a promontory of rock that sticks out of Half Dome's shoulder. It looks like a tiny, dangerous outcropping from every angle, but when you walk onto it you realize it's actually a wide space that's perfectly safe to carefully stand on.

At some point while we were walking around up there, Kevin decided that it was time.

A lot of people have asked us how we managed to get pictures of our actual proposal. All credit for that goes to Kevin. He saw some women taking pictures of each other on the Diving Board and asked if they could do the same for us. We walked onto it and waited for the woman to get to a good vantage point. When she did, I turned to put my arm around Kevin for the shot . . . and there he was, down on one knee, holding up my ring.

I vaguely remember the woman's friends screaming "OH MY GOD TAKE MORE PICTURES TAKE MORE PICTURES!!!" as I stood there with my mouth hanging open for what felt like a year. Finally I said "OH MY GOD YES," and he put the ring on. What happened next varies depending on who you ask.

As I remember it, I gracefully collapsed into Kevin's arms with tears of joy streaming down my face and dulcet laughter flowing from my lips. According to Kevin, I tackled him and almost hurled us both off the Diving Board and into space four thousand feet above Yosemite Valley.

Whatever.

Either way, on June 7, 2012, on top of Half Dome at 8,835 feet Kevin asked me to marry him, and I, of course, said yes.

————◆————

"People enjoy being outdoors, with all of the excitement
of novelty, hazards, and simple physical well-being
which accompany the experience. A few recognize that
the outdoors exertion at high altitude actually helps
in recreating their personhood, helps them find depths
of feeling, emotion, contentment, and inspiration
not conveyed by the term recreation alone."

—Allan Shields, ranger, 1960

7

YOSEMITE HEALS

A Slice of Life on the John Muir Trail

Lori Tierney

W<small>HY WAS</small> I, a fifty-year-old woman with bad knees and asthma, trying to hike the John Muir Trail? I could barely breathe and my knees were killing me in spite of the fact I'd put on braces and was using the hiking poles that almost got left behind.

I have an ongoing love affair with Yosemite since I first stepped onto the Valley floor and worked there as a waitress when I was nineteen years old. Somewhere along the way in my life, I'd lost the young girl inside me. She thrived on adventure and thrill. I wanted desperately to find her again. Maybe this journey was going a bit too far. A woman with a grandmother's face cannot easily revisit her youth in action. But here I was in Tuolumne Meadows heading into Lyell Canyon on the third day of my 222-mile journey in the wilderness. Yosemite was still breathtakingly beautiful and stalwart; it was I who hadn't aged as well.

I was famished and realized the extra thirty pounds I'd packed onto my body wasn't helping me. Like a song in your head that won't go away, I kept remembering the words . . . "You're going to have to get in shape and lose weight if you want to hike that trail." Sean, my rock-solid fire-fighter son, told me this when I proudly boasted I was going to hike the John Muir Trail.

The John Muir Trail is said to resemble a heart-monitor chart. After three days I was exhausted. Perhaps Sean had been right. If I'd followed his foreboding advice eleven months ago, I might not be in my present predicament. Carrying extra weight on my body and a fully loaded forty-five-pound backpack made me feel and look like a turtle—especially when I fell backward onto my pack and lay on top of it. I wished I could pull my head inside my shell. No such luck. Fortunately, my hiking buddy Jane Smilth came over and gave me a hand. It felt good to be upright and moving again.

I surprised myself by trudging along steadily. Lyell Canyon outside of Tuolumne Meadows is a vision of beauty anytime, and that day was no exception. The open emerald-green meadows, the river cascading through the canyons, enormous craggy granite boulders, and a wild tapestry of colored flowers all around made the hike a scenic wonder.

I'd been in the Yosemite wilderness many times and still didn't know the names of most of the flowers. It wasn't something I was proud of. My friend Nan could rattle off the names and species of almost all of them. I could recognize Indian paintbrush and shooting stars. I tend to be a person who likes to let the wilderness soak into me and become a part of who I am. I can tell you what things look like, smell like, and how they make me feel. I often can't tell you my exact location or the name of something. I'm not great at reading maps and even worse with a compass. I wish I'd taken time to become better at both. They're good skills to have.

Rounding the corner, Mount Lyell came into view. Throwing back my shoulders, my footsteps became lighter. The soft wind and the azure sky enveloped me. I felt my mouth curl into a smile.

She was coming back. The young girl was there inside me, fueling me on, reminding me of who I used to be and could still become. Feelings I had at nineteen when I climbed Mount Lyell came creeping back into my soul. It didn't matter that my face was beginning to be laced with wrinkles, that I was dressed in the attire of an old woman with knee pads and hiking poles. The emotions inside of me were real. I was once more in love.

To love a person is one thing, to love a place and have a deep soul connection with it is another thing. I feel this way about Yosemite's wilderness. I'm lucky in love. It comes in the form of my husband, Smiley, and my sons, Sean and Craig. I felt a similar but different connection with Mount Lyell. It jutted into the skyline with a glacier atop it. Thirty years ago, my friends Barbara, Ken, and I had scurried to the top with the freshness of youth and had riotous fun sliding down it on our butts with backpacks lying on our laps. It felt like riding a toboggan chute. Ken said my curly red hair bounced around so much it looked like copper coils dancing in the sunlight. The fierce biting wind on my face and the exhilaration when I signed the climber's book on top of Lyell were memories sustaining me through the more mundane tasks of motherhood and being a second-grade teacher. I always knew that somewhere inside me the wilderness lived.

Arriving at our campsite amid alpenglow I felt a sense of accomplishment. The stars glowed like diamonds and I took out my journal to document my presence in this holy place that had always been my church.

Dear Diary,

It is important to write what you're thankful for. I'm happy to be here. A good day in Yosemite's wilderness. I know why I like it here so much. I didn't hike fast, but I didn't care. Took a peek in the tin mirror and looked like hell when I finally made it to camp. For some reason it didn't matter. Lying atop huge granite boulders while gazing and searching in the dark to see the almost invisible bats flying around was magical. I've never liked bats before now. Their eyes were glowing like embers in the fire. Everything in the wilderness interconnects, and bats eat mosquitoes. They might be my new best friends. The wonder of Yosemite engulfs me. I feel alive.

Butterfly in the Canyon

Bill Heyman

It was a beautiful day in Indian Canyon sometime in the mid-eighties on a warm summer day, as I recall. I had taken my usual route along the creek, staying mostly on the west side, and had made it to the top of the boulder field in about thirty minutes from Church Bowl, stopping here and there to take in the interesting little waterfalls and pools along the way.

I climbed into the little rock enclave, after scrambling up the lower boulder field, then scaled the ten-foot far wall, gripping the familiar handholds and emerging at the orange boulders. These amazing rocks must have contained a larger-than-normal percentage of iron that had oxidized, creating an intricate and masterful pattern of lines, shapes, and designs throughout the granite; nature's magnificent pieces of art.

Here, the upper stream ran along to the right, at points hugging the rock face as it flowed down from above. The stream's water flow greatly diminished here before completely disappearing through a system of boulders only a few hundred feet further downstream from the point where I was standing, emerging below the boulder field in the lower part of the canyon on its way to join the Merced River. While just upstream, a sheer, solid granite shoulder descended from thousands of feet above to meet it.

Just below and to the right of the orange boulders were monolithic rocks, some of which were the size of houses, stacked one upon another, as if some ancient giant had thrown them there carelessly in a fit of rage, and upon which I would occasionally find a quiet place to sit. These were just a few hundred feet or so above the tree line, and so provided an excellent vantage point from which to gaze across the Valley to Sentinel Rock, The Ahwahnee and Leidig Meadow, and an eastward view over the Village and the Lodge areas.

This day, I found a nice vantage point and quickly noticed a small bunch of blue flowers growing right out of a crevice in one of the boulders where perhaps hundreds or many thousands of years of erosion and exfoliation had taken their toll. This was not that unusual, and I had seen many things like this before in other Yosemite Valley canyons, but something just caught my eye that day and drew me in for some unexplainable reason.

I had been aware of a small blue butterfly or moth that had fluttered by, although I took no notice of it at first, since insect life was so abundant here in the spring and summer months. Yet, as I stared out over the green Valley meadows, something drew my eyes to that little bunch of flowers nearby once again. Perched quietly on one of the flower stems was my small fluttering friend. She was a bit lighter blue, as I recall, than the flower she was next to, making a slight, though not imperceptible contrast. With each gust of light wind, the flower would sway, and it seemed that this creature would quickly be blown from her sanctuary, although she was not. To my surprise, as I continued to watch, she decided to take flight, circling around me, and causing me to wonder if she was just curious about what I was doing up there, and if she could have asked me, I think she would have.

Instinctively I put out my hand, and she landed on it. I was astonished. I said something like, "Hello, how are you today?" She sat there, seemingly at peace, and appeared to know that no harm would come to her. After a minute or two, she lifted off and flew all around me again, only to land once more on my finger. This ritual continued for a good long time, probably on the order of fifteen or twenty minutes, at least, and it could have been longer. To this day, I can't explain what was going on there, or why this behavior was being displayed. I wondered if she thought I was some new plant that was conveniently growing here for her to land on. Did she sense that we had some kind of connection that stretched beyond the confines of our species? Could there have been some intelligence at work here, or was I giving off some kind of odor that was drawing her to me? What was it?

I meditated for a few minutes on John Muir's words, who said, "When we try to pick out anything by itself, we find it hitched to everything else in the universe."

I recall feeling happy, and even laughing as this little game went on between me and my unusual flying pet. She'd land, stay for a while, and then fly away, only to land again and again.

Eventually, it was time for me to leave that spot. I said good-bye to the blue butterfly, although I was reluctant to leave, and I thanked her and told her how nice it had been to visit with her. She lifted off in response as I arose, and I could sense that the feeling was mutual. Perhaps we realized we would never see each other again, and this moment in time, while remaining fixed and vivid, would only survive in my memory and in hers, though I felt remorseful for the shortness of her life, as if it were some grave injustice that we could not share equally in this regard.

As I picked my way down the boulders, and then walked or jogged down the lower canyon, I kept thinking about how strange and mystical that day had been, and about my friend, the little blue butterfly. I had a renewed sense of hope that the balance between nature and man was not only achievable, but essential, and that we have a common interdependency upon each other, upon the earth, and upon the universe in which we exist.

Yosemite Falls

Cherise Wyneken

N EAR ENOUGH FOR an outing, you drew our group of siblings to your side. Twelve of us—three carloads—all proudly bearing senior admission cards. We stopped first at the deli for sandwiches and fruit. A long, lovely ride through the springtime Sierra and a view of the canyon from a look-out on the road. Bridalveil Fall was next with its diaphanous spray, then a picnic stop with tables beside the Merced River. The others crossed the bridge; I stayed behind; watched a bikini-clad woman brave the snow-melt stream to an island in the center for a spell of sun; sat and looked up at you—falling so faithfully and far; recalled times when I was young, walked to your feet, felt the spray mist my cheek, stood in awe of your tumbling power. Knew this was good-bye.

There Will Be Another Day

Carrie Gunter

I WAS ONCE TERRIBLY afraid of traveling out of my comfort zone and never left the city area. But, gradually, I ventured farther and farther away from the familiar. I'll admit that it was a tough beginning.

I lied once, telling someone I was going hiking in Yosemite but I parked in a typical mountain area's tourist spot, Glacier Point, and never got out of my car. Heck, I had terrible panic attacks because the mountain drive was stressful with such curvy roads. Afterward, I felt guilty that I didn't see the beauty all around me.

I, like many, have a sad story. My past relationships were full of control, possession, and deceit, which led to my own low self-esteem and insecurity issues.

I've lived in the Fresno area since I was a teen and had never took the time to enjoy what's practically outside my back door. But I wanted change, and I wanted to escape the overwhelming depression. I wanted to be strong.

In 2008, I was struggling with the notion that I had cancer. I felt alone because I did not have proper support. I waited months to have surgery because I didn't know which path I should take. After months of doubt, I finally gave in and had the surgery.

So, with the realization that I did not have a deadly illness after an operation, I gained some insight and inspiration via hiking in and around Yosemite. I worked through the panic attacks by telling myself, if I was strong enough to climb up a mountain, I was strong enough to deal with life's complicated challenges.

I ventured into wilderness areas alone at times. And it was during those solitary adventures that I found peace and self-worth. I'd tackle the toughest paths and take pictures of the trail signs to show proof that I completed a hike. I wanted everyone to know that I was *really* okay.

When I did have company with me, I was told that I had a youthful, beautiful, and confident aura about myself. The pictures I've shared do not show depression or stress lines anywhere on my face, and I enjoy looking at them from time to time.

I began hiking at the beginning of spring and did not miss one weekend for more than seven months. I spent time with bears and many deer, people from different countries, hours next to a beautiful fall, just trying to hike every angle of Half Dome in one year.

My goal was to reach the top on my birthday. Unfortunately, there were too many on the trail with me when I scheduled my birthday hike, and I did not get to celebrate the year's accomplishment on top.

But, I sat with a friend on a mountain's edge just below the massive, but inspiring rock, and revealed all I've shared here with you. I explained the gradual progression after personal heartache and health issues nearly destroying me at the beginning of 2009. I cried just a bit telling my friend how I wanted to hear *Rocky*'s theme song once I climbed to the top. But a storm was coming in and the hour was getting late, so I began heading downhill for safety reasons.

Had I not spent so much time discovering and experiencing all that I had up to that point, growing spiritually, physically, and emotionally, I would have walked away with so much sorrow. Instead, I smiled after revealing my birthday motives and said, "There will be another day."

There *will* be another day . . . and it makes me smile even now retelling this tale because I'm more confident, wiser, and capable of making every hiking season even more spectacular than the last. I am a true fixture within the park these days, and every trail has a new tale to tell.

Yosemite, and all that it has to offer, gave me a new perspective on life. It healed me from my head to my toes!

"The occasional contemplation of natural scenes of
an impressive character, particularly if this contemplation
occurs in connection with relief from ordinary cares,
change of air and change of habits, is favorable
to the health of men and especially to the
health and vigor of their intellect."

—Frederick Law Olmsted,
landscape architect, 1865

A Yosemite Family History

Ellen Girardeau Kempler

As a native Oregonian who grew up exploring the wild Northwest, I did not visit Yosemite until I settled in California in 1982. The following essay about my first visit (published in the now-defunct *Los Angeles Herald Examiner*) describes a far less approachable national park than the one I've come to know well over the past thirty years. My husband's stories probably raised my expectations for a more idyllic valley than the one we discovered back then. Yosemite was where his parents honeymooned in the fifties, and where his family often camped in the sixties to watch the nightly firefall of burning embers dumped over the cliff from the Glacier Point Hotel.

I've since built on the lesson I learned that first visit: to fully experience Yosemite's wild beauty, you must escape the crowds. Back then, getting away meant backpacking out of the Valley. Over the years, it's evolved to mean visiting in fall and, especially, winter. Growing up, our two daughters loved sleeping at Yosemite Lodge and waking up to see if it had snowed overnight. Playing in the snow, eating in the cafeteria, going to ranger programs, riding the bus, ice skating at Curry Village, and learning to ski at Badger Pass all contributed to making winter our family's favorite Yosemite season. With our daughters off to college, my husband and I try to ski Badger every winter. Maybe we'll even be back to camp (with reservations) one September after the vacation season ends. We're overdue.

"ESCAPE FROM THE HORDES OF YOSEMITE"

(*LOS ANGELES HERALD EXAMINER*, 9/4/82)

Through the thirsty fields of the San Joaquin Valley the road to Yosemite's South Entrance runs arrow-straight to the Sierra. There our car climbs and winds into the mountains. The land changes. Flat fields become low-lying chaparral, and scrub oaks give way to giant sequoias. Vacation cabins replace ranch houses, and roadside towns boast fast food from A&W to pizza.

Curves and vacation jitters make me queasy. All through the Valley, I've kept my window closed against dust and withering heat. Rolling down the window now, I breathe air that's cool and curing. Silence and the spicy scent of pines soothe my stomach and quiet my nerves.

It's just the two of us, but we're worried about camping. We thought of reserving a campsite but decided to leave early and take our chances. We aren't going to a rock concert, after all. We're enjoying a spontaneous wilderness adventure.

The first hint of trouble comes at Big Oak Flat. Though it's only noon when we stop to get gas, the cashier says he's been busy all day. "Can't understand it," he says. "A week before Memorial Day. Must be the weather."

A little more worried, we get in the car fast and step on the gas. We're getting closer now. The road narrows, and mountain dogwoods bloom white by its side. We admire the scenery, wondering aloud which campground to try first. Upper River, Lower Pines, Sunnyside: to us they're just names on a map.

Finally at the gate, we ask the ranger what campground he would recommend. "None of them. Try every one," he answers, waving us off and motioning the next car forward.

Anxiousness gives way to frustration, fueling our quick descent into a sea of trees and RVs. With every mile we feel less adventurous and more foolhardy. The Valley's glacier-chiseled rock walls tower higher with every downhill turn. There's not time to stop and sightsee. Instead, we head for Sunnyside, the only campground where reservations are not required. But it's a full house of rowdy rock climbers, their Day-Glo orange tents clustered around communal fire pits.

Racing off again, we gaze out across meadows ripe for napping to a bullfrog's baritone. We try not to notice the hordes of hikers, joggers, and bikers as we near the remaining four campgrounds. But they're all full. The crowds win hands down.

That night we stay in a Curry Village tent cabin far from the whispering river. Next door an Italian couple argues with gusto, keeping us awake late. The next day, thanks to a cancellation, we get a conveniently located campsite downwind of the restroom. For awhile we live like tourists, dodging traffic on rental bikes, taking mobbed hikes, jockeying for position at nature films and standing in line to buy postcards.

On the third day we break camp, fill out wilderness permits, stuff our backpacks and flee to higher altitudes. The trail up to Little Yosemite Valley is steep, with many switchbacks, but we hike with joy in our strides. Our lungs fill with the rich smell of damp earth. Everywhere we find water, dripping off rocks and streaming down the trail. With a sound like surf, the Merced River foams white below us, crashing over rocks, free-falling over cliffs, and rising in thick spray.

Up near the top we spot a hawk circling easily in the thin air. Giddy at this altitude, we celebrate flight with a new sense of freedom.

"Before many years if proper facilities are offered, these hundreds will become thousands and in a century the whole number of visitors will be counted by the millions. And injury to the scenery so slight that it may be unheeded by any visitor now, will be one of deplorable magnitude when its effect upon each visitor's enjoyment is multiplied by these millions."

—Frederick Law Olmsted,
landscape architect, 1865

Darlene and Fayette Part the Crowds

Heather Boothe

IN 2004, I visited Yosemite with three friends, Maggi, Darlene, and Fayette. At the time, I was a park ranger at Muir Woods, and Maggi was a volunteer there. Darlene Wahl was a legally blind park ranger from San Juan Island National Historic Park, and Fayette was her German shepherd guide dog. In 2011, Darlene died after a brave three-year battle against cancer, and Maggi and I decided to repeat our 2004 trip in her honor. The following is a letter I wrote to Darlene's widower.

Dear Ken,

I'm sending you this letter and these photos for Darlene's birthday, to let you know she's still very much in our hearts. To honor her memory as an interpreter, I must tell a story. . . .

In late May 2004, I was working at Muir Woods, and a friend of mine, Maggi Daly, was a volunteer at that park. Darlene came to San Francisco for a week to attend a workshop. While in California, she wanted to visit Yosemite, so we planned for a weekend trip to the park.

I remember using her disabled access card to get us a discount on our reserved campsite at Crane Flat Campground, just outside of Yosemite Valley. The campground was nearly full that first night, and when we arrived, the kiosk was closed and a sign on the window told us where our site was—down a steep embankment off the road. We were fascinated by the fact that the campground staff, knowing we had used an access card to reserve the site, had assigned us a site that required walking down a steep dirt hillside from our car, with lots of logs to trip over. We were concerned that Darlene would trip on the hazards and Fayette would have a hard time guarding her. Darlene, of course, thought nothing of it, refusing any offers of assistance to help her find her way to the restroom in the middle of the night.

Over the next two days we wandered around the park, most memorably visiting the Tuolumne Grove of Giant Sequoias and the Mist Trail.

And it's that hike up the Mist Trail that is fused in my memory. The trail is a very popular one—at no time were we out of sight of other people, and frequently dozens of people. The first three-quarter mile is uphill, but not too bad, partially paved. I didn't know Maggi that well then, but I knew she had asthma, so I was a little concerned for her. It didn't occur to me to be worried about Darlene and Fayette; she never let her disabilities get in the way.

The next section of the Mist Trail goes steeply up to the top of Vernal Fall. The trail is a testament to National Park Service trail building, with hundreds of huge granite steps built in. It's also a well-named trail, as mist from the waterfall keeps the steps perpetually wet. The crowding on the trail adds another element, as people going up take turns with those going down on the narrow sections. Unless, of course, you've brought along Fayette. When you have a guide dog, the crowds part miraculously to let you past. Which is mostly good, except you feel obligated to continue up the steep trail without breaks.

As we slowly worked our way up the wet stairs, with Darlene and Fayette carefully feeling out each unique hewn rock step, it began to occur to me that this might not have been the best choice of trail to take them on. Most significantly, as I watched other visitors pick their way carefully down the stairs, it dawned on me that it might be really difficult for Darlene. Darlene, of course, just laughed and stayed positive, never complaining, though she did express concern for Fayette. I didn't know the trail very well at that time, but I did know there was an alternative way down, though it was about a mile longer. When we reached the top of the waterfall, we decided that we were concerned about Fayette on these rough trails, and we'd take that longer way down—the horse trail, with lots of manure, but no steps. Darlene, horse lover as always, was a bit disappointed that we didn't actually see horses on the trail, just manure.

We made it back down safely, and afterward each of us in turn was saying something to the effect of, "I was scared and tired, but I figured if Darlene/Maggi/Heather could do it, then I could, too."

Since then, Maggi has made a tradition of visiting me at Yosemite for her birthday in June each year. This year was Maggi's fiftieth, and she decided that the way she wanted to spend her birthday was hiking the Mist Trail in Darlene's honor, especially since Darlene had turned fifty the year before. Maggi and I are not in the best shape, but we were determined. We printed out a photo we had of me and Darlene on that hike in 2004, and had people take pictures of us with the photo along the trail. We told anyone who would listen that we were taking the hike in her honor. It was a beautiful day, and we pushed ourselves beyond the top of Vernal Fall and up the to the top of Nevada Fall beyond it, enjoying wine and birthday cake at the top. Then we hiked down the horse trail, of course.

As we came down the very last hill to the end of the trail, there, sitting by the old bridge abutments, was a woman and a German shepherd with a service-dog vest. The dog was in training to become a hearing-assistance dog. It seemed so right, to see Fayette and Darlene's legacy carrying on.

Maggi and I will always miss Darlene and hope this story helps you remember the wonderful place she held in our lives. When we hike the Mist Trail, we will always think of her and Fayette, always ready for adventure.

Love,

Heather

My Yosemite

Jennifer Schooley

THAT SEPTEMBER WAS its normal uncomfortably hot temperature in California's Central Valley town of Oakdale. Looking to escape the heat and to spend a quiet weekend with their nearly four-year-old son and their newly adopted newborn daughter, my parents loaded up the truck and I got to spend the first weekend of my life breathing the high-country air of Yosemite's White Wolf Campground.

Year after year we would return three or four times each summer to escape the heat and to drink in the amazing beauty of Yosemite's high country.

During high school I joined the climbing club, and at the age of sixteen I wrote my name in the registry at the top of Cathedral Peak. Standing on that peak, on that crystal-clear fall day, the world lay at my feet; I looked around silently, unable to express the wonder of seeing such a view.

After graduating from high school I attended Pacific Union College in the beautiful hills above the Napa Valley and joined the business club in its annual fall trip to Yosemite. A group of us rose early and started our one-day round-trip hike to the top of Half Dome via the cables.

Again I found myself standing at the top of a Yosemite landmark with the world at my feet. My mother, who was terrified of heights, would always ask, "Why do you insist on climbing those mountains?" but the answer lay spread out before me, as far as my eyes could see; there was nothing but breathtaking beauty. You had to climb to the top to understand the answer.

After college I lost touch with "my" Yosemite. The six-hour drive was too far for a quick weekend trip and risk of finding a full campground. The years passed by. My parents would write or call, saying they had gone to Yosemite for the weekend, a camping trip here and there, a day trip, once they spent a weekend in The Ahwahnee.

While I lived among the pines and coastal redwoods, I missed the high mountain peaks, the stars you can almost touch, and crystal-clear lakes where you can sit and watch the trout swim by.

Then my parents passed away. I sat in their living room early one winter morning and watched out their huge east-facing windows as the sun rose over the snow-covered High Sierra peaks. Tears slipped down my face. The pressure of the previous year, with its intense stress of trying to care for two elderly adults in failing health while caring for three young children aged from eighteen months to nine years, plus trying to protect everyone from a meth-addicted estranged family member, left me feeling hallow and almost emotionless.

But as I watched the sun rays edge across the sky, the snowy mountain peaks called my name.

Quickly I gathered my three boys and dog into the truck, and I turned the wheels down the familiar roads toward Yosemite.

The sun sparkled on the crisp snow as we rolled into the Valley. Above us the cliffs were hung with snow, while the falls seemed to be frozen in place.

My two older boys were awestruck; the baby slept; I was home.

In the years since my return, I have not lost touch with my Yosemite. This last year I returned four times. Photography is my passion, and now, on a professional level, I share my Yosemite with those whom, for whatever reason, cannot visit the park.

From the ice-covered lakes in the fall to the Valley blanketed in winter snow; from the springtime dogwood in bloom in the Tuolumne Grove, to Gaylor Lakes sparkling in the summer sun; from the Milky Way almost within reach above Olmsted Point, to the Big Dipper nearly touching Washington Column in the purple-black predawn sky; these moments I now capture—pictures from "home"—to take back to share with those who cannot visit and those who simply have not visited but keep thinking that they should.

And in the quiet, especially when I become homesick for my beloved Yosemite, my photography takes me back to the quiet, thin mountain air, sparkling skies, and I am home.

Yosemite with Dad

Laura Young

T RAFFIC WAS AT a standstill arriving into Fish Camp. Visiting Yosemite National Park on Memorial Day weekend is just crazy. Wondering why I ever agreed to subject myself to bumper-to-bumper traffic for hours, I glanced at the seventy-four-year-old man sitting in my passenger seat. The genuine grin on his face had not been seen for a long time. This was the first time spent with my dad since his recovery from major surgery removing deadly cancer from his fragile aging body.

The only thing my dad wanted for his birthday was to visit Yosemite.

He turned to me and said, "I have never seen the traffic so jammed, and at least we have a great view." This was the perfect time to open the sunroof. As the roof retracted, my dad lifted his face to allow the sun to illuminate his face. He looks good today, full of hope and life. My reply had to be positive, so not to make him feel he is putting me out in the dreadful traffic, so my reply was, "It's not the destination but the journey." It took hours to get to the Valley floor. It turns out to be Yosemite's busiest day of the year. The entire trip was full of us saying, "Remember when?" We have so many stories of life in the Yosemite.

As the food and beverage manager in Yosemite in the 1970s, my dad worked day and night. Back then I was forced to live with my dad due to my bad behavior in junior high school. My mom figured I could not get in much trouble in Yosemite, and it was my dad's turn to take responsibility for at least one of his two daughters. I started to remember how happy my dad and I were together. I was fourteen and my parents had been divorced for four years. My mother was a single mom with a full-time job raising two teenage girls. I was more than a handful, and part of the problem was I did not have a father figure.

Living with my dad in Yosemite was a turning point of my adolescent life. I gained respect for my father and could stop and think about what is important in my life. To keep me out of trouble, my father decided to put me to work. That was the best decision he made on my behalf. Working in a restaurant at age fourteen gave me work ethics and a feeling of accomplishment. I was making my own money, and people depended on me to achieve goals. When I was not in school I was working hard and making my dad proud.

Walking into The Ahwahnee with my dad brought back so many wonderful memories. Lunch on the back patio of The Ahwahnee was a remunerable moment. Cancer treatments took dad's appetite. That day he ate his entire lunch. I was a little less worried about my dad getting in and out of the shuttles that would take us on a tour around Yosemite Valley. My dad jumped on and off the shuttle like a champ. A man of few words, his face said it all. I can see fond memories flood his heart. He was truly happy here in the park today and all those many years ago. One memory we do not have living in the park was sitting around watching TV.

I will always remember my dad's face as he remembered some of his favorite times spent in Yosemite so many years ago. I am so blessed to have added joy to my father's life by taking him back to Yosemite on his birthday. Writing this story has allowed me to understand a little of how my personality was sculpted. Thank you, Dad, I love you.

Atop Clouds Rest: A Story of Hope in a Hard Place

Ron Reason

On Saturday, September 8, 2012, I decided to hike up Clouds Rest, in the northern part of the park, despite feeling achy and tired from a week of trekking various gorgeous spots off Tioga Road. From the descriptions and accounts from fellow hikers, it sounded like this would make for an unforgettable experience. That it turned out to be, for more than just the scenery.

At 9,930 feet, Clouds Rest towers five hundred feet over Yosemite's landmark, Half Dome, across the Valley. It's a strenuous, seven-and-a-half-mile uphill climb. (Round trip is more than a half marathon, but at what seems to be a twenty- to forty-degree grade with switchbacks much of the way!) The peak itself is not really so perilous, although about one quarter of climbers seem to halt about five hundred feet short—from vertigo, fear of heights, or wind or lightning or whatever. Hikers are surrounded by deep valleys on all sides and mountains all around in the distance.

At the top, I observed a man, about twenty-four years old, with what I was told was advanced multiple sclerosis, walking shakily with two canes and braces, attempting that final five-hundred-foot stretch, seeking to experience the spectacular view.

Eight men (with a civic or philanthropic group, Rotarians maybe?) had taken turns carrying him up the entire trail in some sort of chair device, just to that five-hundred-foot-short mark.

Helped out of the chair, with the eight guys circling him for safety and clearing a path, he would walk two to three steps with the help of his supports, halt, sometimes fall, but then get back up, rest and catch his breath and balance, and then push on.

Normally a shutterbug, and a journalist by training, I did not take a picture of the endeavor, because it seemed like such a precarious, private, and special moment for all involved, but I cannot get this inspiring guy, and those who helped him, out of my mind. I wish I knew more about the guy and his friends, but just observing them renewed my faith in humanity.

I took a photo from the peak of Clouds Rest on that afternoon. The view faces the opposite direction of the peak; for scale, if you know the park, the huge Tenaya Lake off Tioga Road is in the center background, a small blue dot.

My Favorite Place

Josie Gay

Yosemite National Park is undoubtedly one of my favorite places in the world. I have traveled to Machu Picchu, the Amazon, Zion National Park, the Olympics, the Cascades, the Great Wall . . . and those places are magical and wonderful in their own right, but Yosemite stole my heart many years ago. Now, if I don't go to Yosemite at least twice to three times each year, the year just doesn't feel complete.

My reasons for going vary: Sometimes I just need a little solitude and to clear my head, so I go alone. Often I've gone because the weather was gorgeous and the falls were calling. Once I went and fell deeper in love with my fiancé. And now that we are married, we have started going there with his two children each summer. We look forward to our time there.

Our most recent trip was an interesting one. And I have to say, if I hadn't been in Yosemite, surrounded by the mist of Vernal Fall, the news of a tragic situation in my life just wouldn't have been bearable.

We were there for our annual trip with the kids, hiking the beautiful final steps up to Vernal Fall when my phone rang. Yes—I had the cell phone on. A sin for us, but this time it was on because we were waiting for news of my mom's recent visit to her doctor. I was informed on that phone call that she most likely had an advanced form of ovarian cancer, and they were rushing her to surgery. It was devastating. There was static on the phone, the waterfall was thundering, and I felt like my world had just caved in. Moments into the phone call, my stepson wrapped his arms around my waist, my husband rested his hand on my shoulder, and my stepdaughter held my limp hand. In that moment, I turned to look at the fall and was overwhelmed with the beauty and love surrounding me.

I will forever thank Yosemite for this moment. That park and those trails are powerful, healing, magical, and forever intertwined into my life and my being.

A Yosemite Family Legacy

Ruth Sasaki

WHEN MY MOTHER was a child growing up in San Francisco in the 1920s, there were many more restrictions than there are today. For example, Japanese were not allowed to go swimming at Sutro Baths out by the Cliff House. Vacation destinations therefore had to be carefully chosen, usually researched through the Japanese community grapevine, in order to avoid hostility and disappointment. My family often packed picnic lunches, not only to save money and eat the foods they preferred, but because there were establishments in California that did not welcome nonwhites.

But Yosemite was open to everyone. There are pictures of my grandparents with my mother, aunt, and uncles, picnicking in Yosemite in the 1920s through the 1950s, when I was born.

My father also had memories of being taken on family trips to Yosemite in the 1920s by his father, a Japanese immigrant who ran a grocery store in Berkeley. The Sasaki family "returned" to Hiroshima in 1926—"returned" in quotes because my dad and his sisters had never been to Japan, and they had a hard time fitting in there because they were "different." In 1936, my dad came back to San Francisco on his own, at age eighteen, lured back, perhaps, by those happy childhood memories.

With genes like that, it's no wonder that Yosemite was woven into my DNA. My first trip there was in utero; my mother was expecting me when the family vacationed there in 1952. After the war and the internment of Japanese Americans, Japanese Americans struggled to reestablish their lives, and money was often tight. But it was still possible for a man to take five days off in the summer to take his family of six to Yosemite. We stayed in Cedar Cottage—my mother no longer enjoyed camping out, as it reminded her of internment camp.

I still remember picnicking at a campground one year. We finished our meal and had extra milk left. My dad walked over to the white family picnicking at the next spot and asked if they could use it. They accepted it with thanks. So even families working their way up to the middle class could go to Yosemite and enjoy the outdoors in one of the most beautiful places on this earth.

Our childhood was filled with Yosemite memories: craning our necks to watch Glacier Point from the Valley floor on a summer night, hearing someone call "Hello, Glacier Point!" and an answering call from above, "Hello, Camp Curry!" Then there would be a dramatic pause, and the magic words: "Let the fire fall!" And a cascade of fire would fall from Glacier Point to the Valley floor. I remember seeing a bear for the first time; getting caught in a summer storm while hiking down from Glacier Point and seeing a lightning bolt crackle over Yosemite Falls (I was a city kid, so this was a huge deal); almost drowning in the Merced River and being pulled out by my Uncle Edwin; feeding squirrels (before it was prohibited) from the balcony behind the old cafeteria at the top of Glacier Point.

As my sisters and I grew into adulthood, Yosemite stayed with us. We experienced it in a different way—camping out with friends, or exploring Wawona and the high country. My job at one point involved conducting training programs for Japanese managers, and I always tried to plan a weekend trip to Yosemite. I wanted them to get a sense of the size, beauty, and wildness of this country. In Japan, everything is so controlled and orderly—even nature; so it was always an eye-opener for them to get a glimpse of the wilderness and what it must have taken to survive in it.

When my dad was diagnosed with cancer in 1984, one of his last wishes was to see Yosemite one last time. But it was winter, and by the time the weather cleared, he was too weak to make the trip.

As if to make up for that, we began taking our mom and aunt to Yosemite every spring and fall. In 1987, we discovered that, after many years of closure, the trail to Sentinel Dome had been reopened. We hiked from the Glacier Point Road to the top of Sentinel Dome. My mother was thrilled to make it to the top.

Like clockwork, my sister Susan and brother-in-law Daryl and I took our mom and aunt on twice-yearly trips to Yosemite. Sometimes our sister Joan, brother-in-law Paul, and niece Stephanie came, too. We had our little rituals: stopping for a picnic lunch in Modesto, near where my brother-in-law grew up; walking out to the meadow and the Swinging Bridge (even though it doesn't swing any more); bringing a bento (picnic lunch), and scones for the next day's breakfast; reading or writing postcards on the balcony at the Lodge; going for a serious hike or bike ride while my mom and aunt rode the shuttle bus to the Village, Happy Isles, and Mirror Lake; stopping at the Almond Plaza in Salida on the way home. Vince, who works at the Mountain Room Restaurant at Yosemite Lodge, and Paul Beamer at The Ahwahnee, where we always had breakfast before heading home, would greet us like old friends. My aunt finally became too frail to make the trip; that year, my mom bought a video of Yosemite so that she could watch it after she was no longer able to come.

Now my mom is gone, too. But we still have Yosemite; and now, when we walk through the meadow to the river, the spirits of our loved ones walk with us. Hovering in the brilliant redbud, the flowering dogwood, or flowing under the stoic granite of the stone bridge, there are yet more good memories, waiting to be made.

———◆———

"Who will gainsay that the parks contain the highest potentialities of national pride, national contentment, and national health? A visit inspires love of country; begets contentment; engenders pride of possession; contains the antidote for national restlessness."

—Stephen T. Mather, first director of
the National Park Service, 1920

Wish Come True

Shari Robblets

IN 2003 MY best friend was diagnosed with stage-four breast cancer. She wasted no time writing her bucket list. One of the places she wanted to see before she left this world was Yosemite.

I had the privilege to spend a few days in the park with her in the summer of 2008, only a few months before her death. This trip was truly a magical experience for both of us. I have been to the park many times and have always been inspired by its beauty. Seeing it again through her eyes was so special. She saw her first brown bear and enjoyed the magnificent views from Glacier Point, as well as many other special moments. We were fortunate to stay at the Wawona Hotel and enjoy sitting on the porch watching the wildlife. I will always remember that visit and the joy it brought to her.

Thank you to all the people who love and maintain this beautiful place.

Bracebridge

Tim Aregger

AFTER MY TRUCK was packed, I lifted Dad from his wheelchair into the shotgun-side seat. He was so excited that he didn't even notice the melted glove box that had resulted from my ex-girlfriend leaving the Smokey Joe on the floor with smoldering coals still inside of it.

Like John Muir must have felt when he started his walk from San Francisco to Yosemite, we were exhilarated about beginning our journey across California.

Bracebridge or bust!

For almost forty years, Dad and I got together once a week for dinner and a show. We simply called it "Father and Son Night."

When we started this tradition, we both worked in San Francisco. We'd meet at the terminal and ride the ferry back to Larkspur, where we'd get in our cars and drive to one of our favorite restaurants.

When Dad could no longer drive, I'd pick him up, we'd go out, and I'd take him home.

In his waning years, I'd go to his care facility, wheel him to my truck, lift him inside, and off we'd go.

Long ago, one of Dad's friends waxed poetic about a Christmas event he took his family to in Yosemite called the Bracebridge Dinner. This yuletide pageant was held at The Ahwahnee and featured a seven-course meal accompanied by singing, carolers, and stories set in a seventeenth-century Renaissance-themed era. Dad spoke about it many times over the years and it finally dawned on me: take him to Bracebridge. That would be a Father and Son Night to remember.

Unbeknownst to Dad, I'd been trying to get us into Bracebridge for years. But it'd become so popular that it became a lottery. Year after year I tried to get us in, but we were never selected.

As the holidays were approaching in 2002, I decided to try again and discovered that after seventy-five years, the Bracebridge Dinner became first come, first served. Would tickets already be gone? I called reservation agent Lori Lancaster to find out.

Lori had been helpful to our family over the years in booking reservations and making sure we had a memorable experience in Yosemite. She said there were tickets available, but getting a good table assignment might be tough. I mentioned that Dad was losing his eyesight and hearing, and that any consideration The Ahwahnee could provide would be greatly appreciated. She said she'd do her best.

In our room at the Lodge we slowly got ready for the evening. I bathed and shaved dad, and dressed him in his tuxedo. I showered and dressed in mine.

I poured us each a glass of wine, opened a bag of his favorite goldfish crackers, and we just relaxed—two bachelors dressed like penguins—as we stared through our picture window at the iconic monolith that is Half Dome.

Then, as if The Ahwahnee was in a giant snow globe, and God picked it up, shook it, and set it back down, it started to snow ever so lightly. With Half Dome still visible, it was if I was looking at an animated Ansel Adams photograph. It was beautiful. I looked at Dad and exclaimed, "Look at that!" He softly said, "Fantastic?" He liked the idea of snow, just not being in it.

Since his stroke, speech was difficult for him. So he came up with words that could cover a vast spectrum with a minimum of effort. Words like "Whatever," "That's special," and, of course, "Fantastic."

Dressed in a red tuxedo, our "host" walked to Dad and me to usher us to our table. To my surprise, I recognized the tan face and signature smile as that of Nic Fiore, longtime director of Yosemite's Badger Pass ski school. He recognized but couldn't place me. I reminded him that I taught in Tahoe back in the seventies. Like several instructors I knew, our introduction to skiing was when Nic taught us at Badger Pass. For me, that's when I was seven years old.

Nic taught over a hundred thousand people to ski. By introducing a love of skiing to so many, including some like me who also became instructors, one wonders how many skiers on any winter day trace their skiing genealogy back to Nic Fiore.

He escorted us along the long carpet of the grand dining room toward our table. The room was starting to fill, and I was wondering where Nic would seat us. I was wondering a long time because Nic walked us all the way to the front row, placing us at what must have been the finest table in the room. Lori had come through, big.

Minutes after settling into our seats and introducing ourselves to our tablemates, Nic placed a couple next to me and continued chatting with them. After introductions, I asked the gentleman, "How do you know Nic?" He said, "He taught me to ski when I was a kid."

The performances from "Squire Bracebridge," "the Parson," and "the Jester" were terrific. The seven-course meal was wonderful. The singing was spectacular. "O Holy Night" sung a cappella from a soprano and tenor duet was unforgettable.

Being at this special table, the Parson and Jester came over several times and kidded us. Dad and I weren't just at the pageant; we'd become part of it. Throughout the night, I'd look over at Dad from time to time and he was beaming.

When we headed to the bus to take us back to the Lodge, the light snow had turned to a full-on blizzard. Dad, the one who didn't want to be in the snow, didn't even seem to notice it. He just had the biggest smile I'd seen on him in a long while.

After I got him ready for bed I asked, "So Dad, what did you think?"

"Fantastic!"

Dad passed a couple of years ago, and I miss him, especially at Christmas. But memories of our finest Father and Son Night—The Bracebridge Dinner—helps fill the void.

Rock-Solid Friendship

Wayne Kirkbride

I RECENTLY VISITED A couple of old friends. Not a word was spoken between me and those two. We couldn't, but I was able to renew our old acquaintance just the same.

I thought about how long I had been visiting them. The earliest I could remember was when I was eighteen and had just graduated from high school. I rummaged through some old photographs until I found the one I remembered. Here I was, skinny, tanned, with a full head of hair, sitting on a rock with a big smile on my face and with one of the two old friends in the photo, just over my shoulder in the background.

Since that time, over fifty years later, I have made several trips to revisit them. I, of course, have changed a lot since I first met them. Marriage, kids, divorce, remarriage, death of a child, job changes, grandchildren, retirement, all have taken place and all have played a part of who I am today. In times of uncertainty, or sadness, or lost direction in life, I sometimes have visited them and found strength in their unchanging character, which has, in many instances, lifted my spirit. I look back over the old black-and-white photo. I look at several other photos taken over the years—some with my own children that I had introduced to my oldest friends—and notice how similar the theme of the photo remains. Two unchanging giants and young smiling faces in the foreground.

El Capitan and Half Dome are the names people have given them. From generation to generation, they draw people like me back to their domain to gaze upon their grandeur and to lift spirits in a world that at times seems on the brink of destruction by the current generation of madmen who come and go over the years, only to be replaced by others with the same mind-set; with the changing values of society, the political and social upheavals in the world, with the private-personal successes and failures of each of us in the human family, I found stability in one corner of the earth where one may go to wash away, to some extent, the cares of the world. It is as though these two speak to one's soul to reassure us that they are there as our compass through life's journey. Unchanging. Steadfast. No wonder, then, that the ancient inhabitants of Yosemite Valley revered it as a holy, spiritual place. Those who came after felt the same draw of strength that I speak of. Preserved for generations to rediscover, to refresh their troubled lives, or just to experience joy to be in the presence of these two giants along with the other wonders of the area, the park is holy ground. God's natural chapel. Two of His ministers, El Capitan and Half Dome, have served me well over my lifetime. Their unspoken sermons have whispered quietly and reassuringly to me over the years. I always feel welcomed back in their presence when I visit them. Their wonder and rugged beauty never waver, and after my visit with them, I feel refreshed, rejuvenated. How lucky I am to visit with them frequently.

Yosemite Cannot Lie

Carolyn Montano

IN THE VALLEY where I live, the rain comes in midwinter and stays until early spring. Most days the sky is glaring and hazy, hiding from view anything more than twenty miles away. Often, in the early part of summer and well into autumn, it is easy to forget this is a valley at all. But then all of a sudden it is spring again and one of those rumbly bumpy thunderstorms rolls through from the west, scattering its showers randomly over the farmland, threatening blossoms newly burst forth from buds, pelting the valley floor with tiny pea-sized hail, and in its wake leaves golden stretches of sunlight across freshly washed fields that lead right up to the foothills of one of the world's greatest mountain ranges, the Sierra Nevada. When that happens, the world around becomes transformed, and it becomes evident that, yes, this place is still a valley.

I have parked my car beside the road on a summer night out in the country and lain upon its warm hood while the engine ticked and popped as it cooled. I have listened to the crickets in the tall, sweet-smelling grass and gazed into the marvelous summer night sky. I have put my feet in the cold running waters of the river as it pushed past and through and onward. I have stood in quiet pastures in the alpenglow of evening and listened to the horses around me grazing, chewing slowly; pulling, then chewing more. In those moments, I marvel and think there could be nothing more satisfying to my senses than the pleasure of the moment I am in. Like the moment your car bursts through the north end of the tunnel and there before you, Yosemite Valley. One minute windows down, hair whipping 'round, radio loud and the air abuzz with excitement and then . . . like the shuttle separated from its rockets, seeming nearly weightless and motionless, floating into the quiet of Yosemite. The world behind you, the one from the other side of the tunnel you have passed through, falls away as if you have been launched. No matter how many times I've had that experience, each time I see that view, it feels like I never have seen it before.

Recently, I read that the reason we can't reexperience the emotions we feel the first time we hear a piece of music, or see something beautiful, is because messages sent to our brain depend upon specific details of the moment based on our senses. After hearing a song for the first time, you will not be moved the same way the next time you hear it. Coming through the tunnel, the first glimpse of Yosemite Valley makes an exception of that knowledge for me. Every time I've looked down and into the depth and length of Yosemite Valley from that vista point, I could swear I'd never seen it before. It always feels like the first time. My senses all become sharpened: the sound of gravel crunching under boots, soft and muffled voices of people at a distance, the call of a bird, the hum of the vehicles approaching through the tunnel. The weather is more penetrating, whatever the weather is just then. My soul awakens. In that moment I feel so completely connected to the Universe, the earth, the place where I stand upon it. A rush of spiritual wisdom comes over me. Everything is reset once again. It is the first time. In that moment, all is truth, for Yosemite cannot lie. Before my eyes and tangible, Heaven. Nothing, no other natural experience, has ever touched me more deeply or been more profound than that of Yosemite.

8

MY DUTY STATION

Xmas Greetings From Q. G. Patterson

My Summer at Glacier Point

Jim Salisbury

As the summer of 1951 neared, I had thoughts of earning enough money to purchase a reliable automobile before the start of my high school senior year. That all changed when I heard that summer jobs were available in Yosemite. I was hired at a Yosemite Park and Curry Company interview in Los Angeles, and soon bused to the park.

My first view of the Valley was one I'll never forget. What beauty! Originally, I was assigned to The Ahwahnee, then to laundry duty in the Valley. Before my first shift at either place, I was reassigned to the Glacier Point Hotel. I had no idea where or what that was.

I wasn't very impressed with my first glimpse of the old hotel. However, I soon began to really appreciate its charm. As for the view from the point . . . WOW!

Seven or eight of us male employees were housed in tiny ground-floor rooms on the downhill, or view side, of the hotel. Two fellows to a room. Female employees had rooms on the upper floor in the hotel. From our doorways we had an unobstructed view of Half Dome, Nevada and Vernal Falls, and the vast high-country panorama beyond. I have never seen anything to compare.

My duty was to work the early shift in the cafeteria. Get-up time came at 5:00 a.m. in order to help prepare breakfast for the hotel guests. My shift usually ended about 3 p.m.

We took turns getting the firefall ready. Midafternoon, two of us loaded the old pick-up truck with fir bark pieces from the huge pile at the south end of the hotel. The bark chips were then piled at the rim push-off point and ignited. The firefall was always a much-anticipated nightly event.

Glacier Point visitors and employees began gathering at the point about dark. We enjoyed the ranger talks, storytelling, and impromptu group singing accompanied by my roommate's ukulele. By then, the chips were a mass of glowing red embers. At exactly 9:00 p.m. someone from Camp Curry called out in a loud voice, "Hello, Glacier." The greeting was barely audible at the point, over a half mile above. The call was returned from us, "Hello, Camp Curry." Then it went back and forth. "Is the fire ready?" "Yes." From below, "Let the fire fall." Finally we responded, "Okay." Immediately, our two 'fire pushers' began pushing the glowing embers over the edge. We pushed from the sides in alternating strokes. Because the heat was tremendous, long-handled push-type rakes were used.

After the firefall, on most nights, some of us would pile into someone's car and head to the Valley for the rest of the evening. Sometimes to the dance pavilion, sometimes just to visit with our Valley friends. If I was driving my rusty 1941 Chevrolet, it was necessary to fill the radiator at the midpoint, going and coming. That place being the now long-gone service station at Chinquapin Junction. We appreciated that they left the water faucet available. That holey radiator plagued me all summer.

Another of our rotating duties was dumping the garbage. The dump was a few miles from the point, not far off the main road. The trick was to find a dumping spot away from the half dozen or so resident bears. We'd dump the barrels, jump back into the truck, and watch the bears run toward us for their fresh meal.

Near the end of summer, I fell asleep while driving back from the Valley alone one afternoon. My car ran off the road and sideswiped a large tree. No damage to the tree, but my poor Chevy lost its right headlight. No problem driving during the day, but night driving was a challenge. Nearest repairs were in Merced. Not wanting to take the time (or expense), I got the bright idea of taping a flashlight on the fender in place of the missing headlight. My friends were impressed, but the park ranger wasn't. He warned me in no uncertain terms to not drive that car in the park at night.

All in all, 1951 was a great summer. Did I save enough money for the car upgrade? NO. At seventy-two and a half cents an hour, almost nothing was saved. Room and board were provided; however, tax was withheld for our housing. But how could I complain about a summer spent in surely one of the most beautiful places in the world?

———

"Regulation 53. When teams, saddle horses, or pack trains approach, automobiles shall stop and remain at rest until the former have passed, or until the drivers or riders are satisfied regarding the safety of their horses. If the approaching animals manifest signs of fear the engine must be stopped."

—Mark Daniels, Yosemite superintendent, 1914

Oh, Those Volunteers!

Robert Campagna (volunteer in 2005, 2006, 2007, 2009, 2010)

BUT WHY?"

That question is often asked of Yosemite Association (now Yosemite Conservancy) volunteers. "Why do you volunteer?"

Some volunteers take leave or vacation from work. Many abandon the comforts of home and retirement. Some travel thousands of miles to report for duty.

Most volunteers come from California. Others have come from Virginia, Iowa, Colorado, Oregon, Washington, and Nevada.

It's not for the pay, though a minor stipend helps pay for food or fuel.

Volunteers live in tents or campers. They randomly assemble to become community, a gathering that resembles Woodstock and M.A.S.H. blended.

Bathrooms are shared. The nearest shower is over half a mile away. Campground neighbors can be noisy. Laundry is a dicey prospect. Random visits by bears and other forest creatures punctuate the night. (One particular bear visit resulted in Lower Pines campers chasing it with an air horn.)

The meals of volunteers can be a hodgepodge of foods cooked in the campground. Sometimes they enjoy finer dining at Curry Village, the Yosemite Lodge, Degnan's Loft, or in a daring moment . . . The Ahwahnee or Mountain Room.

Proudly wearing the Yosemite Association shirt, bedecked with pins illustrating their years of service, they operate a variety of stations: the yurt, the membership booth, the Nature Center at Happy Isles, or the Yosemite Museum Gallery.

They daily face thousands of visitors from dozens of countries and from all over the United States. The questions are often repetitive, sometimes humorous, and always answered professionally:

- Why can't I drive to the top of Half Dome?

- Where can I catch the shuttle?

- Do Indians still live in the Indian Village?

- Is curry sold ANYWHERE in Curry Village?

- How can I take a speedboat from Tenaya Lake to the Valley?

- Where are the geysers?

- Is there a restaurant on the Four Mile Trail?

- The waterfalls are dry. Wasn't the water bill paid?

- Must I drive to the Wilderness Center?

- Where can we see rattlesnakes? Or bears? Or mountain lions?

The most common question of all is "I only have two hours here, what can I see?" That also is the saddest question. Yosemite is too large to trivialize.

Through it all the volunteers patiently handle visitors one at a time.

Each month a new volunteer crew assembles. Each month that group forms its unique collective personality.

Underlying that diversity of volunteers are recurring elements: passion and commitment.

Those elements help volunteers endure challenging conditions and unpredictable situations. Passion sometimes makes volunteers drive each other a bit crazy. Passion and commitment link all to a great life adventure. Consider these perspectives:

Bill Love (Reno, Nevada), a retired teacher of music, finds an "unexplainable inner connection with the Valley." The wind in the trees and the pine smell enticed him to return a second time.

Marianne DeLuca (Reno, Nevada) is enlivened by walking through meadows and satisfied when she helps tourists who donate to Yosemite Conservancy after being helped. "It's then that I know I did a good job!"

Like all first-time volunteers, she has the nickname "newbie." Her warm, caring approach is appreciated.

Mary Jane Johnson (Santa Clara, California) has volunteered for five months per year for seventeen years. "I realize I have spent over six years of my life living in this camper!" Her husband, Vern, often joins her. They first met while in service to the park. Yosemite is in her blood.

First-year volunteer Neila Stewart (Santa Rosa, California) sacrifices a month's work as a corporate graphic designer. She came to "meet people, to hike, to be in nature, and to be in this stimulating environment." Her high energy and sense of organization prove effective.

Nine-year volunteers Mary and George Sutliff (Ontario, California) honeymooned in Yosemite. Mary appreciated the "sense of community" among the volunteers. "However, if we weren't volunteering, we'd still come to Yosemite," she once said. As for life in the woods, George exclaims "I love it!" adding, "animals do their thing, I do mine." (George has continued to volunteer since Mary's death in 2010.)

Carol Harris (Sacramento, California) became the monthly campground coordinator in her seventh year as a volunteer. She recalls the adjustment period when she returns to her "other life." "My friends want to know about how I live in a tent, it's a curious source of humor for them."

Bob Campagna (Loveland, Colorado) has volunteered five times, four times in the summer and once on special assignment in February 2007. He always drives from his homes in Colorado and Iowa. "As a photographer, I wanted to visit this sacred shrine of Yosemite. It has a sense of aliveness. I like to balance time between helping visitors and exploring the park."

Suzy Hasty joined the Yosemite Association in 2009 as volunteer coordinator after retiring as an art teacher. She moved to Mariposa to be close to Yosemite. "My first season has been physically challenging, dealing with driving, altitude, temperature differences between the Valley and Tuolumne Meadows." Hasty adds that working with volunteers is quite satisfying. "I see volunteers who keep giving, in or out of uniform, to help people have the best experience in the park." Seeing Yosemite every morning is an "incredible gift" Hasty added.

Yosemite is indeed a gift. Much as volunteers love the park, they also must let it go. There isn't always a certain return. There is no sense of entitlement.

High-energy second-timer Phil Rocha (Fairfield, California) always concludes his service to tourists by saying "my pleasure!" And so it is with volunteers, "our pleasure!"

Yosemite Fire

Brian Galle

In the summer of 1991, I had the pleasure of being a part of the Yosemite Fire Team based out of Wawona. What a great group of people I was able to grow with. As a team, we responded to several backcountry fires. My first experience was a "raging" fire, a whole one-chain, or sixty-square-foot smolderer. Another firefighter and I were flown by helicopter by a Vietnam veteran pilot and inserted somewhere above Chilnualna Falls. With a one-skid landing, this combat pilot dropped us right into the fire fight, literally. Using backpack pumps, Pulaskis, and McLeods, our team of two fought hard to contain the flames. After a long, four-hour fight, we contained the inferno and settled in to ensure that our protective lines preserved the pristine backcountry. The peace and pride I felt at that moment recharged my soul. We enjoyed lunch and took in the spectacular view. As the flames died to smoke and smoke died to coals, our need to stay died with it. Clearly, we were successful, and the fire could be declared out. About the time my adrenaline was wearing off, our peace was interrupted by the crackling of the radio on my partner's hip.

"Are you all ready to come back? We need you at the station, there's more strikes out there." It was our red hat Lisa's voice. "Can I send a bird to get you guys?"

"No," my partner said, "it's too windy."

I looked blankly at him, wondering if the light breeze I felt constituted "too windy."

An hour later, as we wound through the beauty of Yosemite, hiking our way out, being bathed by the mists of Chilnualna Falls, I understood the reason for his response. That summer, I was blessed to enjoy some of the most beautiful sites known to man. That summer changed me forever and gave me an appreciation for the gifts nature has to offer.

What About the Aspen?

Beverly Combs

On-the-job" training—the best kind, especially when made up of a combination of "book learning" and "in-the-field" study. As month-long volunteers with the Yosemite Association, now Yosemite Conservancy, we were privileged to work in the museum of the Mariposa Grove of Giant Sequoias, Wawona, one home of the largest living entities in the world. During the earlier years, we did book sales as well in the museum, so had at our fingertips the latest in research on these vast trees, as well as the opportunity to actually walk among them.

As the Augusts, when we volunteered, passed, I became complacent, spouting out the statistics of the trees being larger (in bulk) than two dinosaurs, one stacked on the other, or three whales in the same position. And yet, way in the back of my head, almost buried under Mariposa Grove tree statistics, was one other tree name: aspen!

One summer day in the Grove Museum began as all the days did—beautiful sunny weather, tourists hanging on our every word, and many people wandering through the grove. That was when the dreaded question unexpectedly came. It was what appeared to be a sixth- or seventh-grade boy who asked it: "What about the aspen?"

My mouth stopped spewing statistics, and my brain found itself at a loss. It had come—after several years, the dreaded "aspen" question had been asked. Being a year-round mountain dweller, I, too, had seen the aspen groves—each tree connected by its roots to its neighbor, whose roots in turn produced its duplicate trees. Yes, the huge grove could, indeed, be construed as one great organism.

Unwilling to stand there and just glare at the boy, I had to agree that he had given the only argument that could possibly be made against all of my statistics: can we count the aspen grove trees as one?

I roused myself to congratulate him on his botanical knowledge and on not being too shy to challenge the volunteer docent when he knew he had facts with which to back up his claim.

Never again since have I been asked that iconoclastic question, "What about the aspen?" But, I hope to be, again, as more middle school kids open their minds to learning and to solving more mysteries in this world of nature yet to be unraveled.

The Queen and I

Anne Cannon-Graviet

I STOOD AT MY Ahwahnee maid's cart early one morning . . . and I just couldn't help it—I had had enough and I burst into tears. "This is NOT fair!" I said to myself, miserably. See, I was an Ahwahnee front desk clerk and cashier, not a maid! That was true up until a couple weeks ago, up until the winter layoffs came around.

After deciding my summer job was going to be year-round (five years), it was my turn to "pay my dues." The former maids who were transferred to the front desk this summer, the ones that I helped train, had more overall seniority than I, so they got to stay, and my choice was between the housekeeping department or unemployment.

That same morning, the general manager's secretary was wondering why the hotel had a maid crying in the mezzanine, so she kindly stopped to ask what was bothering me. Through my tears she heard me say that I was a fully trained secretary back in Iowa, and a desk clerk here, not ever a maid, and I wasn't enjoying manual labor at all.

As fate would have it, she was going on vacation for a few weeks and needed a temporary replacement. Later that week she was showing me her desk, phone, and filing cabinets, and I was freed from being expected to imitate Wanda Wackerman's training technique in hand-scrubbing a toilet with bare, ungloved hands. ("Make sure you clean out the little hole in there too!" she said, poking a finger vigorously into the little hole, and then her whole hand went inside the larger toilet hole like a plunger. We had brushes, but Wanda didn't train us how to use them.)

My temp work as secretary for the GM earned me a roving hotel position thirty days later. What a relief and what fun for me!

So that winter, I worked at the Sweet Shop scooping ice cream, I delivered buckets of ice for a dollar, I "portered" the lobby (whatever that meant, but I decided removing the cigarette butts from ashtrays was a part of my duties, being careful not to overdisturb the running-Indian design (or was it an "A"? I've forgotten, it was so long ago. It might have been an A. . . .) stamped into the fine white sand of the hotel's ash-stand containers from back in the day when you could smoke inside the hotel), and I was grateful that I'd never be a maid again!

Never again would I have to sit with my legs under a hotel bed, grab the front end rails and drag the bed away from the wall, pulling the bed with, and over, me as I leaned back, tugging and pulling with the weight of my whole body in order to vacuum under all the beds that week. (It was vacuum-under-the-beds week, one of the hardest weeks of all!)

It was spring of 1983, and we were preparing for Queen Elizabeth's upcoming visit. We scrubbed, painted, and polished every inch of The Ahwahnee in anticipation of her arrival, and many memos were written that month. (Don't paint, said the Queen's travel-memo writer, she's tired of smelling fresh paint everywhere!) But we painted the Tressider Room anyway. I got the happy memo that management decided I was to be the pool attendant/hotel porter the week of her visit, so I donned the black-and-white porter's uniform, thinking it looked a lot better on me than housekeeping's drab brown.

The Queen and her entourage arrived and their vacation began—no speeches, no functions to attend; she went to Yosemite to relax and enjoy its beauty, same as any tourist does, and she probably puts on her hiking boots the same way we do, too.

Management's new memo asked all the employees to leave the lobby and front desk area during the time when the Queen returned from her motor tour of the Valley. They decided only management should be seen and heard during this important and very special time, apparently.

What a disappointment! We had worked hard to make her visit perfect, and I wanted to see the Queen! "This is not fair!" I said to my soon-to-be-banished self, as I "portered the lobby" some more, waiting to be told to leave.

Management was busy straightening their ties and shirt cuffs, not noticing me, so I decided the pay-telephone booth, next to the gift shop, needed some portering.

"She's back!!" a bellman called to the lobby from his position outside in the porte cochere.

"Okay, everybody! She's here! Let's get in place! Line up! This is it!" a manager barked to his peers as they all took their places in the receiving line.

But I had no place out front; according to the memo, I was supposed to be "in the back of the house," but I wanted see her so badly! I am from small-town Iowa, and we never see anybody there! I'd never seen the Queen before, and I doubted I ever would—this was my once-in-a-life-time chance!

I tucked myself into the shadows, out of sight of the row of managers lined up parallel to the front desk to greet her (and ready to berate me if they saw me). Neatly and quietly, I pressed myself up between the massive wooden phone booth and the corner of the gift shop entrance; I found the perfect place to hide!

The Queen returned with her handsome Prince Phillip, and together they entered the front door. No trumpets announced their arrival but I could hear quiet excited gasps from the row of suited managers, holding their breath in anticipation of meeting her face to face, maybe wondering and mentally rehearsing what they were going to say if she spoke. (An earlier memo explained that we were not to speak to her unless spoken to, you see.)

All eyes were on Her Majesty as she entered the lobby room . . . but then, she went off route and did the unexpected! She decided to stop by the gift shop for a look around, and there was no memo for this excursion!

Suddenly, it was us three—Her Majesty Elizabeth II, by the Grace of God, of the United Kingdom of Great Britain and Northern Ireland,

and of Her other Realms and Territories, Queen, Head of the Commonwealth, Defender of the Faith, her Prince Philip, and me at the gift shop entrance!

I didn't know what to do or say! It was surreal!! No one expected this would happen! It was the Queen, live and in person right in front of me! I could have reached out and touched her! But even in the thick of my insubordination, I remembered the "don't speak" memo and so I smiled broadly at the Queen and she smiled back at me . . . and with a small nod toward me, the prince gave me a smile too!

Now, I don't remember much about the lecture management gave me afterward for doing that; but I'll never forget when the Queen and Prince Philip shopped The Ahwahnee gift shop. They were our very best guests ever! And if you want to experience Yosemite one way that she did, request "The Queen's Table" at the dining room.

Never Call Your Wife as a Witness

Don Pitts, U.S. Magistrate, retired

WHILE STOPPING AT the Visitor Center in Tuolumne Meadows, a husband and wife saw a drawing and writing by John Muir and asked for more information. There was no interpretive ranger available so the couple continued driving to Crane Flat, where they saw a ranger speaking to a passenger in a car. The ranger had already arrested the driver for DUI and was determining if the passenger was also drunk. The couple approached the ranger (Steve), asking him about John Muir. Steve asked them to go back to their car, as he was obviously busy. The woman complied, but the man insisted that as an American citizen he had every right to blah, blah, blah. He would not stop, nor would he return to his car. Finally, Ranger Steve had no choice but to arrest the man and take him to the jail in Yosemite Valley.

When the man appeared in my court for arraignment, I determined from the National Park Service that the case would be a minor fine, probably one hundred dollars. But, Mr. America insisted that he was innocent and wanted to go to trial. I explained that a trial would involve his returning for a pretrial conference as well as another trip for the trial, plus time off work. He was not dissuaded of his right as an American citizen!

The day of the trial, Mr. America, armed with his best Perry Mason persona, acted as his own attorney. He called Ranger Steve to the stand and had him diagram the location of the drunk-driver car and the ranger car. Steve had made the point that by walking between the two cars and approaching him as he was questioning a suspect was suspicious behavior, and could be threatening to an arresting officer. He diagrammed the cars at about twenty feet apart. Next, Perry Mason called his wife to the witness stand. Looming over her and pointing at her he said, "The

Ranger locates the cars about twenty feet apart, but I say they were more like sixty feet, so he shouldn't have felt I was interfering in any way."

"Oh, no, dear. I'm sure they were less than ten feet apart!"

"Well, hang on to your seat," I said to myself, "this could get interesting!"

Undeterred, Perry Mason continued his examination of his wife. "The Ranger says I swore at him, which is not true, is it."

"Oh yes, dear, I'm sure I heard a 'you bastard' and a 'son of a bitch' as well!!"

Some days in court are simply lots more fun than others! And keeping a judicial manner becomes really challenging!

Managing to stifle my mirth, I found him guilty. The penalty? One-hundred-dollar fine.

I have often wondered what the four-hour drive back home was like for this couple.

"In addition to the 5 regular rangers heretofore employed, 10 temporary rangers have been engaged to do the work formerly done by the soldiers. The employment of these men will terminate on October 31, 1914. With this small force the work of protecting the park was as well done as could have been expected. . . . It is recommended that this force be increased."

— Mark Daniels, Yosemite superintendent, 1914

The Falls Creek Snow Surveys

Mark Fincher

THE FALLS CREEK snow surveys have been conducted every winter and spring for many decades. The lowest course was established in 1931, the rest just after World War II. The snow is measured at the end of January, February, March, and April. For decades the surveys were conducted by a contractor working for the California Department of Water Resources, but since the late 1980s they have been skied by park rangers. I've been doing these surveys since 1992.

We start at Hetch Hetchy and hike and ski about forty-six miles over four days, staying in cabins that are stocked with food in the fall. The lower cabin was built when the courses were established; the upper one was rebuilt in 1990 after an avalanche destroyed the original one.

I'll admit that for a while I started feeling bored. I have to go up these switchbacks again? The novelty of a new discovery around each corner faded with repetition. But after a few more years, I found a new rhythm to the trip. It became more like a pilgrimage; each turn in the trail another ring of a familiar bell.

Sometimes patience is rewarded. I saw river otter tracks along the creek for six years before finally seeing otter. The landscape becomes more animated when seen over the course of decades. The way the forest evolves after a fire, the comings and goings of killdeer and bear and porcupine, the patterns in the ways the streams open up in the spring all give the country a new vibrancy; an old friend who has learned a new song. The human landscape also evolves—sections of trail fall apart and get rebuilt, a cabin decays and is repaired—and we snow surveyors age, learn, and alter our patterns of work over time.

The snow hides the summer trail and demands greater attention to one's surroundings. I've always liked being out in front, finding the way.

The increased attention that's required changes the focus from what one experiences when merely following tracks. Instead of drifting off into a reverie about last week's work dilemma or that nagging pain from a blister on a heel, one is always looking ahead. On skis, the game becomes even more fun, finding the best route through changing snow conditions and tiny variations in topography, or guessing where the best creek crossing is going to be. Skiing the same route for so many years has changed the scale of the game. I know where I am at all times, but anticipating the small changes in snow type or coverage is always a challenge. The familiarity takes the edge off the experience but adds a certain glow. The years have incised the route in my memory, the trail as furrowed into my brain as it is on the countryside.

Sometimes when I can't sleep, I'll hike and ski the route in my head and see if I can remember each bump and rill, each willow and gully. The names roll by as I ski along—the formal names: Beehive, Moraine Ridge, Vernon, Jack Main, Paradise, Wilma, and Grace; the informal names—Tin Shack, the Frog Pond, the Slabs, the Golden Stairs, Water Horse Lake, and Tim's Camp; and the personal names—Death Cookie Hill, Killdeer Crossing, the Swamp, Foulk's Folly, and Porcupine Hollow. Each spot on the trail tied to a memory—a spectacular crash, a great wildlife sighting, or a place of confusion during a storm.

A day of unexpected magic, one of many: The previous day we had hiked and skied to the Lake Vernon cabin. The weather had been unsettled—a little rain, a little snow, some sleet, with some gusty winds. The new day dawned clear, and we hiked up the slabs to Jack Main Canyon and enjoyed some nice skiing on the way to our snow course. About a half a mile short of Paradise, we skied across Saddle Horse Lake, a small pond that is formed by the natural levee along Falls Creek. At its east end is a small copse of aspen.

We had left the cabin fairly early that day, and our arrival at the pond coincided with the sun touching the tops of the aspen as it came over the shoulder of Andrews Peak. Aspen in winter have a somewhat skeletal aspect—the pattern of the chalky gray-green branches shows in its full dendritic complexity, the sensuous texture deceptively suggesting warmth. On this day, however, there was no such illusion. The previous day's weather had left every limb, branchlet, twig, and bud coated with an eighth of an inch of shining, clear, crystalline ice.

The effect, with the treetops backlit by the rising sun, was blindingly beautiful. The upper branches were outlined, in every detail, in brilliant, glowing gold against the shadowed north side of the peak. We threw our packs down, stuck our skis into the snow as backrests, and enjoyed the spectacle. As we watched, the ice at the tops of the trees started to give way with the sun's warmth. Each falling cylinder would break more below, creating a bright, sparkling, tinkling, ringing pachinko cascade of glassy ice bells, the crescendo fading to a whoosh in the soft snow beneath. Soon the ice was falling from all the trees, moving across the grove as the sun migrated across the levee, and for the ten minutes it took to melt all of the ice we were bewitched by this illuminated alpine symphony.

Good things happen when you stay at something long enough. Attachment to a place not only grows stronger through the years, but evolves, sometimes in unexpected ways. Those of us who work in Yosemite's wilderness are not full-time residents, yet we can achieve a kind of phenological intimacy with certain places. Our wanderings carry us across a large expanse, but there's a recurring geographical rhythm to our paths. It's a more diffuse sense of home, but home nonetheless.

The Best Job in the World

Nancy Fagerstrom

For thirteen years, I had the best job in the world! Now, I'm not sure if my bosses would agree, but I still believe it to be true. You see, I drove around in circles and got nowhere. Those were my orders, and I got paid to follow them. The real fun part happened when I'd get to stop every few minutes and tell someone where to get off. When they asked, I would tell them where to go! As a bonus, I did this in Yosemite National Park.

As a school bus driver from San Diego looking for summer work, I arrived in Yosemite June 1991. I had been notified by Yosemite Park and Curry Company that they had me scheduled for an interview. I went by the Yosemite Transportation System office to check in. I told the guy with his feet on the desk my name and that I had an interview appointment for the next day. A voice from the next office said, "Go across the street, get signed in, and pick up some uniforms." I replied that I had arrived early for my interview. The man with the voice stood up from his desk, came around the corner, saying, "You did fine on the interview. Now go sign up and get your uniforms." I'd been HIRED!

After a few days of Yosemite orientation training, I began driving a bus around the "loop." It did not take long to figure out that even though I now drove in one of the most "AMAZING" places in the world, it could still be a four-letter word, you know the one, yeah, WORK! As with all jobs, there is a certain amount of the mundane that is going to exist, but as a shuttle driver, you drive around the stops numbered one through nineteen, for eight hours a day. As you arrive at each stop, you make an announcement. You make pretty much the same announcement as you did the last time you stopped there and that you will make the next time. You tell the passengers where they are and what is available there . . .

food, hikes, camping, bathrooms, you get the idea. Don't get me wrong. I loved ALMOST every minute of it, but being ADHD, my mind began looking for things to do.

The shuttles are the way most folks move around in Yosemite Valley. The trailheads for several popular hikes are at stops on the Happy Isles section of the loop. Only the shuttles are allowed to drive in this area, and only from 8:00 a.m. to 8:00 p.m. I had been driving for only a few days when IT happened.

At 6:45 a.m., the two starting shuttles would head out of the bus yard for their respective start points. This day I would start from Curry Village, Stop One. The other bus started at Stop Eight, the Lodge. To stay equally spaced, we would meet in Yosemite Village, exchange passengers, and drive toward where the other had just come from, completing the loop. Other buses were added as the day progressed. I eased into Stop One to start my day. Just across the street at Stop Fourteen, a large family group stood waiting for a bus to the Mist Trail, Stop Sixteen. As I stopped, a male from the group started yelling, demanding to know why I had stopped on the wrong side. "Don't you see the large group waiting for the bus?" As I tried to explain that another bus would be there in half an hour, he interrupted, shouting, "Just how do you expect us to get an early start on the hike if we have to wait for a different bus?"

It was seven o'clock in the morning. I had worked until ten thirty the night before, I slept in a tent with a snoring bunkmate, rose to find the ground frozen as I walked a quarter mile to the toilet, had no breakfast, now this guy wanted to yell at me. IT just happened! I opened the driver's window, leaned out, and asked, "What are you going to do when you get to Stop 16?" He answered, "We are going to hike!" I yelled back, "That is how you get there." I never heard what he said, because of all the laughter coming from the group with him and the few folks on my bus. I do hope they had a good time.

When I stopped in Yosemite Village, an elderly gentleman walked up from the back to exit the front door. As he stepped down the last step, he turned, with a big smile, and said, "You are pretty ornery, don't you think?" As I tried to apologize, he laughed telling me how much fun he had over the exchange. He and his family had been coming to Yosemite for years and had many a laugh over all the folks that stood at a bus stop, complaining about the time lost waiting, instead of walking less than a quarter mile to where they would be "starting" their hike.

After that incident, I knew how I would enjoy my time on the shuttle. Whenever someone asked, "How are you?" I answered, "Ornery." Often, when asked "Where is . . . ?" I would reply, "Are you asking me to tell you where to go?" Even though I would announce each stop, I would be asked, "Will you tell me when we get to . . . ?" With a huge smile, I would say, "Sir/Ma'am, I would be tickled pink to tell you where to get off!"

I had fun; I tried to make it fun for those that rode my bus. The laughter seemed to make everyone happier, AND I still think I had the best job in the world.

Hail El Capitan

Fred V. Cota

IN 1962, AFTER graduating from El Capitan High School in Merced, California, my friend Joe M. asked me to go work in Yosemite Valley. He would work at Degnan's Loft as a night porter whenever we were on vacation from school. His aunt Pearl was a house mother of the dorms behind the restaurant. Joe and I were assigned a room on the second floor, which was also the same floor where the female employees stayed. The hall had a door that separated us from them. Our room was on the left side, the same side as Yosemite Falls. It took time to get used to the roar of the falls that went on night and day. We would work the night shift cleaning the restaurant and would take a break to watch the firefall every night. On some nights we would borrow a co-worker's 1957 Ford convertible and drive up to Mirror Lake. We would all squeeze into the front seat because of the bats. They would dive down on us, and some would hit the top of the windshield and land on the backseat; no one wanted to sit in the backseat (I wonder why?).

The highlight of my time in Yosemite was when President Kennedy visited and stayed overnight at The Ahwahnee. I will never forget that day. On the way to the hotel, the Valley was packed with people wanting to get a glimpse of the president. Security's worst nightmare. The area where I was standing was close to the road. The crowd surrounded the president's maroon Lincoln convertible. Everyone wanted to shake his hand. I managed to reach up and shake his hand. I then went to the front of the car and took his picture. Unfortunately, over the years that picture was lost.

That night, the firefall was kept flowing longer than usual to honor President Kennedy.

The next day, the president flew out in a helicopter. The president was on his way to dedicate the San Luis Dam.

It was only fitting to be in Yosemite Valley and see El Capitan when I was a member of the last graduating class (1962) of El Capitan High School (Go Gauchos). It is now called Merced High School.

In 2012 we had our fiftieth high school reunion. My granddaughter Giavanna Cota will be attending high school in 2014. The new school is named "El Capitan," and the mascot is a "Gaucho" just like we had back in 1962. Go figure.

Yosemite, 1933 till Now

Chuck Holcomb

Dad taught me to swim and fish when I was six. He worked on the highway under construction from the Wawona Tunnel to Wawona. Dad, Mom, and I lived in our tent on the South Fork of the Merced River near Chilnualna.

When school started, I walked downriver and crossed over the covered bridge to the one-room schoolhouse that had eight students. I looked for it in later years and the ranger said it had been sold and moved. Too bad—it could have been an item of interest in the Pioneer Yosemite History Center, which is there now.

The next summer we lived in a construction camp on Bridalveil Creek while Dad worked on improving the road to Glacier Point. The fishing was good and scenery beautiful. I returned forty years later and could not find any sign of this camp, not even a bent nail. We moved to Mariposa, where Mom renewed her teaching career, but summers were still spent in Wawona. I worked as a caddie at the golf course. There were no golf carts, not even hand carts. It was carry your clubs or hire a caddie. Some days I would carry doubles for eighteen holes in the morning, and then again in the afternoon. Slow days would find us caddies swimming in the river in the evenings.

In 1940 I started Mariposa High School. The Yosemite students also went there. It was a forty-five mile bus ride each way, morning and evening. Yosemite Park and Curry Company was short of help during the war, so some of us students would ride the bus to Yosemite Friday afternoon, work Saturday and Sunday, and ride back to school Monday morning. This gave us the inside track for summer jobs. At fifteen I was driving a truck for the maintenance crew—the start of my life's career as a builder.

One of the high points of this job happened one weekend when I was assigned to the Glacier Point Hotel as a relief worker and told to build a fire on the point and slowly push it over the edge on cue at 9:00 p.m.

Another great memory was playing in the high school orchestra led by Bill Lintott, a senior student who lived in the Yosemite Valley. He played the accordion, the trumpet, the piano, and kept the rest of us in check. We played for the Girls State Convention in Yosemite Valley— over one thousand girls and only seven of us boys in the band. Also, the 1942 junior/senior banquet for Mariposa High School was held at The Ahwahnee in the Great Lounge, and the high school orchestra entertained.

The following year, 1943, the junior/senior banquet was again held in the Great Lounge, but most of the orchestra members had enlisted in the armed services, including our leader, Bill Lintott. In 1944 the navy had turned The Ahwahnee into a recovery center.

Upon high school graduation in June 1944, I enlisted in the U.S. Navy, except they said come back when I reached eighteen. So, I took a job with the Standard Stations in Yosemite, now called Chevron, and I worked relief in all seven stations: Government Center, Camp Curry, The Lodge, Chinquapin, Wawona, Crane Flat, and Tuolumne Meadows. Later I was assigned to Tuolumne Meadows because Standard's contract required it to be open when Tioga Pass was open, even if few cars had enough gasoline to reach there. I had a tent cabin, running water, stove, and generator. Friends would visit, we would fish, hike, and explore the most beautiful part of this world.

High in the California Sierra, east of the divide near timberline lives one of nature's rarest and most beautiful native species. Where glaciers end in deep blue lakes and sheer granite peaks stand guard, the home of the golden trout can be found. Like the pot of gold at rainbow's end, it awaits the hearty, adventurous angler. The puritan fly fisherman's greatest prize! The sight of its golden sides and blood-red underbelly when it jumps clear of the water causes disbelief.

Below the lake, the stream runs through a meadow and then dives down a rugged canyon into a dark pool. I knew he would be there, but it was a risky climb for me. The approach to such a quarry must be in silence and caution, for the fish will be quick to hide and slow to reappear. The presentation of the fly must be true and soft, for seldom is there a second chance. The retrieve must be slow, like a struggling bug on the water's surface. If the angler is skilled, the water clear, the moon on the wane, and God's in his Heaven, the fish might strike. The moment of truth is at hand—the preparations forgotten, the sore muscles ignored, the concentration intense, and Lady Luck is in charge. The bump is felt, the line goes taut, the strike is swift, and the fight is on. The fish goes deep toward his lair but the line holds fast. Next, he surfaces to shake the hook. He jumps, flips, cartwheels, tail walks, and dives to no avail. The battle is ended, the prize is won, the angler can boast. His prowess is clear. But! Reliving the deed on the long trip back brings forth a touch of conscience and growling remorse. Such a creature is to be admired, respected, and allowed in his domain.

The rod and reel are carefully stored away with a lifetime full of memories of Yosemite.

TENAYA LAKE
TRAIL

TENAYA LAKE 2.1 →
TUOLUMNE MDWS 21.0 →
GLEN AULIN 8.7 →
WATERWHEEL FALLS 22.5 →

9

KEEP WILDLIFE WILD

Rattlesnake Panic

Bob Roney

ONE WARM LAZY day in camp near Hetch Hetchy, I was sitting leaning against a log reading when I caught a movement out of the corner of my eye. When I looked up I didn't see anything at first, just my electric-blue nylon sleeping bag lying on the ground nearby. Then I saw it—a big fat rattlesnake gliding along the edge of my sleeping bag. While we don't kill wild animals in Yosemite, I didn't want it crawling into bed with me either. I grabbed my tripod and a piece of cordage. I tied the cord in a noose at the end of one of the legs, extended it as far as it would go, and gently slipped the noose over the snake's head. I pulled the cord tight. The snake writhed wildly for a moment and then relaxed. I didn't. My heart was pounding at the thought of the venomous creature slipping out of the noose and biting me.

Now what to do? I wanted to move the snake away from my campsite far enough so that it wouldn't come back. Fueled on adrenalin I began walking back down the trail toward the dam. How far to go? I really didn't know how far to take the fanged beauty, so kept walking until I passed the first drainage to the west. "This is far enough," I thought and then hiked on. I don't know how far I had gone when I finally let the poor creature go, but it was a long way and at least two drainages away.

It was so hot that night I slept in my undershorts with the sleeping bag unzipped and lying loosely on top of my legs. Sometime after midnight I was awakened by a strange sensation. Something had gotten under my bag and was moving up along my thigh to my rump. I was lying on my right side. I had lifted my head about two inches off the ground when I first sensed it, and now my neck muscles were beginning to shake with fatigue.

I felt its cold body slither along my back until it was even with my shoulder blades, where it stopped and seemed to coil up. Paralyzed with fear, my mind raced, trying to figure out what to do. I finally decided I couldn't just get up because it could bite me on the face. I would have to grab the snake with my hand and fling it away. I hoped I could do it fast enough that the scaly devil wouldn't have time to sink its fangs into my hand.

I practiced the maneuver in my mind over and over until I thought I had the timing down—now for real. I let out a scream as I moved my right hand in one continuous motion around to my back, scooped up the cold-blooded thing, and flung it away from me! I was so pumped with adrenalin, my whole body shook violently. No bites. I turned on my flashlight to see that it was a very large but harmless garter snake. I laughed uncontrollably.

———

"As a rule predaceous animals should be left unmolested and allowed to retain their primitive relation to the rest of the fauna, even though this may entail a considerable annual levy on the animals forming their prey no step [should] be taken to diminish the number of . . . predators, except on the best of grounds."

—Professor Joseph Grinnell and Tracy Storer on their multiyear survey of Yosemite animals, 1916

In the Bear's House

Susan Swanson

Several years ago I participated in a Yosemite Association (now Yosemite Conservancy) backpacking trip. We stopped near the Lyell Canyon/Evelyn Lake Trail intersection to camp the first night, and along about sunset, a "redhead" of the bear species showed up to check us out. I was about one hundred feet from my tent putting my bear canister behind a fallen tree when I turned around to see him inspecting my "home" for the night. I wrote this poem that night:

IN THE BEAR'S HOUSE

There's something about a bear
in the woods
at sunset
his burnt orange jowls
lit up
by the last golden rays
of the setting sun
like a second fiery orb
just beginning his day
with a short visit
to my tent
which stands in his house.

Scare the Bear

James Schlotthauer

LAST YEAR WAS my seventy-first summer trip to Yosemite, plus there were many off-season trips in between. My first trip in 1941 is one that my sister has told me about many times, and I have no reason to think that it isn't true. In those days almost everyone camped in tents, mostly tents that were of the army type, very heavy, smelled like some kind of oil-rubbed canvas, which made them somewhat water resistant. My folks always stayed in the same campground because it was very close to the river, but the bad part was that it seemed to be the bears' favorite also, and every night the bears would search the campgrounds for the site where some foolish camper may have left some goodies out by mistake. One night we were all fast asleep in our cots when my mother let out a bloodcurdling scream because a curious bear had stuck its head in their tent. My mother threw a black cast-iron frying pan at the bear, but my father timed it perfectly and sat up just in time to have the frying pan hit him right in his head, and the scream that he let out was so overwhelming that the bear took off running in the opposite direction.

Pika Running over My Feet, Bears in the Office, Lovesick Toads, and Other Yosemite Wildlife Tales

Beth Pratt

IT IS A TRUTH universally acknowledged among national park visitors that you visit Yellowstone for the magnificent wildlife and Yosemite for the breathtaking scenery. Having worked in both parks, I feel somewhat qualified to pass judgment on this unofficial pronouncement. Yes, Yellowstone deserves to be crowned champion of the charismatic megafauna, as during my time there I dodged elk herds to get to the post office, and claim a personal record of seeing eight grizzly bears in a single day. Characterizing Yosemite as a wildlife wasteland because of a lack of bison herds, however, misses the "story behind the scenery," so to speak, and omits a rich part of the experience.

Like countless others, I became instantly captivated by this awe-inspiring cathedral of granite on my first visit. And I am still filled with a surge of joy when the mighty rock sentinels greet me as I drive through Yosemite Valley. As Muir remarked, "this grand show is eternal," and I never become weary of Yosemite's charms. I live near its west entrance and spend most of my free time losing myself in the comforting embrace of its backcountry.

And in my over twenty years of wandering in the park, I've been lucky enough to encounter many of the remarkable wildlife that call Yosemite home, beginning with my first trip in 1991. I had driven into Yosemite Valley during a major snowstorm and almost had the place to myself, as the road had been closed behind me. I took full advantage of the gift of Yosemite as a private winter playground and enjoyed making snow angels and constructing a snowman in El Capitan Meadow, all while a lone coyote regarded me curiously. Snowflakes speckled his luxuriant winter coat and his tracks made their own snow art alongside mine. For over an hour we seemed like the only two living things in Yosemite Valley until he finally trotted away and disappeared into the storm.

From that first coyote encounter, all my memories of granite and water also vibrate with the living world of the park.

For instance, each year the Gaylor Lakes basin comes alive with a chorus of amphibian song. I recall first hearing the symphony—and being a bit baffled at the noise—as I strolled down to Lower Gaylor Lake and caught the sonorous trilling of one creature in particular, a song rising above even the boisterous shouting of the Clark's nutcracker. After consulting the guidebook, I reckoned this was my introduction to the Yosemite toad. Once the snow melts—or even before, as the critter has been observed tiptoeing over snowfields to reach its breeding grounds—the males emerge from hibernation and start singing for a mate. Their distinctive "love song" can be heard up to one hundred yards away, and as the naturalists Grinnell and Storer noted in 1924, "its mellow notes are pleasing additions to the chorus of birdsongs just after the snow leaves."

Another musically inclined animal of Yosemite, the almost unbearably adorable pika, emits an unmistakable high-pitched chirping. For me, watching the pika scurry over talus fields is as essential to the beauty and character of Yosemite's alpine landscape as the towering peaks. Pikas can be elusive, and more often seen than heard, so imagine my astonishment in meeting not one, but several very social pika ambassadors over the years. Once while stopping for a water break, a scampering over my boot startled me, and I looked down just in time to see a pika dashing up the slope, perhaps thinking me just another rock in the rock pile. And on another excursion I shared a picnic with a friendly pika. As I took my meal break near Mount Dana, the little critter remained with me for an hour, dashing back and forth to gather a nice alpine salad of lupine stalks. Pikas do not hibernate, but dry vegetation in the sun to create a "haystack" for winter consumption. The mischievous pikas have also been known to loot their neighbors' haystacks, but this one made no move to try and steal my Clif Bar.

The animals with an infamous reputation for looting in Yosemite—black bears—hold a special place in my reminiscences, as I worked on a project aimed at curbing their appetite for human food and their propensity to destroy cars in pursuit of said tasty cuisine. Yosemite Conservancy teamed up with the National Park Service to create the Keep Bears Wild campaign and even enlisted the help of the late Phil Frank, who had penned many a cartoon in homage to the bears' insatiable appetites (bear incidents remain greatly reduced to this day as a result of the successful project). Although I prefer my wild bear encounters, my most entertaining bear story involves a lone youngster surprising a staff person in the Conservancy's offices. Lou Carter, a longtime El Portal resident, called me frantically one morning to the copy room. I just assumed the copier had broken down yet again, so did not expect to see a bear emerge. Just another day in the office in Yosemite!

I could add so many other wildlife moments, like discovering the tracks of a mountain lion with ranger Dick Ewart on the Granite Divide, or hearing the soft patter of a bobcat trailing me on the boardwalk near Happy Isles, or relaxing by the Tuolumne River one evening as a great blue heron swooped out of the dusk to catch a fish.

Yet my favorite Yosemite wildlife tale comes from rock climbers scaling El Capitan, who report seeing tiny Pacific chorus frogs hanging out on the cliffs. Perhaps even the smallest of creatures aren't immune to seeking out a good vista point. People will always flock to Yosemite for the scenery, to feel the spray of Yosemite Falls, or peer down from the dizzying heights of Glacier Point. Certainly let us cherish and enjoy the grandeur of the landscape, but we should not neglect the wonderful array of life that calls this "noble park" home.

———◆———

"The national parks . . . should be looked upon as open books of nature, repositories of knowledge, on which every plant, herb, tree, animal, bird, insect and reptile forms a page . . . Life histories, habits and behaviors of animals and birds should all be completed within these parks, and not solely within the four walls of the schools and colleges."

—M.A. Badshah, wildlife officer, 1962

A Brave Coward

Kenda Haro

COMING DOWN THE John Muir Trail, I walked peacefully in awe of the morning mist and quiet. I was afraid; the forest has always been so eerily quiet and yet active with unfamiliar sounds. I'm a city girl from Los Angeles, shopping at REI for gear, Costco for food, and making sure I have mosquito repellent. Despite my urban upbringing, my parents always made sure we made it to a national park to camp and learn about Nature. This year, I was with friends and had decided to go down the trail ahead of everyone else. Going from top to bottom on each of the switchbacks, I picked up my pace to a brisk walk—watching out for rocks. As I rounded the switchback and was at the top of the next, I heard a rustling sound amid the quiet of the morning, I stopped. My feet, heart, and breath stopped as I quickly focused in on the source of the sound. Ecstatic and profoundly afraid of what I saw because my mind and heart raced at this next realization: the bear cub I saw had a mother—and she would be near. My heart pounding in my ears, I remembered everything I had learned about bear safety. I scanned to see if I could jump without crossing the cub's path and listened intently for the mother. Jumping was not an option, I was too high from the next switchback, running would put me in direct path with this adorable bear cub. Then I heard a noise that made me decide faster than ever before. I raised my arms, completely self-conscious of how stupid I might look and sound, as I stomped and attempted to yell. Opening my mouth only released a meager squeak. I tried again. "Go away, bear! GO AWAY!" I said as I stomped, raised my arms to appear larger than five feet and yelled as loud as the fear that gripped me would allow. It worked; I scared the cub enough to make it run into the trees and out of the trail. As I ran by, tears streaming down my face, I warned other hikers, the ranger, and anyone who would hear my tale of enhanced cowardice.

Lessons from the Alpine Mammal Survey

Brian Whitehead

I CAME TO YOSEMITE to be a park ranger. However, my path to get there was not as direct as I had hoped. It turns out that they don't just give those jobs away. You have to earn it. Volunteering was my ticket to the green and gray.

I came to Yosemite to be a volunteer. It was the spring of 2012, and I had a place to set up my tent and a bucket load of enthusiasm. My number-one rule: never pass up a chance to volunteer. I was going to say yes to any job offer to help with any project and get as much experience as I could while I was there. It might have been skill, it quite possibly was luck, but I was able to help with a tremendous number of projects. From wilderness restoration to ranger programs, from wildlife management to trash pickup, it seemed like the opportunities were endless. I had the chance to work with so many amazing people that all care about this place so much. The experience I've gained from working with those people and on those projects has been invaluable, but some of the things I learned were surprising. Let me tell you about the alpine mammal survey.

As we travel through Yosemite National Park, most of us try to fit in as much as we can. In a park the size of Yosemite it can be overwhelming to try to see it all. Just the same, we rush from one scenic vista to another in an effort to make our limited vacation time go further. There is another way to experience Yosemite, but you have to slow down. My work on the alpine mammal survey took me to locations far and wide around the park. Part of this survey required that I stand in one place for fifteen minutes and be as observant as possible. I was looking and listening for only four species of alpine mammals, but I saw and heard much more. I found that if you take the time to get to know a spot, it doesn't have to be the best view you have ever seen to be rewarding. Truly knowing something, something intimate, about any particular place is very powerful.

Take the time to notice how the spiderwebs that are between the ridges in the bark of the red fir in front of you have collected pollen and appear as though they are dozens of little golden hammocks, moving gently in the breeze. Observations like this connect you in a deeper way to this great park and they may be the best memories you have when you leave. I encourage everyone to spend a little time using all of their senses to observe something somewhere on their journey through Yosemite. You may be surprised where it takes you.

Hiking in Yosemite is a great way to see the park. More than 94 percent of this park is designated wilderness, and there are many adventures and great views to be had. Hiking will take you off the road, but you still won't see much of Yosemite if you are staring at your feet. This is something I noticed during the alpine mammal survey. I was required to walk sections of trail while constantly watching for the target species we wanted to record. In order to do this you had to have two things, a good pair of shoes because stubbed toes were common, and patience. Walking slowly was the best way to observe the wildlife and, with quick glances at the ground, the only way not to trip and fall during the survey. Normally, I would be hiking much faster to get to a destination, and not seeing much in between. The adjustment to my pace opened up a whole new world to me, the trail itself became a destination. It allowed me to marvel at the seamless transition from exposed granite to forest to meadow and back, to enjoy the changes in plant communities that were growing along the trail, and to see much more wildlife than I would have otherwise. The miles of trail between you and your next scenic view should not be a barrier or an inconvenience. They are a story of their own, waiting for you to take the time to read them.

By the end of 2012, my story had led me to an awards ceremony where I was honored as the Individual Volunteer of the Year. The best part was that I didn't feel as though I had worked a single day. One thing I know, it doesn't matter if you are a visitor, a volunteer, or a career ranger, you will always get much more from Yosemite than you can ever give. I, for one, feel as though I owe Yosemite a great deal, and I plan on trying to repay that for a long time.

I Was Only a Visitor

Kathleen Lindman

I WAS ONLY A visitor, he was The Bear.
I only wanted a picture, but he didn't care.
"Get out of my space, please, and give me some room.
If you must take my picture, put your camera on zoom!"
Everyone was leaving and how I was shaking.
This is a very big mistake I was making.
Remember, the forest is not like the zoo.
Here, wild animals always should rule.
Yosemite is beautiful beyond any dream.
Take pictures of waterfalls, mountain, and stream.
And remember to respect every living thing there.
The forests, the wildlife, and especially The Bear!"

Damselfly Emergence at Lower Cathedral Lake, Yosemite

Lisa A. Murphy

"The most beautiful thing we can experience is the mysterious. It is the source of all true art and science. He to whom this emotion is a stranger, who can no longer pause to wonder and stand rapt in awe, is as good as dead: his eyes are closed."
— Albert Einstein, "The World as I See It," 1954

I have been spending my summers in the high country of Yosemite for eleven years now, and I am still fully enchanted by it. I try to spend my time off in the summers learning more about this place and exploring its wonders. Sometimes that means reading or sitting by the river drinking my tea and journaling; other times I'll be found climbing the rocks or hiking up one of the many peaks in the high country.

* * *

On this particular day off, my friend Renate and I headed out on a hike to Lower Cathedral Lake. We hiked the six miles of trail through the lodgepole pine forest, looking forward to the opening in the trees when we would see the subalpine meadow and the deep blue lake backed by an impressive wall of granite. We had no idea of the magical experience we would encounter on this sunny High Sierra afternoon.

As we emerged from the forest and crossed the meadow, our pace quickened, as the mosquitoes were swarming around us. The maddening buzzing around our heads and the piercing bites through our gossamer hiking shirts driving us on. We had hopes of escaping these pests by diving into the chilly blue waters of Cathedral Lake. However, as we stepped onto the granite rock, our attention was diverted. We heard rattling sounds that brought our gazes down to the rock upon which we now stood. What we saw there was a magical spectacle taking place all around us. We slowed our pace, stood still in fact, to witness this mesmerizing transformation that was occurring at our feet. We saw damselfly naiads crawling out of the lake, making their way up the granite. They began to jostle and jolt, each apparently attempting to catch its exoskeleton on the irregularities in the granite. There were thousands of them, vibrating on the surface of the granite slab at the edge of the lake. These naiads, looking like prehistoric creatures; green insects, long and slender with bulging eyes on either side of their head, and little green wing buds on their backs. They were everywhere. Thousands of them were crawling up from the lake, splitting their outer covering at the upper section of the thorax—their exoskeleton breaking open behind their head. Each damselfly was fighting its way out of its old skin and emerging into the terrestrial world in its new form, then sending blood pulsing through its body to fill its wings and abdomen so that the flies themselves would extend, seemingly growing in a matter of minutes, into their adult size and shape—their adult form so different from the body of their youth. Then they were twice the length, their bodies a vibrant blue, their heads still prehistoric or alienlike, but now with lacey wings, both delicate and beautiful, a complete metamorphosis.

As we watched, the air began to fill with blue movement fluttering about upon the light breeze. It was mesmerizing, I was no longer aware of any of the earlier annoyances, totally captivated by the mystical experience unfolding around us.

After watching this event and enjoying the beauty of Upper Cathedral Lake, Renate and I began our journey back to Tuolumne Meadows. As we walked around the edge of the lake, through the trees and meadow, we found the number of mosquitoes had dwindled to just a few. This was a pleasant surprise. We wondered if they might have been affected by this recent emergence of damselflies. We were still surrounded by these dazzling creatures in flight. As we watched, as if to answer our questions, we saw the chase of damselfly and mosquito, the damselfly the victor (and our defender!) in this display of aerial acrobatics.

The damselfly naiads dine on mosquito larvae in their aquatic form, and the adult damselflies feast on the adult mosquitoes in their terrestrial form. As adults, their life is short, usually emerging midsummer, then mating, laying eggs, and dying before winter arrives. A fleeting moment of time, this instance of transformation, and this short terrestrial life.

What an amazing day. Experiencing this transformation; being present for the emergence of thousands, maybe millions of damselflies. These opportunities to experience and learn from our natural environment firsthand. How often do we slow down our pace enough to notice, not only the amazing waterfalls, cliffs, lakes, and megafauna, but also the tiniest of creatures? Do we notice the amazing natural occurrences, changes, and grandeur of the world we travel through? How lucky we are to have these wilderness places to explore, these intact ecosystems that protect even the creatures we may not notice except on these extraordinary occasions. It is all here, all around us, when we are ready to engage and "stand rapt in awe." And when we are fully present, we are welcomed into a magical, even mystical experience.

Muir's Bird

Steve Peck

Above the churn and curl
Of the backcountry stream,
He heard it. The liquid trill
Of the water ouzel,
The solstitial act of a solo vocalist.
Its ringing song floated clear
Beyond the agitation of the bouldered rill.
Under water it becomes an aquatic acrobat
Of incomparable agility.
Wings become flippers,
Tail a sure rudder,
Bill a probe to pick
Caddisfly larvae from graveled places.
But it was the sweet fluty song,
Wrenlike, that so enraptured Muir.
Perhaps while sitting in this short-haired meadow
Fringed with racemes of red penstemon,
He first heard it,
His bird of "blooming waters."

"The songs of the Yosemite winds and waterfalls are
delightfully enriched with bird song, especially in
the nesting time of spring and early summer. . . . But the
most wonderful singer of all the birds is the water-ouzel
that dives into foaming rapids and feeds at the bottom,
holding on in a wonderful way, living a charmed life."

–John Muir, 1912

10

MAGIC OF YOSEMITE

I Am on a Bridge

Elizabeth Wengrin-Rohrbaugh

THE STORY OF Yosemite is so great, so beyond measure, because it is a shared and collective understanding of how a place can be so powerful, so provocative and transforming on an individual level as well as a social function. We reconnect to something we harbor within ourselves that is so primitive and honest it can only be described through images of massive glaciers, iconic monoliths, shallow rivers with deep secrets, and valleys with colors so intoxicating you blink your eyes to readjust, assuming it's your vision, that this valley can't possibly be speaking to you in such a palette that seems it could have been devised by DaVinci himself. Yet here it is, a little pocket of scientific wonder, natural extremes tangled in an embrace dancing before you, falls crashing down, pine needles bathing in amber, and light playing a child's game of tag with shadows. I am a native Californian, and my story is one that is by no means unique, but special because it is common of many.

My first memories are found in old photographs. A mommy and daddy holding little baby me wrapped up in baby-girl coat and winter hat. We are standing on a bridge near Curry Village. Bonding, Yosemite encouraged the little baby girl to hold tight to her parents and snuggle in to find comfort and protection from the cold winter elements. Bonding, Yosemite enticed me to look out onto meadows, down at rocks in dry creeks, and up, up so high all the way to the top of Half Dome. Bonding, Yosemite showed me how to tilt my head to one side to hear the soft hoot of an owl and the rush of a near trickling fall, how to hear quiet far away from the big city. As a little duckling imprints to her mother, I, a small baby, imprinted Yosemite. I am wired to know her, to return to her, and I can find this young heart of wonder as an old woman, standing on the same bridge, looking up at that same big rock.

Returning ever so often, I grew up to appreciate Yosemite National Park. The solemn and noble way I felt as we drive into the Valley didn't even compare to the first time I entered into Notre Dame in Paris. Yes, she was and is the most majestic cathedral I will ever have the privilege to enter. One cannot deny the power and care of the great creator. This is where the great ones live, the ancient trees that bear witness, and have endured countless experiences we can't comprehend. They know and feel in ways we can only imagine. Yet, these ancient organisms communicate with us, through growth, illness, and even death. They articulate their meaning in the way they stretch their branches, in the way the sun shines through their needles, and in their constant praise as they lift up to the heavens. Sometimes we listen and do the same, realizing they are so right. They are guardians of so many, from chipmunks to insects and ravens. When I am close I feel compelled to reach out and pet them, to rest my palm against the soft furry bark. And then I have to sniff the tree because the earthy clean smell is pure goodness. And if you're lucky enough to sit under them at night, they really open your mind.

As I became older, nothing was more special than a family trip to the park. One Christmas I decided my family had so many blessings that gifts seemed pointless. We drove two hours to the park to spend a cool December day enjoying each other. For what I would have spent on gifts, I treated my family to lunch at The Ahwahnee, which was decked out in signature traditional Ahwahnee Christmas decor. This is one of my favorite memories, Christmastime at The Ahwahnee with my mom and dad and brothers. Yosemite had unknowingly set the course of my life; the way the Merced coursed through the canyon and the Valley had somehow set into motion a direction in me.

* * *

I am twenty-two and am driving up to visit my twenty-year-old brother who is living in Hodgdon Meadow. He is living in the park as a volunteer working on a tree crew. He is a young man, and we are from a middle-class home, and he is volunteering for no money. The park supplied him with a modest cabin with a wood-burning stove, no heat, and a ten-dollar-a-day food stipend that he has to make cover his food and gas expense. He is there for months, working and giving in solitude. He started doing backcountry work with the California Conservation Corps, then winter work for the park, then he volunteered at Tioga Meadows working in the backcountry. For a young man to spend his time in the park this way—I will never know how much this means to him.

That is his story, but it permeates into my story. Inspired by Yosemite, I craved to see her sisters, the other national parks. I spent ten months, collectively, working in Denali National Park living my life as wild as the animals that call Denali home. I played guitar under the midnight sun and raised my glass in a toast to the northern lights as they twisted and moved above. I spent a summer working in Yellowstone National Park, where I discovered the origin and history of all of our parks, and the amazing gift that is the National Park Service. These events have given me a sense of stewardship, a guardianship to care and protect our most vital resources.

Eventually I returned to California, living in our Sierra Nevada Mountains when I met my future husband. Before the wedding, the house buying, and the birth of our son, there was a road trip. As a Virginia native, I had the honor to take him to his first visit with Yosemite. We shared, and connected, again we bonded. Soon we will be planning our next visit—a date with my baby, my husband, and a bridge near Curry Village. I will be snuggling them close, and our baby will have a warm baby-boy coat and a winter hat. When he is older he will look at this picture and remember his first trip to Yosemite.

It's Yosemite

Robert Slusser

GUARDED BY EL Capitan
an ice-carved valley wonderland
cradles the soft Merced.
Mellow sky—Mirror Lake's home
lies just below Half Dome
near lofty Clouds Rest.
Beautiful water falling far
from hanging canyons in the air;
soft thunder is their voice.
Follow any pathway out,
emotion wants to make you shout
the beauty of the land.
Up Mist Trail or Snow Creek,
wander without haste and seek
the tidings of the wild.
Beautiful Lyell Fork so near,
Tuolumne Meadows high and clear,
gateway to the north.
Expansive silent woods abound
with ear-soothing natural sounds
of wind, birds, and streams.
So many things to see and do
and I have touched but a few,
ever so briefly.
It truly is a wonderland.
Intense beauty on every hand.
It's YOSEMITE.

A Day in the Yosemite Valley, 1950

Charles Peradotto

LOOKING BACK ACROSS over sixty years as if through the wrong end of binoculars, the details are faded but I remember an overall amazing experience at Yosemite.

YOSEMITE FALLS

Ten years old and with an untested sense of adventure I traveled with my family in our 1946 Nash as it labored up El Portal Road beside the crashing Merced River and into the Valley. It was a rare late summer vacation just after Labor Day.

We settled into a tent cabin, a compromise blessed by my mother and exciting for my younger brother and I.

After a day checking out the sights of the Valley with my family, I decided I wanted to explore alone. Late the next morning I told my parents I was going out for a hike on my own.

They said. "Fine, just be careful." (Remember it's 1950.)

I crossed the road to a clearing and looked long at Yosemite Falls. I would head up that trail and see how far I could go. I had no food, no water, and, of course, no map. There were few people at the base of the falls, as it was after "vacation time."

The lower switchbacks were above me and I started winding my way up. The falls were on the right, but the flow was weak at that time of year. When I got thirsty I drank from any spot that had clear water running over rocks. I continued climbing, meeting no one on the trail.

It became cooler in the shade as I made my way around the steep cliffs. The mist off the falls added to my concern as I had on only a light jacket. My ambition began to grow. I became determined to make it to the top. I was going to finish this adventure that I had started.

The trail went behind rocks, and the falls were hidden, although I could still hear the cascading water. The hike was becoming more of a challenge, even for my strong young legs. I reached the upper, seemingly endless, switchbacks about midday.

Finally, I met another hiker. The man resembled a mountain man from a hundred years ago. He was bearded and devilish with a huge pack and looked like he had been in the backcountry for weeks. Where had he been? What had he seen? We looked at each other silently. The man smiled, nodded once, then strode on down the trail.

At the top, I was actually on granite rocks above Yosemite Creek looking down on a pool and the banner of water blowing off the falls into the Valley, over 2400 feet below. I wanted to drink from that edge, so I carefully made my way down and then crawled on all fours to the ledge. Luckily, I am not prone to vertigo. I dipped my hands into the pool, scooped up the freezing-cold water, and drank until my thirst was quenched.

The view was unbelievable. The entire Valley, other falls, and all those tremendous mountains were before me. The trees looked like grass, the few buildings, roads, and cars, like miniatures. I watched as the people moved silently below.

The sky was coloring to a soft pastel. I could feel the chill creeping into me and decided to head back down. To a ten-year-old boy the switch-backs were boring, so I began to run, leaping and jumping over obstacles. At least I warmed up some.

As dusk crept quickly down the Valley, it dawned on me I was in black bear country, three-hundred-plus-pound monsters I did not want to reckon with. Luckily, I had seen none, but as darkness approached my mind started seeing shapes and imagining that they were more than what was really there. Full night was descending, and that spurred me on.

I redoubled my effort and exploded down the trail and onto the flat of the Valley, and did not stop until I reached our tent cabin.

Needless to say, I had stretched my trust. But as I was safely back, it ended well. My mother's spaghetti and garlic bread were sure welcomed.

But the day was not over.

FIREFALLS

We all bundled up and found an open spot on the meadow to gaze at the massive cliffs above. Soon there were calls back and forth between the peak of 3,000-foot Glacier Point and Camp Curry. Then the most spectacular thing happened. Against the coal-black wall, beneath a sky full of stars, a glowing firefall streamed down the face of the monolith. I had never seen anything like that before and couldn't imagine how this awe-inspiring event could happen. When it was over, flashlights darted in the inky night as folks made their way to their lodging or tents.

But . . . this day was still . . . not quite over yet.

THE BEAR

Just as we reached the tent cabins, we heard shouts and my father, with our light, went ahead. He came back and motioned the family forward. In the beam of a dozen flashlights was an enormous bear scavenging in the tin garbage cans. Even with the lights and shouting, the old bear just casually went about picking out his evening meal. I'm glad I hadn't met that big boy when I was alone high on the trail.

* * *

This experience stayed with me all of my life. I deeply appreciate the unbelievable beauty of Yosemite. When times seem their worst it helps to remember that there are places in this world like Yosemite.

Whenever difficulty arises, as it has a habit of frequently doing, I recall that hike and thinking, "I will never ever give up. The end result is worth it. I can do this, I can do this."

My warm sleeping bag inside a secure tent cabin with my family sure felt good that night.

Lost Arrow Wind, 1968

Steve Lake

As a full-time resident of Yosemite in the late 1960s, I was able to fully enjoy all of the seasons of Yosemite, from the cold nights filled with the rustle of snowflakes falling to the hot summer days full of tourists and smog. The summer evenings in Yosemite were warm and soothing, full of campfire smoke and the cacophony of campers camping. Our neighborhood, near the base of Yosemite Falls in the north corner of the Valley, away from the tourist areas, was a quiet refuge where the full experience of Yosemite Valley permeated the soul.

Late in the summer at about nine or ten o'clock in the evening, when all was quiet, a faint whisper of the wind could be heard coming from the north. And in a few minutes, a steady warm wind would fall from Indian Canyon, just east of the Lost Arrow Spire and, after stirring the pines for ten minutes or so, would be on its way. Now, forty-five years later, this experience of a fifteen-year-old young man stays with me today. My dad called it the "Lost Arrow Wind."

Scout Camp in Yosemite

Vahl Clemensen

IT WAS APRIL 2002. I had just arrived in the Valley as a national park volunteer assigned to the Wilderness Division. I settled into campsite D on the western edge of North Pines Campground for the duration. Having spent most of the last thirty years camping and hiking the Yosemite High County, I had spent little time on the Valley floor. I decided to take a walk and get reacquainted. My campsite was facing Tenaya Creek, which was hidden from my view by underbrush. Just down the road I discovered the Backpackers Campground Trail along the creek and over a bridge.

I stood on the bridge for the longest time looking at the Backpackers Campground on the north side of the creek. Something looked very familiar. Déjà vu! That's where I had spent two weeks in 1949 in my first Boy Scout summer camp. The Backpackers Campground used to be the Valley's Group Campground. Our Boy Scout Council in Stockton had sold its camp and bought new property, which wasn't yet developed in that summer of 1949, so Yosemite became our summer camp for Troop 14.

I experienced a sudden overwhelming flood of memories. Back in those days, you drove to the Group Campground on the Northside Drive leading to Mirror Lake, which was now a bike path. We used to head up that road to the "Indian Caves" any chance we got, when not working on scout craft skills for Second Class. Oh what fun we had climbing all over those wonderful boulders, which formed caves, playing hide-and-seek or Indian. We marveled at the smoke deposits on the rocks made by real Indian campfires hundreds of years ago. The parking lot and signs for the "Indian Caves" are all gone, as the area is a sacred heritage site of the Ahwahneechee.

We would hike on up to Mirror Lake and play along its shore, throwing in pebbles to watch the concentric circles they made, rippling across the glass surface, making the reflections of Half Dome shimmer. That beautiful lake is now an alpine meadow with Tenaya Creek meandering through it. The lake permanently silted up when the National Park Service stopped dredging it each year, allowing it to take its natural progression toward becoming an alpine meadow.

Still standing on the bridge, I remembered the wonderful campfire programs in the amphitheater in Lower Pines Campground. We Scouts would all sit down front and heartily lend our voices to the singing that started each campfire. No one sings at the park campfire programs any more. It's too bad. Something has been lost.

A couple of nights we all went with our leaders to the meadow south of Lower Pines Campground to see the firefall. What an amazing sight that was! No one said a word as we stood in awe, transfixed. It was always great fun going back to camp because we got to take our flashlights out of our pockets and use them to see our way home, and shine them in each other's eyes, and put them in our mouth so our cheeks lit up, and put them under our chins and make weird faces.

One night we were put on our best behavior and we went all of the way to Camp Curry to the campfire program. At the end of the program, one of the guys who worked there yelled at the top of his lungs, "Hello, Glacier Point." Then everybody was real quiet and listened real hard and we heard way in the distance, "Hello, Camp Curry." Then the guy down here yelled, "Let the fire fall." Again, everyone had to be real quiet and we heard in the distance, "The fire falls." And there in the black of night, at the top of the cliff, a huge glowing mass appeared and it began falling down the face of the cliff from Glacier Point like it was in slow motion, a waterfall of fire. Then they played the "Indian Love Call" over the PA system. Wow, was that neat! That was even better than watching it from the dining-room porch of The Ahwahnee on my honeymoon many years later. But, of course, there is no longer a firefall. It isn't ecologically acceptable.

Oh, then one night, just before dusk, we hiked all the way over to Southside Drive and part way up toward Happy Isles to the garbage dump. The rangers had the dump roped off and there were bleachers to sit on, but they were all full, so we just stood. At dusk, bears started coming out of the woods, and the rangers started dumping the garbage. It was great fun to watch the bears eat, and they would fight with each other over the garbage. Of course, that practice is long gone. A lot of my time as a volunteer has been spent educating the public about protecting the bears from people. Do you know what happened to that dump site, now that all garbage is hauled out of the park? It is the backpacker's parking lot on Southside Drive, which has been closed to regular traffic for years.

Looking back into the campground, I saw myself, that twelve-year-old in 1949, trying to stuff everything he owned into that huge, 1928 alpine pack of his dad's in preparation for his first overnight backpack trip. I was so excited as I proudly hoisted my pack and headed for Camp Curry with my fellow Scouts. We were going to climb the Two Mile Trail to Glacier Point. There was hardly a switchback on the whole trail. You took two steps up and slid back one. I was so hot, tired, dusty, and thirsty, but we all finally made it. That trail has been closed for years because it was too dangerous, difficult to maintain, and long ago wiped out by avalanches.

Once on top, we went into the campground just at the head of the trail and set up camp in the beautiful sugar pine forest. You say there is no campground at Glacier Point? There was then. A nice one. We all walked out to Glacier Point, and you could look right down at Camp Curry and the swimming pool. Wow! On our way back to camp, our leader took us by the beautiful, white, Victorian Glacier Point Hotel. It so impressed me that I would spend the first night of my honeymoon there years later. The hotel burned down several years after that and was never rebuilt. It stood where the new amphitheater has been built.

Back in camp we burned our dinner, of course, but ate it any way. We were hungry. After dinner there was a special treat. Our leader took us back out to Glacier Point for a ranger-led campfire. We watched a ranger light a big pile of bark on fire and then watched it during the campfire burning down into a pile of glowing coals. At nine o'clock the ranger ask everyone to be quiet, and then I could hear it, a voice from way down in the Valley yelling, "Hello, Glacier Point." And sure enough, when they stopped yelling back and forth, the ranger, who had been watching the coals, got a great big rake on a long metal handle and started pushing the coals over the edge. I had a hard time going to sleep that night, even though I was so tired, thinking about all of the great things we had seen and done that day. The next morning we packed up and headed down the Four Mile Trail, because the Two Mile Trail was only one way. That hike was the beginning of a lifetime of backpacking for me in the Yosemite wilderness.

A few days later, camp was over, and we headed for home. Boy, I'll never forget that first Scout camp. But there I was, standing on that bridge not forty yards away from my new campsite and so close to all those memories of so many years ago.

"All the world was before me and every day was a holiday."

–John Muir, 1890

The Old Woman in the Volkswagen Beetle

Bill Grewe

It was a red Beetle. It had been parked in the lot in front of the Tuolumne Meadows Store all night. Overnight parking was permitted in the 1970s. It was just before 8:00 a.m. I was just opening the store, and as I ran the register I watched through the door as an elderly woman got out of the Bug. She had slept in it. The car stayed in place and, later that day, I saw the woman return to her car, and I struck up a conversation.

She was just shy of eighty. Her Bug could have passed for the same age. She told me she was from Milwaukee. Widowed. Her kids had lives of their own. She had, for a lifetime, seen pictures of Yosemite and wanted to visit. There was never a chance, an opportunity, or an offer. The dream would die with her, she thought.

She was sitting around a table with her lady friends earlier in the week, as they did every week, playing cards. It just struck her that everyone was complaining. Complaining about health, finances, family, or whatever. She said she just stopped. She put down her cards, walked out, and got into her Bug and began driving. She followed her dream and for the first time in her life made it to California and to Yosemite. She had a bag of clothes in the back, a board to use as a cutting board across the passenger seat and a collection of food items, blankets and such, and a little spiral book for notes. Her hair was long and gray, partially pinned in the back. She smiled broadly as she recounted her "foolishness" and what tomorrow might bring. I have never forgotten her.

A Boy's Memory of Four Seasons in Yosemite

Allen Berrey

Spring
Was water
Booming and smashing down Indian Creek
Falling silver and white from shimmering blue sky
Then resting in meadows, soft and warm and green
Hiding pollywogs from searching little boys
Summer
Was rock
Towering high and hot in godlike mystery
Rising bronze and gray into the monumental above
But also cracked and ledged and bay-treed
Beckoning us sirenlike to high fearful places
Fall
Was leaves
Black oak, willow, and white alder yellow
Painting mirrored pools in the slow Merced
Then crunchy incense, sleeping on the Valley floor
At dusk I run through them, to home on wind-tumbled trials
Winter
Was snow
Sparkling cold magical happiness
Falling at night in mesmerizing silence
In morning the Valley a shining white cathedral
I fly on my skis down slopes of rainbow-crystalled beauty
I am the luckiest boy in the world

Indian Love Call

James Schlotthauer

IT ALL STARTED for me when I was about five years old, back in 1946. Every night, just after dark, the event that everyone waited for occurred, the firefall. In Camp Curry just before the firefall, they would have a talent show, and then someone would call to the person at the top of Glacier Point to proceed with sweeping the beautiful red-hot coals over the edge of Glacier Point. While the beautiful glowing coals were coming over the edge of the cliff, someone with a voice like Nelson Eddie or Janette McDonald would sing, "Indian Love Call."

That was so inspiring to me, even at that young age, that to this day whenever I hear that song, it brings tears to my eyes. One of the many lovely memories of what I consider to be the most beautiful place on Earth.

Falling for Yosemite

Daniel Marengo

Yosemite sparks magic-wand memories for me. They rocket from the wand's tip like the streaking water comets of Yosemite Falls, powerful and potent as turbocharged pixie dust.

In my Yosemite, water plays the leading role. Holding my new daughter tightly, as we waddle into the granite bowl of Tenaya Lake, her tiny dangling toes skimming its surface, my wife at the waterline snapping pictures that take me back in a heartbeat.

A dozen winters later, ice skating on the same, now-frozen water during the record-setting dry winter of 2012–2013 that allowed Tioga Road to stay open well into January.

My son and I, not quite wading, more like really slowly inching into the Merced River from the sandy edge of El Capitan Meadow. Within seconds, ankles aching from the swirling April snowmelt, shoulders red from the warm spring sun.

I have traveled to Yosemite many times, most of those trips originating from the San Francisco Bay Area (but no, never on foot like John Muir). My first time, I was thirteen, and my middle school had the vision (and courage) to take a class of freshly minted teenagers to Yosemite National Park for a week of 1970s-era "Ecology Now" environmental education.

Our yellow school bus shot across the Central Valley, its engine winding and whining up the Sierra Nevada's western grade. When the bus turned the corner on Tunnel View, the rattling din inside the bus fell, hushed by the panorama before us. By then, I was a High Sierra regular, but I had never seen anything like the arresting, high-definition majesty of Half Dome and El Capitan.

Our days were split between Yosemite Valley and Crane Flat. We hiked and munched on gorp and Space Food Sticks. Up at Crane, we bunked in rough-hewn cabins and sloshed through cold puddles the color of French roast. Park naturalists led us on a hike under an inky night sky, flashlights off, across an alpine meadow torched by starlight. With a hand on the shoulder in front of you, we walked gingerly, tentatively, until we found our stride.

Down in Yosemite Valley, the trip's main event beckoned: Yosemite Falls. From the Valley floor looking up to Lost Arrow Spire, hiking to the Valley rim appeared to be an audacious goal. With waterfalls turbocharged by a warm and early spring, the upper and lower sections of Yosemite Falls were raging, wild and free. Kind of like us.

Though, as a group of semisoft suburban Bay Area kids, we might as well have been climbing El Capitan's Nose. The patient park ranger dispatched to brief us delivered clear directives. (No switchback cutting! Everyone in front of the sweeper! Do not stray off the well-marked trail!) Since this was 1973, I do not recall being basted in sunscreen as kids would be today, but my favorite teacher did have a cool green Sea and Ski tube in the back pocket of her bell-bottoms.

And we set off for the top of North America's tallest waterfalls, propelled by adrenaline, hormones, and intoxicating levels of mist-infused alpine oxygen. High we climbed, the rhythmic mineral crunch of our Vibram soles taking us up the trail. The torrential thunder of the falls filling our ears and wetting our hot faces when the trail curled near the falls' foaming cataracts—by far the most fun I ever had in "class."

We arrived at the top and wandered close to the terrifying edge of Upper Yosemite Fall. We watched, wide-eyed, as Yosemite Creek raced over the edge and into the foaming frenzy below.

At lunch, I brandished a brand-new scarlet Swiss Army knife. After devouring the best peanut-butter sandwich ever made, I angled the Ibach-factory-fresh stainless-steel blade into the thick top of an orange and sliced off a nice section of rind, fruit, and the inside of my left forefinger. The blood that pulsated out of the cut was bright red and hard to stop.

I hunkered on a granite slab close to the water's edge and extended my hand into the water. The neat, red cut bled into scarlet clouds that instantly atomized into the fast flow of Yosemite Creek, my bloody DNA soon to join the launch party at the top of Upper Yosemite Fall.

I stayed there for a few minutes, bleeding underwater and cursing my carelessness. Fortunately, by now my finger was essentially in an ice bath and quite numb. Word got around and a group of concerned teachers and chaperones kneeled beside me. Sea and Ski reached up and removed my bandanna-tied headband. She soaked it in the icy water and wrapped it around my turning-blue hand. And so, my kind core teacher saved me from the embarrassment of bleeding out at the top of Yosemite Falls.

Forty years now since my first date, Yosemite has aged well, its legacy burnished by the National Park Service and the philanthropy of stewards like Yosemite Conservancy. My grandmother would recall, as a girl, witnessing the Yosemite firefall and feeding black bears as if they were roadside theme-park attractions. In her day, sightseeing was considered a full-contact sport. Concepts of sustainability that we now embrace were decades away. Today, Yosemite at 150 is restored and preserved as a place John Muir would recognize and still tramp across California for, which is an amazing thing considering the many millions forever changed by its magical realm. Long may it thrive.

"Beautiful falls. Oh! Beautiful falls. Singing so sweetly again and again."

—Park visitor commenting on Nevada Fall, 1873

In Search of Nature's Temple

Karen Bowerman

High in the Sierra Nevada, carved by glaciers and sculpted by time, are the giant granite cliffs of Yosemite, topped with domes that look as smooth as enamel and pinnacles that reach for the clouds.

The Valley, once home to American Indians, means "gaping mouth" in the Ahwahneechee dialect, and as you turn the corner and see it for the first time, it stretches far and wide: swathes of forest sloping down to the wide Merced river which, corralled by three-thousand-foot walls of stone, weaves deep through green meadows, woodland, and a wilderness that's home to chipmunks, coyotes, and bears.

Yosemite National Park has long been a place that's inspired wonder, poetry, and a sense of the sacred. John Muir, the nineteenth-century Scot who sought to protect and promote America's open spaces, described it as "the grandest of all the special temples of Nature."

And yet, on the approach road, when I first took in that classic Valley view: the towering rock face of El Capitan on one side, the iconic Bridalveil Fall on the other, and in the distance, the polished granite of Half Dome, sliced in two by the force of a glacier, there was that nagging feeling I should have been more impressed.

Maybe it was the pre-trip hype or the familiarity of the image—the subject of so many posters and postcards—or, ironically, the fact that everything was so vast.

Faced with such magnitude, scale was deceptive. The mountains, which I thought would dominate the view, seemed insignificant, and Bridalveil Fall, which was no doubt crashing into the Valley, looked, as its name suggested, delicate and fragile—a streak of mist or a swirl of smoke unfurling absentmindedly over a precipice.

I drove on, anticipating the "great reveal."

There are three main approaches to Yosemite: the coach-crazed Highway 140; the scenic 120, which skirts along the northern edge of Mariposa County, home of the gold rush; and the Fresno road from the south.

I flew to San Francisco and drove four hours through the endless orchards and flat, sprawling farms of California's Central Valley to Tenaya Lodge, outside Yosemite's South Entrance.

After awaking early to a view of dew-drenched pines, their tips disappearing into a morning heavy with mist, my first stop was the Mariposa Grove, home to some of the country's most spectacular grand sequoia trees.

I stood in a maze of cinnamon-colored pillars, craning my neck as I tried to trace a trunk, any trunk, to the point where it touched the sky.

These beautiful, gangly giants with soft, spongy bark enjoy an eight-hundred-year spurt to full height (around three hundred feet) before settling down to enjoy the next two or three millennia in relative comfort—their girths, much like humans', widening with the passing years.

Among the five hundred sequoias at Mariposa, there's the famous Tunnel Tree with a gap in its trunk wide enough to take a stagecoach, and the Grizzly Giant: a monstrous beast heading toward his three thousandth birthday.

Back on the road, a traffic jam signaled my approach to Yosemite (the park attracts four million visitors a year). I arrived to find the tourist-oriented Yosemite Village packed with people: hardly conducive to feeling at one with nature.

But once I'd left behind the hordes of picnicking families, gangs of children, and whizzing cyclists, my focus shifted back again—to the granite monoliths and massive waterfalls for which this seven-mile long Valley is known.

For those keen to learn more about the park's history, geology, and fauna, rangers offer guided walks. I joined a group at The Ahwahnee—a quirky, 1920s Flintstone-style building, topped with towers and green tarpaulins.

It's where the rich and famous stay when they visit the park; guests have included Charlie Chaplin, Walt Disney, J. F. Kennedy, and the Queen of England.

We cut across the hotel's lawns, under the cupped, yellow flowers of dogwood trees and hiked through woodland where a tufty-eared douglas squirrel was retrieving a cache of nuts. It was so engrossed in discovering, sorting, and nibbling its treasure that we were able to observe it at an arm's length.

At the river Merced, our guide, Mynard Lutts, told us how the valley was regularly reshaped by rockfalls and the river.

"In the Great Flood of 1997, the bridge we're standing on disappeared underwater, trees were uprooted, and the park's campgrounds swept away," he said. "The sewage system was also ruined. The stench was foul, but the spill gave rise to a stunning display of wildflowers the following spring!"

At the end of the walk, I set off again, this time alone, heading uphill, through the puzzle-piece trunks of ponderosa pines, incense cedars, and California black oaks, whose acorns were once the staple diet of American Indians.

Centuries ago, the Ahwahneechee used to burn the Valley to make it easier to hunt and to encourage black oaks to thrive. But when Yosemite became a national park, the authorities did their best to prevent wildfires.

Their well-intentioned efforts changed the entire look of the Valley. In Muir's time it was 80 percent meadow; now it's 80 percent forest. Prescribed burning has been reintroduced, but the black oak is still struggling to survive.

I pass evidence of a recent, controlled fire: scarred trees, blackened roots, and a soot-stained earth that crumbles beneath my feet. It's hardly a picturesque spot.

There's a climber, I think, in the distance: a speck of red clinging to a near-vertical drop. And a waterfall that's hurtling into a dark, wet chasm, as desperate to reach the bottom as the sportsman is the top.

I recall the words of John Muir, "It's by far the grandest of all the special temples of Nature I was ever permitted to enter."

In this scarred, forgotten forest, nature's cycle finds its source. From this dark, distorted wilderness, an age-old Valley looks to life. This is Muir's temple, and I have it to myself.

"The Valley has been cleansed."

–Julia Parker, 1997

The Tunnel Tree

Klaus Penning

WHEN I WAS child in Germany, I collected pictures. They came in cigarette packs and showed places or buildings of interest, like the Leaning Tower of Pisa, the Eiffel Tower, Grand Canyon, and so on. But the picture that fascinated me most was of a tree so large that it had a tunnel cut through it for cars to drive through! I always liked forests and trees, but the picture of that Tunnel Tree fascinated me, and I never forgot it.

World War II came and raced over Europe. It affected everyone's life, and I was no exception. After becoming a soldier, I was sent to the Eastern Front and captured by Russian troops. The war came to an end in 1945, but I returned home in 1948. I was twenty-one years old then, and life was difficult in Germany. At this time, it even looked like there could be another war on the horizon. It was at this time I got married and my daughter Dagmar was born.

In 1956, we decided to immigrate to the United States. There was a program under the Eisenhower administration that made it possible for people from behind the iron curtain, also for ex-POWs from Russia, to build a new life in the U.S.A. I applied for a visa for myself and my family. After filling out dozens of questionnaires, we were asked to come for a personal interview to the American consulate in the town of Düsseldorf. Everything seemed to be okay; we were accepted and could make plans for our immigration. But when the consulate employee asks me where we would like to live, I was not prepared to give an answer. In fact, neither I, nor my wife, knew much about the U.S.A. I had to say something, and in my desperation the only thing that came to my mind was that Tunnel Tree I was so fascinated by. "Oh," he said, "you must be thinking of the Tunnel Tree at the Yosemite National Park. I have driven through this tree myself." Then he looked through his papers and mentioned there was a chance he could find a sponsor near Yosemite. After the interview we returned to the town of Bochum where we lived, and two weeks later we were informed a sponsor was found in the town of Fresno, located about sixty miles from the entrance of the Yosemite Park.

In February 1957, we started our trip into the new world on a former troop transporter to New York with many other refugees. After twelve days of mostly stormy weather, we arrived in New York. We spent one night there, and the following day we flew to Los Angeles and finally to Fresno.

In the beginning, life was not easy in our new country. My first job was working on a turkey ranch. I bought my first used car about eight months later, and the first trip we took was to that Tunnel Tree! Yes, the tree was all I had dreamed about! Even more, I was fascinated by the beauty of the park. The beautiful Yosemite Valley with all those fantastic rock formations. It was love at first sight!

Later on, my wife and I divorced. Again this was a difficult time, and I was thinking of returning to Germany. Surprisingly, a job was offered to me in Yosemite, working at the maintenance department as a painter. I took the job and now I could live right in that wonderful park. During this time, I also met my (future) wife, Gail, who was working at the front desk at the Yosemite Lodge. After two years we got married. We left the park, returning to Fresno, where I started a sign-painting business. I did well and we were looking for a house to buy. But since we both were in love with Yosemite, we wanted to live closer to the park.

We found a home in Oakhurst, only sixteen miles away from the South Entrance of Yosemite. I also found a nice shop in the center of town. I was doing very well with plenty of work. Surprisingly, one of my best clients was the Yosemite Park and Curry Company: I did all the sign work for Badger Pass, Wawona, Camp Curry, and signs for the High Sierra Camps. After retiring from the sign business, I worked at Badger Pass as a ski instructor, and for four more years as a tour guide, showing tourists the beauty of Yosemite. Sorry to say I could no longer show off the famous Tunnel Tree, as it fell to the ground in 1969 after reaching the age of 2,300 years! Now it is known as the Wawona Tree. This tree guided me to a wonderful life. Who said dreams do not come true?

More Seeds Taking Hold

Jack Walston

It was on a late morning in mid-August 1943 when the Southern Pacific San Joaquin Daylight train arrived in Merced, California, to connect passengers with a green eight-door Yosemite Park and Curry Company Packard touring car. Detraining the Daylight were a mother and her two sons on their way to Yosemite National Park. It would be the very first visit to the park for the brothers—Carl, eleven years old, and me, Jack, age eight. The first stop on the way to Yosemite via the "All-Year Highway" 140 was at Midpines for a late lunch, where a bear was chained to a tree in front of the restaurant—a totally unexpected scene that neither impressed nor pleased the passengers in the touring car.

When the Packard finally arrived at Yosemite and the view of the Valley opened up, it triggered the genesis of a transformational experience for three future generations of the Jack Walston family. That initial Yosemite visit was followed by countless additional park visits over the next seventy years. Indeed, there have been so many that it would be difficult to exactly recall how many, other than to say that Yosemite has been "a lifetime of returning" for family members, loved ones, and special friends.

For those who have been captured by the magic of Yosemite, one of the most rewarding personal experiences is to "see" Yosemite vicariously through the eyes of another who views the park for their very first time. I have been most fortunate to have shared such opportunities with my children (Jennifer, Jill, Leslie, Bruce, and Wayne) and grandchildren (Cole, Charles, and Tommy), as well as with my five stepchildren and many friends. In particular, I recall a Yosemite visit during early June of 1971 with Tenzing Norgay (who made the first successful climb of Mount Everest in 1953 with Sir Edmund Hillary), his first and only park visit. When

Tenzing, his wife, Daku, along with Apollo 8 astronaut Bill Anders (who took the iconic Earthrise picture from the Moon on Christmas Eve, 1968) and his wife, Valerie, and Lenore (mother of our daughters), and I hiked to the top of Sentinel Dome, we were caught up in the magic of Yosemite and the 360-degree incredible view of the High Sierra while sitting on the famous Jeffrey pine tree. In fact, as Tenzing looked out upon the breathtaking vista, he said, "It is so free, open, and magnificently beautiful" (indeed, quite a reflective perspective from someone who had stood on the top of the world eighteen years earlier, almost to the day).

Our family, particularly the girls and their husbands, have been true stewards of Yosemite. Jennifer, my oldest daughter (who worked a summer in the park when in college) and her husband, Gregory Johnson, were engaged in Yosemite and have been very involved for several years with Yosemite Conservancy by generously donating their time, talent, and resources to the Conservancy mission. They currently are cochairs of the Mariposa Grove project, and Jennifer is serving as the cochair of the November 7, 2013, gala.

My middle daughter, Jill, two days after her graduation from college, became an employee of the Yosemite Park and Curry Company, where she had a successful career working in various positions, including key assignments at The Ahwahnee and in group sales. There she met, was engaged (at the top of Sentinel Dome), and married a third-generation National Park Service ranger, Cameron Sholly, in the Yosemite Chapel. Cam had lived in Yosemite as a young boy and has had a very distinguished career in the National Park Service. He is now an associate director of the National Park Service in Washington, DC.

Leslie, the youngest daughter (who has twice camped overnight on the top of Half Dome when it was permissible to do so) and her husband, Tom Watson Jr., a retired naval aviation officer and graduate of the United States Naval Academy and the Naval Fighter Weapons School (Top Gun) frequent the park when their schedules permit. Like her sisters, she learned to ski at Badger Pass (under Nic Fiore's tutelage), and recently she and Tom introduced skiing there to their four-year old son, Tommy—a Walston right of passage.

Personal passion for the park has opened many doors for our family, including a treasured friendship for me with the late Horace M. Albright (indispensable assistant and often acting director for Stephen T. Mather, the founder and first National Park Service director), a six-year appointment by Rogers B. Morton, secretary of interior, to the National Park Service Western Regional Advisory Committee, and early involvement in the initial formation (a coming together of economic and educational objectives) of the Yosemite Institute in 1971, as its first chair (identifying key and prospective board members), and interfacing with Don Rees, executive director (former headmaster of Cate School in Santa Barbara and the founding Yosemite Institute executive), as well as with National Park Service personnel and Robert Maynard, vice president of operations for Yosemite Park and Curry Company. Retrospectively, it is truly exciting to reflect on the importance of stewardship that has been instilled in the one million participants (predominately schoolchildren) who over the last forty-plus years have attended weeklong field science programs of the Yosemite Institute (aka Yosemite National Institutes and now known as NatureBridge) in its five different national park locations!

Also, it has been a privilege to have had a long-standing affiliation with Yosemite Conservancy on both the council and board of trustees, which has provided more than $80 million in private-sector funding to complete park projects that the National Park Service has had a moral obligation to undertake but has lacked the necessary budgetary funds to do so. In this regard, one hastens to add that the impressive accomplishments of the Conservancy in cooperation with the National Park Service are the direct result of the dedicated efforts and commitment of the present and past staff members and all those who serve or have served over the years on the council and board—all truly outstanding individuals.

How Yosemite inspires and brings out the best in people is both a testament and ongoing gift to humanity. As an example, in July 2012 my three daughters and their husbands accompanied four couples (hosted by Jennifer and Greg) that were chosen by the Special Operations Warrior Foundation for a seven-day High Sierra Loop Trail outing. These were seasoned Special Operations military personnel along with their spouses and a guest. The warriors had never been to Yosemite. In fact, they had no idea that such an exquisite place even existed. Indeed, they have been superbly trained and are true patriots defending our country and individual freedoms. In fact, one of the warriors, at the conclusion of his Yosemite experience, was going to be deployed to Afghanistan for the fifth time!

These soldiers and their spouses and guest were extremely appreciative of their introduction to Yosemite. They openly expressed that they had been extraordinarily "touched" by the experience and the incredible beauty of the park, and said, "It was truly rewarding to experience the beauty of the country that we spend so much time defending." Indeed, and in actuality, my three daughters and their husbands were unquestionably "touched," too. Like so many others before them who had "seen" and shared Yosemite vicariously through the eyes of others, they would always remember what they shared with their very special guests whom they were so proud to know.

Such is Yosemite! A "SEED" that truly nurtures the betterment of mankind!

Unexpected Amazement

Tom Caverly

IN AUGUST 2009 my beloved and I were vacationing in San Francisco when suddenly I was presented with an idea. A thought entered my mind, direct and deliberate, almost as if it was an order being given, from something much bigger. "Go to Yosemite National Park," it said. Being from New Jersey, and never having been to California or a national park before, I had no idea what we were in for. We set the alarm for 5:00 a.m. and set out on the road to Yosemite before sunrise the next morning. As we got closer to Yosemite, the weather became much warmer, and before we knew it, the top on the Mustang was down, and we were peeling off layers of clothing. Lucky for us, we wore our bathing suits under our clothes!

We came upon a quaint western town named Mariposa and decided to stop in and say hello. It wasn't long before we found out Mariposa meant "butterfly" in Spanish, and because of my wife's spiritual attachment to butterflies, we knew we were in the right place, and on the right track. Onward to Yosemite!

As we approached the park, the landscape became more and more beautiful. I have never experienced anything quite like it. And once we entered the park, I was blown away. We decided to pull over and take a little swim in the river. We pulled into a little parking area, and it seemed we had the whole park to ourselves. The Merced River was crisp and inviting on such a warm summer day. I took the water bottles out of the back of the convertible and they were hot, so I decided they were going to soak in the river with me. They cooled off for drinking in no time! You could see right to the bottom of this crystal-clear riverbed, and it had to be ten feet deep. My wife and I swam out to a flat rock in the middle of the river and decided to relax there for a while. After about ten minutes of lying and drying on this cool piece of granite in the middle of the river, I noticed what looked like a big trout swimming in the cool water before us. It was amazing! The silent breeze caressed my skin, and the scent of the trees that surrounded us delighted my sense of smell. I was embraced by something I've never quite known before, and I liked it! I knew we had much more to see, so after another little swim in the river, we climbed back into the car and headed farther into the park.

Having no idea what was around each bend, we kept being unexpectedly amazed by the beauty of this place. Next, we stumbled upon El Capitan, a gigantic vertical rock formation of pure granite. I couldn't believe my eyes! I pulled over again and ran down into a field of wildflowers that grew in the shadow of this towering wall of majestic stone. We were like kids in a candy store, laughing and playing, and posing for pictures. I tell you, it was the time of our lives. . . .

Next, we came upon the most amazing scenic overlook I have ever seen in my entire life: Tunnel View. You must experience this amazing turnout and view of Yosemite Valley to believe it. What an awesome road trip this has been so far, and little did I know, the best was yet to come! The arrow pointing up to Glacier Point was a street sign I couldn't resist! All of a sudden, we found ourselves heading even higher up, into the awe-inspiring Sierra Nevada of California.

We happened upon another incredible place to pull over and get out of the car on our way up to Glacier Point. This is where my Yosemite experience suddenly moved beyond physical experience to spiritual revelation. There I was, standing on top of a rock, gazing out over Yosemite Valley, with what I now know to be Half Dome directly across from me. I stood there paralyzed by the pure power of this magnificent natural landscape, and God was there with me. I knew it. I felt it. I wish I could describe it, but it is lost in the words. You must go there, my friend. Whoever you are that is reading this, just go to Yosemite. Make yourself a promise, and then keep that promise. You will not be sorry.

Finally, we continued the rest of the way up to Glacier Point, where we explored the grounds, met some extremely cool, laid-back people, had an ice cream bar from the gift shop, enjoyed the view, and took a slow ride back down into the Valley, and back to San Francisco. The next morning we got back on our plane, and five hours later we were back in New Jersey. I will never be the same since my trip to Yosemite, and I must say, out of all the national parks I've been to since, it holds a special place in my heart and continues to call me back. Some day, Yosemite . . . someday!

Time Stands Still

Chris Waldheim

A FAWN FOLLOWS HER mother through a dewy meadow on a
cloud-covered morning
Children laugh as they splash in the Tuolumne
The click-clack of mule's hooves echo on a path taken countless
times before
Footsteps lead to new destinations, sights beyond belief,
otherworldly views
Mountain peaks salute peering eyes with stature and grace
A tree lies felled by a howling windstorm, a thousand more lie
in silent memory
Golden trout swim in a granite trough on the Merced
Thunder claps time and time again, applauding the magnificent
scenes below
The pitter-patter of raindrops falls on trees, leaves, lakes, rivers,
and earth
Light rain foreshadows hail, waterfalls come alive on dry
granite walls
A bear, startled from a misty afternoon slumber, bounds over
the natural steeple of nearby logs
Half Dome glistens in the distance while drizzle, sun, and clouds
dance across the sky
The dinner bell rings in camp, calling the tired and hungry in
Sunset is a blaze of pinks, purples, and reds, as shadows climb
the steep walls
Bats come out, fish jump, a ranger tells his tales, knee-deep
in Merced Lake

A sky so black that the Milky Way looks as infinitely vast as it
     really is
Uncharted destinations are firmly etched in our memories
Friendships are forged, bonds are strengthened, awareness is
     heightened
No one goes home the same
Yosemite is nature and nature is life. Yosemite is life renewed.

Conquering the Fear of Heights

Rebecca Kerley

LAST SUMMER I planned a trip to visit my girlfriends in California. Yosemite wasn't supposed to be on my trip itinerary. Half Dome certainly wasn't on my list either. At the last minute, I booked a room at a small hostel outside the park for three days. It was supposed to be a relaxing trip. No plans.

I was sound asleep in a hostel outside of the park when I was awakened by a 6:00 a.m. phone call. My friend Aaron, who lived nearby, had applied (on a whim) for two last-minute permits to hike Half Dome. He received an email that our names were picked. My reaction via phone call was part excitement, part giggling, and part a let's-do-this attitude. Inside, I felt like I was going to vomit. I was scared and sick to my stomach. I've read *Off the Wall: Death in Yosemite*. I've heard horror stories about the cables. There was no way I was going to do this. However, Aaron showed up that evening with every piece of gear imaginable and plenty of food and water for the hike. We started out of Curry Village at 6:00 a.m. feeling energized and ready to go.

The hike to the cables was nothing short of spectacular. The views were incredible, inspiring, and my pictures will never do it justice. As we crept closer to the saddle and the cables came into view, my heart was pounding. My stomach was wrecked. However, everyone that we encountered coming the opposite direction was smiling, laughing, and wishing us well. We were prepared. As we finished up the sub dome, we realized we forgot something important. Gloves. We FORGOT gloves. The most important piece of gear had been left in a van. We both knew there was a pile at the base, and I was hopeful to find a pair that worked. As we got to the saddle, I started to lose some composure. Fear of heights and the reality of climbing the cables began to sink in. I looked at Aaron, and through my tears said to him, "I don't think I want to do this any-more." He very calmly put his hands on my shoulders, looked me directly in the eyes and said, "Stop crying, go put on the gloves, and get on those cables . . . now." It was all I needed. I couldn't leave here with regret.

There wasn't a line, so I went up first. The first few steps were easy. That didn't last long. I learned not to pull up on the posts as they come OUT of the granite. Aaron talked me through every step of the way, and we reached the top quickly. I am forever thankful that I didn't quit. The sheer beauty of everything surrounding us was overwhelming. I cried tears of happiness and pride. The trip down the cables was just as intense, except there were more people and waiting is difficult when your knees are shaking. At the end of the day my feet were destroyed with blisters, I smelled and looked terrible, I was soaked with sweat, but at that moment I was happy. Content. At peace.

That night I went to Tunnel View alone to watch the sunset while sit-ting on a rock. Looking on Half Dome as the sun set, I kept thinking that just a few hours earlier I was sitting on the Diving Board. Yosemite steals a piece of your soul when you visit. At the age of thirty-seven, I still cry when I turn around and take my last view of the Valley before leaving. Yosemite is the most magical place on Earth.

A Birthday Sunset on Sentinel Dome

Billy Hurst

I RODE MY MOTORCYCLE up along Glacier Point Road in the early summer evening and parked in the dirt turnout just where the road starts its winding descent to the point. I walked solo up the old service road to the base of Sentinel Dome as the sun lowered in the west. Swiftly up the steep granite slabs; I didn't want to miss the actual sun setting. Huffing and puffing at eight thousand feet, I made it to the rounded top of the dome where a mild breeze cooled the day's end. It was the park's birthday, June 30.

As I caught my breath, my spot on the earth slowly pivoted away from the sun. The tall conifers on ridges beyond the park boundary rose to obscure the shining yellowed disk. We say that "the sun sets," but really it's the horizon rising. I'll see that bright star again when my part of the planet spins around to face it again in our morning.

Thin clouds toward the Pacific coast caught filtered sunlight and glowed gold, orange, then pink. To the east, there were cumuli over the Sierra crest; these dissipated while they went from bright whites to tinted yellows to various grays. The slopes and forests toward the foothills were dark in the shadow of the brighter western sky, while the thousands of acres of bare granite toward the high country were pale with reflected sky glow.

It was very quiet; one last Steller's jay squawk, then no sound but the intermittent breeze. At certain moments the white roar of Yosemite Falls drifts up from the canyon below.

As the light faded, I saw the bright star Vega overhead, then the Triangle and more summer stars. The dim wash of Half Dome, Mount Starr King, and the Clark Range kept the view east punctuated with gray regions. Sunset's glow lingered for a long time in the atmosphere to the west. Having watched our own good star moved out of sight by the earth's rotation, I now got that sense not that space was out there, but that we were in space, on our little world.

Sunsets like this have been happening for eons, whether someone watched from atop Sentinel Dome or not. One hundred and some years ago, did anyone stand sentinel from this prominence on June 30 as the faraway president signed legislation protecting some of the landscape below? The top of Sentinel Dome marks part of the boundary of that protected parcel. Sunsets like this will continue for ages into the future, and with our care, so will Yosemite.

Your Own Cathedral

Hannah Hindley

"I had nothing to do but look and listen
and join the trees in their hymns and prayers."
—John Muir, *Travels in Alaska*, 1915

When he caught the orange-gold light reflecting from those impossible granite walls and felt the mist from those rocketing white falls, John Muir did well to describe Yosemite as a cathedral. How apt to think of this place—with its ancient groves of skyscraping sequoias, its gravity-defiant rock faces, and its thundering towers of water—as a vast and shining, unroofed shrine. What better place to worship, you might ask yourself, as you idle in bumper-to-bumper traffic in the heart of Yosemite Valley, searching for the scent of pines through the slight smog that has settled over the one road that leads into Muir's "great temple."

Someone up ahead has slowed down to take a picture of deer. You can see the driver with his camera out the window, foot still on the gas as he rolls forward, eyes diverted from the road. This is an era of multitasking, after all. Across the meadow, on the other side of the Valley, you can already make out the dark throngs moving as one toward the base of Yosemite Falls. Cars are double- and triple-parked along the Merced River. The traffic ahead slows down again, this time to a stop: a black bear has been sighted, strolling in the direction of the tent cabins in Curry Village. He has the swagger of a well-fed bear who probably learned from his mother what an ice chest looks like.

The whole place thrums with restive, bustling humanity. It is a day of comings and goings. Many of the vehicles up ahead won't stop longer than a few minutes to snap photos before they continue along the loop that will carry them back out of the Valley. The average visit to Yosemite National Park—all 1,200 shining square miles of it—lasts about four hours. I'm not a religious kind of girl, but this seems to me kind of like strolling into a church, snapping a shot of the angels on the ceiling, and hurrying out midway through the first sentence of the sermon.

For me, this is one of many commutes I've made into the Valley. Some mornings, like today, are frenzied with fair-weather traffic; others, hushed and holy. I have the luck and luxury to have worked in Yosemite. I have had time and seasons to savor this cathedral. I've watched the crowds thin and the haze of summer traffic dissipate. I've stood alone in the Valley, with only the pines for company, and listened to the wind. I have waited, in perfect silence, till the setting sun turned the waterfalls red with its last light. Unhurried, I have laid down in the snowy trail and willed the tall mountains to speak to me. I have learned that, though the attention here can't help but wander outward and upward—toward the tallest, the shiniest—the "holy" here is less about magnitude than about perspective. All 2,425 fluid feet of Yosemite Falls are impressive in any context, but it's hard to savor that rumbling power amid the jostle and shouts of hurried photographers. But step away from the trail anywhere in the Valley, close your eyes, and lean back into any warm granite rock. The power of this whole place will electrify you. It needs only a little silence and solitude to break through.

You don't need to have lived here to know Yosemite's magic. Neither do you have to be a rock climber or a winter mountaineer or a backcountry explorer to find those little moments of solitude that can transform this place from souvenir snapshot to sacred. My favorite little cathedral is just minutes from the bustling Valley floor. It is a place where most of the famous, towering batholiths are hidden from view. There are no big trees here, no seething torrents to shock and awe. It is a quiet place that smells like summer. A little snowmelt creek runs down over rose quartz and glistening mica. Sometimes there are wildflowers. Often there's a breeze. And almost always, I am alone with just the sound of water and the comforting stretch of wilderness on up the trail beyond me.

You, too, can find your cathedral here. You don't have to stay for long. Maybe, the next time you go hiking, you will slow a little and let your gaze and feet stray. Just off-trail, you will find a hidden little meadow waiting for you. Where the river bends, maybe you will bend, too—sit for a moment, watch the water roll past. Where the rocks lie jumbled at the edges of the Valley, tuck yourself into their cool shadows. Maybe you will find a cave there where, without sight, you can listen more carefully to the mountains, to those "songs and sermons preached and sung only there," as John Muir wrote.

Do not be afraid to love the high rocks and the mighty falls. They speak to the soul, and this place was set aside in their honor, so they could always be tall, free, and witnessed. But this, too: love the little things. Look for the secrets. We protect this park not only for its landmarks, but also so we can always have open spaces to roam and solitude in which to reacquaint ourselves with our own hearts and the heart of the land. Every trail and every creek here harbors its own cathedral. Pay attention. And for gosh sake, don't take pictures with your foot on the pedal.

A Winter Afternoon Spent in the Grove

Jennifer Nix

WE DID NOT feel like intruders in the peaceful, silent grove of ancient giants, the air hushed and heavy with rain and mystery. Even with our gay laughter bouncing off the shining rocks and echoing down the leaf-strewn trail stretching out before us, she welcomed us with watery arms. No, there was no stern disapproval in the air as our joy disrupted the solemn silence of the trees, our joy-filled faces uplifted to catch the cold rain on our skin. The soft gray light, muted in a kaleidoscope created far above, washed down our bodies, infusing us with the primordial story of nature, one we unconsciously recognized and rejoiced in with equal fervor. In the gentle wind-driven movements of branches, the drip of raindrops on the soft ground underneath, in the furtive shadows and light that moved in the secret hollows of the soft, fallen logs, the secrets of the earth were whispered to us for safekeeping.

"The ice and snow of a thousand winters have wrapped
them around in chilly embrace. . . but neither fire,
nor frost, nor winter's furious storms, nor summer's
glowing heat, have done aught but reveal their sturdy
strength, their majestic and awe-inspiring character."

–Charles Augustus Stoddard on
giant sequoias in the Mariposa Grove, 1894

Yosemite Falls

Ann Muto

On one of our nearly annual visits, we encountered a photographer who told us to make sure to get to the bottom of Yosemite Falls at 8:30 a.m. to see the rainbow. We did, and we saw the gorgeous rainbow.

Yosemite Falls
Torrents of water
Thundering thousands of feet
Rumble into the day,
The roar a room around me.
Morning light lends its aura
To boulders and conifers.
In the spotlight,
A river rainbow.

The storm-driven fog
Swirls over me
Blankets the granite bridge.
Glacial beads flee
The explosion of water on rock
Settle into emerald effervescence
Edged with foamy froth.
Clumps of ice captured
By pebbles and branches
Nestle in nooks along the shore.

Wind whips
my legs.
Icy spray stabs
my face, numbs
my cheeks,
freezes
my fingers.

Rainbow warms
My eyes.
No longer earthbound.

Silent Beauty

Pat Ballengee

It's been many years since I have actually lived and driven in snow. I've been to the snow when it was sitting politely on the roadside while the road itself was clear, unchallenged pavement. On a cold February day, when I saw that Yosemite Valley was full of fresh fallen snow, I had to put my hesitation aside and just go.

As I leisurely make my way into the Valley, not far from the Arch Rock Entrance, powdery snow gradually accumulates until I am surrounded by a winter wonderland! The nostalgic feelings and smells of cold and damp build, even inside my car as I steadily increase the heat. Blue, gray, and white colors sink into my vision as I take in the pale blue-white glow of the shadowed, tree-lined road. The silence of snow-covered earth still astounds me; it penetrates my senses until everyday thoughts temper, and I become consumed by the tranquil composure of winter. My whole being becomes serene and in the moment. I am embraced by Mother Nature's winter.

Carefully moving over the crunchy, packed snow, I quickly remember how it feels to drive in winter. With one mile behind me, I feel more at ease.

I meander my way along the narrow riverside road. Glaring beauty meets me at every turn. The shimmering river is full of immense boulders of various shapes and sizes. I enjoy watching the water jostling past them only to meet another colossal boulder creating more waves, whirls, and turmoil. After the long, lazy, dry summer, the river is so happy to be cold and flowing and alive! Further down the road the snow depth thickens and the massive boulders camouflage their usual mystique of mighty sentinels of the river, and playful ogres of snow appear wearing silly caps of fluffy, cotton snow. Snowcapped boulders create humorous shapes, prompting a game of "What does that one look like?" I spot a gnome, a duck, a gremlin, Santa, and a swan.

The narrow two-way road opens to a one-way two-lane road. I can now slow to an even more relaxing pace without concern of hindering others, few that there were. Sometimes I'm looking around so much I forget to step on the gas. Soon I learn that people are parking just anywhere ON the road to get photos. I understand that, as most turnouts are not cleared and traffic is light. If there is no one behind me, I, too, stop for a quick, can't-miss-that photo through the car window.

The sky above is translucent and blue as blue, defying the accusation that just hours prior it was dropping white sheets of hushed, serene chaos. Everywhere I look, white dominates. The classic scenes of Yosemite Valley are dressed with new light and color. It is all so familiar, yet unfamiliar. I see the sheer granite wall of Half Dome rising behind the chapel, turning iridescent. It glows brilliantly under its speckled coat of white. The Inspiration Point view is splattered with tufts of snow up and down the towering vertical cliffs. Waterfalls are framed with built-up ice along their waterways. The river is acknowledging the crystallized, leafless trees that bow to it, perfectly reflected in the water's undisturbed rest. The entrance of a tunnel is protected by stretched, strong, thick icicles, like a line of tall, armed soldiers. Walking underneath them could result in a bad day.

I see a photo I want to take. It requires walking through the soft, giving snow. Luckily, someone earlier saw the same photo opportunity and I am able to follow in their footsteps. Each step feels like a long journey as I sink two to three feet deep all the way to the ground! I am doing an extreme marching exercise, having to raise those knees as high as I can to clear the top snow level to reach the next boot-made hole. The old hips will object later, but this is well worth it.

My attention is frequently darting toward the crackling and thundering rumbles of avalanches echoing from nearby cliffs. They seem close, so I can't resist looking for them, even knowing they are hidden among a hodgepodge of snow-covered granite walls. Every branch and needle of every fir tree is enveloped by heavy frosting, bending them low. On some pines, the frosting drips from their very top, snakes in and out over each branch, down along the trunk, and then drops to the ground, where it finally collects in a soft heap. Other firs are billowing steadfastly with their collected masses, refusing to let them go.

I wade in the soft, deep snow, take lots of photos, and, in the still air, I never get cold. I wonder and marvel at the surreal paradise of Yosemite Valley in winter. And I feel most fortunate to be allowed to witness such splendor.

"No temple made with hands can compare with Yosemite."
—John Muir, *The Yosemite*, 1912

Lift Thine Eyes

Pauline O'Briant

From 1952 through 1955, I had the honor of being a member of College of the Pacific's A Cappella Choir under the direction of J. Russell Bodley. During those years, Mr. Bodley and the choir were invited to participate in the annual Easter Sunrise Service at Mirror Lake in the park.

Members of the choir would arrive at the park on Good Friday and were lodged in the cottages at The Ahwahnee. Meals were provided, and after rehearsals we were given free time to relax or enjoy the park.

On Sunday morning we were awakened at 5:00 a.m. and hustled to the chapel for vocal warm-ups. Then it was up the hill to Mirror Lake to await the break of day.

The women members of the choir, clad in maroon robes, had to hop across some stepping-stones and get into formation on a small islet in the lake. Mr. B would remain on shore from which point he could conduct and keep an eye on the crest of Half Dome. This was usually around seven o'clock. The moment the sun peeked over the granite monolith, we would break into Mendelssohn's setting of the twenty-first psalm: "Lift Thine Eyes, Oh, Lift Thine Eyes to the Mountain." The effect was dramatic and, indeed, it captured the congregation's attention. There were oohs and aahs from the crowd gathered around the lake as the mountain and solar ball of fire over its crest reflected in the pristine water while our voices echoed through the Valley.

Each time I visit Yosemite nowadays, I take a trip down memory lane and hike up to Mirror Lake to relive those Easter Sundays so long ago. I lift my aging eyes to the mountain while all the time the familiar anthem plays its tune in my head.

Reflections of Yosemite, Mirror Lake, February 2012

Carole Siska

W HEN MY BROTHER asked me to go to Yosemite in February, I was reluctant to say yes. I don't like the cold, and I don't ski. But when he told me that Yosemite is quite beautiful at this time of year and that we would just do some short hikes and take photos, I said okay. The few times that I have been to Yosemite I have taken a lot of photos—those great memories are date stamped and put into a photo book. But there are also those great memories that have no photos. They're those little motion pictures in your head complete with sound, all of those things that touch the senses. This trip was no exception.

We did a number of hikes. This is a reflection of one hike at the end of a day.

Our last hike of the day was to Mirror Lake. I protested that it was too late in the day to do another hike, as it was going to be dark fairly soon. My brother insisted that he wanted to take some photos and gave me the big-brother ultimatum to go or not. So I went.

We started on the trail just outside of The Ahwahnee. The trail was matted with yellow and brown leaves and ran alongside a forested hill to the left and down a gentle hill to the right to a road packed with snow. The road seemed to run parallel with the trail. We followed the trail that lopped up and down through dense forest, always hugging the hill to our left. A group of college students appeared, tromping through the snow on the road below going back to The Ahwahnee. Soon the road below started to disappear, and our trail became narrower and denser with trees and brush. As we made our way, we found ourselves stepping over slick black rocks and jumping over tiny little streams that seemed to be coming from the hillside alongside the trail. I looked up through the thick canopy of trees to a blue sky that was now being joined by large clouds, and the light that filtered through the trees was becoming dimmer. The forested hillside to the left was home to giant boulders, some the size of cars, and they were sprinkled with pockets of moss and dark patches that looked like bruises from years of unmerciful winters. My urban-girl psyche started to take hold, and I found myself peering to the left and right, my ears pricked to any crinkle or rustling of leaves in the brush. When I was just about to reassure myself that animals were hibernating during this time of year, the thought occurred to me that one might decide to go against the hibernation rules and come out looking for food. And wouldn't that animal do so close to dusk? I started to complain to my brother that it was getting too late and that we should turn back. He assured me that it was just a bit farther and to keep going.

When I was just about to complain again, the trail started to go up a slight hill to what looked like a sharp turn to the left. We got to the turn and directly to the right, down a hill, was a white wall of mist that rose upward for at least thirty feet. I stopped and looked again. The white mist appeared to extend along a corridor to the left over white ice and clear shallow water that trickled around flat gray and black rocks, a vision so surreal I expected to see a snow queen dressed in silver and white come gliding over the water. This was Mirror Lake. I sprinted down the trail that wound around to the bank of the lake, and there in the distance to the left was Half Dome, dark against the light pink evening sky. It was stunning. It was very quiet here except for the gentle sound of the water trickling around the rocks on its way to the Valley. The beauty, the stillness, the serenity of the place was magical, and I just stood on the bank taking it all in while my brother's camera clicked in the background. We stayed just a bit longer, and then we started back. It was a brisk hike, and we made it to The Ahwahnee with only a few minutes of daylight to spare. I was happy to get back to civilization, but I was so happy to have added this wondrous place to my little treasure of motion pictures. Mirror Lake, Yosemite National Park, February 2012.

11

YOSEMITE
BY NIGHT

Chasing Moonbows

Debbie Croft

THE CLIMATE CHANGED abruptly, and a storm raged all around us. We had felt the drops when first crossing the road to walk up the trail. By the time we reached the viewing area the light spray had become a shower. Pulling our hoods over our heads, we stood, watching. Numbing wet winds whipped this way and that as tons of water plunged from the cliff above.

Our family had driven two hours, sacrificing precious sleep for a late-night adventure, to witness a rare occurrence of nature: a bow in the mist under the light of a full moon.

"Couldn't we just stay home and try the experiment in the backyard with a garden hose?" my husband asked when I suggested the idea several days before.

"Nope. We're going to Yosemite."

Earlier that evening we packed the car and headed for the mountains.

We had lived in the foothills of Central California only a few years when a photographer friend told me about one of nature's most enchanting wonders.

"Ever seen a moonbow?" he asked.

I hadn't. Didn't even know such a thing existed. But after he explained, I did some research.

During the months of late spring and, sometimes, early summer at Yosemite National Park, visitors flock to the base of Lower Yosemite Fall long after the sun has set.

To watch a moonbow.

The conditions have to be just right: a full moon in a dark, velvety, star-studded sky, a waterfall, and lots of watery mist below. A university astronomy professor developed a means of predicting the appearance of moonbows in Yosemite and posts the data on a website.

So began my quest to see this elusive moonbow for myself.

When we arrived, the parking lots were full. Voices carried on the night air. I was surprised at how many people roamed the Valley floor in the dark. Young parents pushed strollers. Several people walked dogs. Those not on foot rode bicycles. Children ran around, pointing their flashlights into trees, stopping on a bridge to watch the rushing water, or pausing to count tiny lights dotting the wall of El Capitan from climbers tucked in for the night.

And of course, there were photographers. Dozens of them had arrived before dusk, positioning themselves and their equipment along Southside Drive near Cook's Meadow for a view of the fall. With a snack or cup of coffee in hand, they talked, swapping stories, comparing cameras . . . all the while patiently waiting, and hoping, to get that perfect shot.

At the base of the fall it was standing room only as people crowded for a glimpse. To make matters worse, the roar was deafening.

"Excuse me. Excuse me, please," I yelled as politely as I could.

The man looked my way.

"Excuse me. Could we just slip through here, please?" I asked.

"Oh, yes. Go right ahead." He stepped back to let us pass.

"Thank you."

The moon was still hidden by the south rim. Only a faint glow hinted at its presence behind the shadows.

For the most part, darkness obscured our identities. Thankfully, my husband's blue-and-white coat provided enough contrast for me to find him in the crowd. My daughter and I clung to each other, partly to stay together and partly for warmth. When she wasn't at my husband's side, she was looking through the lens of the camera owned by our friend.

A few brave photographers stood on the bridge. Plastic sheeting protected their investments, and rainproof ponchos covered their shivering bodies.

The number of spectators continued to increase, crowding us even more. I craned my neck to see the water. It felt more like a sporting event than a wilderness adventure.

There was a commotion behind us.

"Do you think you all could walk behind the tripods?" one agitated photographer asked.

"Maybe you guys could move forward to give us more of a walkway," was the response.

Almost comical. There we were, chasing moonbows and tripping over tripods.

We kept checking the time. The moon would soon reach the correct position. We could tell as the glow behind us grew brighter. We waited anxiously. Just a few more minutes. . . .

High above us the celestial orb of lunar rock would make its appearance, casting light on the base of the fall. Voices quieted, and we held our breath.

Finally, moonlight peeked above the shadows, illuminating the spray in front of us. And there it was—a moonbow.

As if on cue, the crowd exhaled in hushed awe.

Astounded by this wonder of nature, nothing else mattered. All eyes gave witness to the manifestation of beauty taking place almost within reach. For the next several minutes the moon continued to rise, until it completely broke free from the shadows.

As if making her appearance in an outdoor theater, the silvery diaphanous arc increased in brightness. Spanning the creek, she took center stage and simply glowed.

I stood, spellbound, with eyes wide open. It was almost midnight and long past my bedtime.

Our teenage daughter was mesmerized and declared Yosemite to be her favorite place on earth. She wrapped her arms around me and put her head on my shoulder.

"Yosemite is so beautiful! The moonbow is so beautiful! I've never seen anything so beautiful!" she said over and over.

On the way home my husband agreed, it was better than the backyard garden-hose experiment.

Some memories remain with us for a lifetime. Like every time I see a moonbow. In the middle of the night when normal folks were asleep in their beds, crazy people like us wandered around in that great expanse of protected wilderness, looking for beauty in an unexpected place. And we found it.

So began my lifelong romance with one of Yosemite's hidden wonders.

Nighttime Journey to the Top of the World

Nicole DeFazio

THE SUN WAS setting as the alpenglow cast a beautiful pinkish hue on the granite scenery before us. My sister, Kim, and I were standing at Glacier Point on a humid July evening. Our journey that we were about to embark on in a few hours was laid out in front of us. Far below us, we could see Vernal and Nevada Falls, still roaring due to the above-average snowpack from the previous winter. We could see Little Yosemite Valley and Liberty Cap. And, dominating the landscape was the mighty Half Dome. It towered over the Valley below with unsurpassed grandeur. This was our mission. We were going to hike through the night and watch the sunrise from the summit of Half Dome. We would hike past the waterfalls, through Little Yosemite Valley, and finally up the subdome and infamous cables to the summit.

After the sun had set, we returned to the car, made some final preparations, and attempted to rest, despite our overload of adrenaline. We then found a parking spot, grabbed our gear, and made our way to the Mist Trail trailhead. Our gear consisted of multiple layers of clothing, ponchos, headlamps, flashlights, water, granola bars, gloves, and the always-essential glow sticks (these were more for our entertainment, I suppose).

The first thing I noticed was that my senses heightened. I remember the fresh smell of the forest and the mist. I remember the sound of the breeze through the trees, the roaring Merced River, and thundering waterfalls. I remember looking up and seeing what seemed like a million stars through the treetops. And I will never forget the feeling—the feeling of unsurpassed excitement and complete solitude at the same time. We did occasionally meet some friendly hikers that were making their way down the trail after watching the sunset, but, for the most part, we were all alone—all alone in the pitch-black wilderness in an area so different from what we are accustomed to.

There were times that we would hear a noise, and we would be reminded of the possibility of running into a bear. Bears in Yosemite do not have a strong history of being dangerous to humans (although they should always be assumed to be so, if you happen to see one), but the darkness and isolation from civilization brought out the fear in us. We began making noises when passing through sections that we felt bears would likely be located. We would clap, and we eventually came up with our own chant—"Bad Bears, Bad Bears, whatcha gonna do . . ." (to the tune of the COPS theme song). I think the lack of sleep combined with the adrenaline may have been getting to us at that point.

The hike itself went through stages. It began with the Mist Trail. I remember two things about this section: the waterfalls and the steps—lots and lots of steps. We could start to hear the waterfalls long before we got to them. As we would get closer, we could begin to feel the mist and the roaring would get louder. Vernal Fall was the first of the waterfalls. As we climbed the steps along the fall, the noise was deafening and we were getting drenched by its mist. The mist was refreshing, as the air was still warm and humid, but we decided to put our ponchos on partway up the fall. It was so dark that we could only see the fall if we shined our lights at it. It was then that we could see just how mighty this fall was.

After crossing a bridge over the raging Merced and climbing up along Nevada Fall, we soon entered Little Yosemite Valley. This provided a nice break from the climb, but it seemed to be prime bear country. We did a lot of clapping and singing during this section.

The trail then began to climb steadily. The grade increased as the trail went on until we finally arrived at the subdome. The subdome is the smaller dome before the "big dome," but it is just as challenging in my opinion. It starts with steep steps, but the steps eventually disappear and you are left to find your own way up a steep slab of granite, which can feel like somewhat of a mean trick in the dark. At some point, I turned around to look behind me. This was one of the few moments in my life that took my breath away. There was just enough light that I could begin to see the outline of the mountains. It was then that I realized how high up we were and the exposure and steepness of the trail we were on.

Once we reached the top of the subdome, we could see the outline of the summit. Our goal was in sight. There was just one obstacle left—the cables. We could see a couple of tiny lights partway up the dome. We soon realized that those were actually headlamps of some other hikers. The nervousness really set in for me at that point. As we approached the cables, it was getting lighter out and we were able to see just how great of an obstacle this was going to be.

After taking a moment to catch our breath, collect our thoughts, and take some words of encouragement from some veteran climbers, we put on our gloves, grabbed a hold of the cables, and began the climb. I went first. There are boards to rest on every ten feet or so (although some were broken or missing, which made us not want to rely on them too much). We climbed the cables one board at a time. I kept looking back at my sister to ensure that she made it to the next board before moving on. Each time I looked at her, I could see the start of the cables getting farther and farther below us. As we got higher and higher, it was evident that, if we were to fall, there was nothing to stop us until the Valley, which was roughly 4,800 feet below. My sister's eyes were glued forward. She would give me a nod when she was ready to move on to the next board.

It was bittersweet as we reached the top of the cables. I was relieved, but I also knew that we had to climb back down. All of the worrying went away as I came to the realization of where we were. We were there. We were at the top of Half Dome in Yosemite National Park, and the sun was about to rise over the mountains.

The sun rose right on cue and gave light to the unbelievable scenery surrounding us in all directions. I was in complete awe, but there was one more thing I needed to do to make this journey complete. As I approached the edge and I saw the Valley below, I paused to take in the moment. I have never in my life felt small yet so large at the same time. I felt as though I was on top of the world. A very large beautiful world.

Half Dome and Yosemite National Park will always hold a special place in my heart.

In the Shadow of the Blaze

Kathy A. Pippig

Amber light rings the rich brown earth. Flames of the campfire reach up, as if grasping for the dark canopy of spreading tree limbs.

Low noises come from the periphery of the camp. The night-stirring creatures tread the forest floor or amble about on their perches in the trees. The fire hisses and crackles; a piece of wood splits in the heated pit and tumbles to lie up against the stone circle containing the blaze.

Down the slope, a small creek whispers up against the shallow embankment, then winds a course away from the camp.

The old folding chair creaks as I settle down into it, put my feet up on the footstool close to the fire. Firefly sparks of rust-orange leap from the sheets of flame. They dance in the smoke before winking out in midflight.

The air is crisp, with a bite to it. I lean back in my chair, tilt my head up, and gaze at the patch of black, black sky, pierced with glitters of pin-pricked light. I pull in a breath, heady with the perfumes of wood smoke, evergreen, loam, and the early autumn night.

Small stones and the dry fallen pine needles crunch in the shadows of my fire. I turn to the sound. Behind me, two spots of light bob in the dark and move from side to side. Then, I make out the contrasts of white and black; tan and gray. Two tiny, delicate paws pad out and stop at the fringe of light. The glowing spots blink; then the raccoon lowers its chubby back end to the forest floor and quietly stares at me. It begins to idly work its tiny front paws back and forth in the dirt and needles.

I smile. High above, the trees drag to and fro in the wind; the shuddering of their limbs like a low moan. The blinking eyes follow my gaze upward, then veer off to the side; exploring the shadowed depths of the campground. Clever paws mindlessly pick at the earth.

The raccoon dips its head up and down, sniffing in the direction of the iron storage box. Shuffling in the rim of the shadows, the forest bandit waddles over to the iron box.

Stretching up on her hind legs, she inspects the box. Her paws move quickly over the doors of the box, then linger on the latch. And as if performing a magic trick, the paws move furiously on the latch, prying and lifting; a blur of movement; a slight of paw. But the mechanism does not give way, and clearly this frustrates her.

She then trundles over to me. She stops at what she feels is a safe distance from me, sits up, and stares impatiently. She is sending mental pictures to me.

I watch the fire, then reach into my coat pocket and fish out an apple. From another pocket I withdraw a pocketknife. Placing them on the footstool, I cut the apple into four slices. I sample one of the pieces, enjoying the tart sweetness. As I gaze into the fire, the black-and-white figure quickly approaches and a slice of my apple disappears.

Fingering the treasure in her paws, the raccoon regards me for a quiet moment, then lowers herself to the ground. She stuffs the slice of apple into her mouth, turns, and toddles away, toward the stream.

I watch her retreat, until she and the shadows become one. (I know feeding wild animals poses a threat to their lives—but this was many years ago. It has since become illegal, and rightly so.)

Somewhere in the dark, someone is softly playing a guitar. In another corner of dark, I can hear someone chopping wood. Faint snatches of conversation twist in the wind and carry over to me.

I stare back into the flames and listen to the snapping discourse of burning wood. It is getting chillier by the moment.

Overhead, I hear the high piping squeak of a bat, as it dodges in and out of the illumination from the blaze: grabbing a meal on the wing.

I finish the apple and decide to call it a night. At the entrance of my tent, I take my shoes off, shake them free of debris and place them inside. In the tent, I change clothes quickly and slip into my sleeping bag.

As the warmth from my body heats up the confines of the bag, the smells of wood smoke and pine waft up from the flannel lining, and from my hair and skin. The air is cold on my face and I snuggle deeper in.

I rise to the songs of a multitude of birds; in the trees above my tent, on boulders that line the campground, on wooden rails that front the meadow to the west. After dressing in jeans and a sweatshirt, I step outside and glance through the trees, into the meadow.

Though the columns of light that pierce through the forested Valley are warm, it is still cool in the shadows and I prepare to make a fire. I have only the weekend here to savor the out-of-doors. But I have those two days well planned. I am looking forward to my hike to "Indian Caves" and Mirror Lake.

And that is just the start. Yosemite Valley holds many wonderful sights to explore.

The Lunar Rainbow

Carol Ann Hironymous

YOSEMITE WAS BECKONING
Each season calling more
Every month approaching
Summer made it harder to ignore.
So when I got a few days off
I called my mom to say
"Let's go up to Yosemite
I'll stop by on the way."
Our reservations were secure
We didn't have to worry
Our cozy home was waiting there
At Housekeeping, Camp Curry.
We ate our dinner on the way
As it was getting late
A picnic by the river
Just outside the granite gate.
We finally got there, tired
From a long exhausting day
I glanced at the small newspaper
They give you when you pay.
I read through all that day's events
I really don't know why
But when I got down to the end
One of them caught my eye.
There'd be a lunar rainbow
At Yosemite Falls this night
A ranger would be waiting there
At midnight at the site.

Though my sleeping bag awaited
Something told me I must go
I knew it wasn't often
One could see the moon's rainbow.
I grabbed the small red flashlight
And awoke my mom to say
I was going to Yosemite Falls
I'd see her the next day.
My mom looked at me smiling
Then alarm shone on her face
She hoped that I was joking
But she jumped up just in case.
"You can't go through the woods alone."
She felt it wasn't right
"Wait and I'll go with you
It's the middle of the night."
Protected by huge granite cliffs
We started on our way
Walking slowly through the shadows
On the pathway where they'd play.
As we got closer to the falls
Their rumbling voice was calling
The peaceful night was shattered
By the thunderous water falling.
We soon arrived at Nature's stage
The sound effects were loud
The moon, a giant spotlight
Shone down on the waiting crowd.
We stood there in the spraying mist
A mother and a daughter
And watched a giant rainbow
Stretch across the crashing water.

We stood there staring up in awe
At this amazing sight
Embraced by gorgeous colors
As they shimmered in the night.
Nature must have been quite proud
Of her lunar creation
Which filled the night with beauty
And unceasing admiration.
I knew nothing could replicate
The wonder of this night
And that I'd never feel the same
About another sight.
Our visit soon came to an end
Reluctantly we parted
But little did I know
A new tradition had been started.
Each month that followed after
When the full moon came in view
I'd be sure to tell my mother
And she'd answer right on cue.
Her reply would be a question
One that I would always know
"Want to hike up to Yosemite Falls
And see the lunar rainbow?"
I only saw the rainbow once
On that late-night endeavor
But memories still linger on
And magic lasts forever.
I still think of that wondrous night
And every full moon after
When I would gaze up at the sky
And share my mother's laughter.

A Pot of Gold

Emily Croft (age seventeen)

For years after I moved to California, I wished I still lived in my previous home in Phoenix, Arizona. There was a mall, a grocery store, and a gas station half a mile down the road. Now, we do have modern conveniences here, but those places are half an hour to an hour away.

When I first moved to California, if you had asked me if I enjoyed living here, I would have said that I didn't. I had very few friends for the first few years in Mariposa. In moving, I had to leave the home I grew up in, the people I felt comfortable around, and three best friends, whom I had known since I was old enough to recognize faces. Plus, I was only seven. So it's understandable when I say I really wanted to move back to Phoenix. Although, you'd think that I would have gotten used to living in California sooner than I did. I've lived here for ten years! That's why I surprised even myself when I decided that living in California was worth it. Here's how that happened:

It was a Thursday night, May 7, 2009, around 10:00 p.m. We were in Yosemite, on the trail that led to Lower Yosemite Fall. The going was tough; the force of the fall alone was creating a wind that was hard to push against. Amazingly, even though we were still quite a ways away, and even though there were several bends in the trail, we were being misted by the spray from the fall.

What were we doing? Looking for a moonbow. What's a moonbow, you might ask? It's when the full moon, as opposed to the sun, shines on a waterfall, creating a rainbow. In fact, Yosemite is one of the few places in the world where this phenomenon, also called a lunar rainbow, can occur. What's interesting about moonbows is that children are usually the only people who can see the colors. Most adults can typically see only a white bow. As you get older, the cells in your eyes become unable to pick up the colors in a moonbow. The reason for this is, since rainbows reflect more light than moonbows do, the colors in a moonbow aren't as easily detected by our eyes.

No one in my family had seen a moonbow before, so by the time my mom and dad and I reached the bridge across the Lower Falls, which was our destination, I was itching with excitement. We couldn't wait to see it! We made our way to the middle of the bridge. The walkway was very narrow, so it was hard to not trip over the many camera tripods set up all over the viewing area.

I'm pleased to say, though, that the main attraction was well worth the hassle. Because when we got to the middle of the bridge, the sight of the waterfall, viewed by the light of the full moon, was enough to take my breath away!

Suddenly, I saw it. A white bow was stretched across the water. But what thrilled me was the fact that I could see faint color! Come to find out, my mom could just barely make out the red, yellow, and green, also!

There wasn't a pot of gold at the end of this moonbow. No, the treasure was strewn about all over the bow, making it a sight I would never forget. And that's how I decided, even though Phoenix has its conveniences, living in California is definitely worth it.

The Perseids

Elizabeth Blair

T HERE WERE SIX of us, on our second trip to Yosemite, in August 2010. That evening we were back at our cabin, very tired from our long hikes over the past several days. After dinner each of us grabbed a pillow and blanket from our beds, loaded into the car, and made the dark pilgrimage to Glacier Point. There was no moonlight, and we couldn't see our feet to watch where we were stepping, but we reached the point, and as our eyes adjusted, we could see the Yosemite Valley below us, lit dimly by the starlight. We spread out our blankets on the ground and sat there as a ranger spoke quietly to a group of visitors, and several groups of people around us chatted. Within a half hour or so, about one hundred people had gathered up there, and soon we were all quiet with anticipation. As we all looked hopefully and deeply into the night sky, into our beautiful galaxy and beyond, we, like so many humans before us, were overcome with the knowledge of how brief a time we are on this earth and how insignificant in the grand scheme of things our little lives are. We were grateful to be spending this awesome moment at one of earth's most beautiful spots. We pulled our blankets up to our chins and huddled together, lying flat on the ground and looking straight above us as the night turned colder. Suddenly, someone called out, "There's one!" And then another meteor streaked across the sky, followed by cries of "Wow!" and deep sighs of awe. The Perseids were at their peak, and we were watching them from Glacier Point in Yosemite, and we were going to remember this the rest of our lives!

"When we contemplate the whole globe as one great dewdrop,
striped and dotted with continents and islands, flying through
space with other stars all singing and shining together as one,
the whole universe appears as an infinite storm of beauty."

–John Muir, 1915

AFTERWORD

THE STORIES AND poems in *Inspiring Generations* capture fond memories and love of Yosemite from a tremendous diversity of individuals, spanning decades. We hope these accounts will not only entertain, but also inspire you to come join us in the park, and to consider helping us provide for the future of Yosemite.

We have gathered these stories to honor the 150th anniversary of Abraham Lincoln's signing of the Yosemite Grant that set aside the Yosemite Valley and the Mariposa Grove for all people, and led to the idea for the national parks.

I had the great privilege to serve as the superintendent of Yosemite National Park for six years, and in that time I developed a deep love for Yosemite and an enduring commitment to help preserve and protect it. After my retirement, I am delighted to serve as president of Yosemite Conservancy.

Through the support of donors, Yosemite Conservancy provides grants and support to Yosemite National Park to help preserve and protect Yosemite today and for future generations. The work funded by Yosemite Conservancy is visible throughout the park, from trail rehabilitation to wildlife protection and habitat restoration. The Conservancy is dedicated to enhancing the visitor experience and providing a deeper connection to the park through outdoor programs, volunteering, and wilderness services. Thanks to dedicated supporters, the Conservancy has provided more than $80 million in grants to Yosemite National Park.

Yosemite Conservancy provides a terrific way for individuals to become stewards of Yosemite by supporting essential work that would not happen without help from our donors and friends.

No matter the season, it's time to visit Yosemite—go for a hike in the Mariposa Grove, feel the mist from Vernal Fall, gaze up at Half Dome. Join us on this journey. Help us provide the margin of excellence, and become a steward of Yosemite for the future.

Mike Tollefson, President
Yosemite Conservancy

A THANK YOU FROM
YOSEMITE CONSERVANCY

Yosemite Conservancy is made up of individuals whose spirits are tied to Yosemite. We salute Dave and Dana Dornsife for their ongoing support of our programs and projects, and here honor their own memory of serving the park. Dave and Dana have a special tie to Yosemite's back-country, and through the Conservancy they pair their passion for the park with good works that help ensure Yosemite's future. They shared their story with us and we now share it with you:

> For twenty-five years I spent most of my recreational
> time in the backcountry of Yosemite. I was thrilled when my
> wife, Dana, joined me on my hiking adventures in 1999. One
> of our most memorable trips in the Yosemite backcountry
> was spending a week with a National Park Service/California
> Conservation Corps trail crew working out of Virginia Lakes.
> We had just agreed to co-chair and launch the Campaign
> for Yosemite Trails and needed to experience trail work first
> hand. We spent time with the crews while they were working,
> learning about the process of building and maintaining trails.
> We quickly gained respect for the dedication and hard work
> required by the crews every day. They were able to restore the
> trails—many installed during the great depression—using new
> and improved techniques. We took some day hikes, returning
> to the trail crew camp in the evening. The food was excellent

and plentiful, the camaraderie was strong, and the experience invaluable. Our most memorable observation was that we were glad someone else was doing the work!

—Dave and Dana Dornsife

CREDITS

Sources for display quotations added by the publisher are listed below.

CHAPTER 1

Joseph LeConte. *The Autobiography of Joseph LeConte* (New York: Appleton and Co., 1903) 273.

Theodore Roosevelt. Speech before the Colorado Livestock Association. Denver, Colorado. August 29, 1910.

Josiah D. Whitney and Geological Survey of California. *The Yosemite Guide-Book: A Description of the Yosemite Valley and the Adjacent Region of the Sierra Nevada and of the Big Trees of California.* (Cambridge: University Press, Welch, Bigelow and Co., 1869), 67.

Claire Marie Hodges. Letter to Yosemite Superintendent W. B. Lewis. 1918.

James Mason Hutchings. "California For Waterfalls!" *San Francisco Daily California Chronicle.* (August 18, 1855).

John Muir. *The Yosemite* (New York, The Century Company, 1912), 1.

CHAPTER 2

L. R. Tulloch. *Biennial Report of the Commissioners to Manage Yosemite Valley, 1889–1890.*

Will Neely. "Notes from my Tuolumne Journal." *Yosemite Nature Notes*, vol. XXXVI, no. 1 (January 1957): 6.

Galen Clark. "A Plea for Yosemite." Reprinted in *Yosemite Nature Notes*, vol. V, no. 2 (February, 1927): 13–15

CHAPTER 3

Carl W. Sharsmith. "Tuolumne Meadow Wildflowers," *Yosemite Nature Notes*, vol. XXIX, no. 7 (July, 1950): 64–67.

Cora A. Morse. "Yosemite As I Saw It." (San Francisco: San Francisco News Co., 1896), quoted in Robertson, David. *Yosemite As We Saw It: A Centennial Collection of Early Writings and Art* (Yosemite: Yosemite Association, 1990), 94.

James Mason Hutchings. *In the Heart of the Sierras: Yosemite Valley and the Big Tree Grove.* Reprint of 1886 edition. (Lafayette, CA: Great West Books, 1990), 16.

CHAPTER 4

Senator John Conness on the proposed Yosemite Grant. Congressional Globe. 38th Congress, 1st session. May 17, 1864.

William Cronon, quoted in Duncan, Dayton. *The National Parks: America's Best Idea.* A book based on the film by Ken Burns and Dayton Duncan (New York: Alfred A. Knopf, 2009), iv.

Freeman Tilden. *The National Parks.* Edited by Paul Schullery. (New York: Alfred A. Knopf, 1986.)

Thomas Ayres. "A Trip to the Yohamite Valley." *Daily Alta California.* (August 6, 1856).

CHAPTER 5

Jack London. "Dutch Courage." With an introduction by Gerald Haslam. Yosemite National Park, CA: Yosemite Association, 2006. Reprint of the story in "The Youth's Companion." November 29, 1900.

Edward Abbey. *The Journey Home: Some Words in Defense of the American West.* (New York: E. P. Dutton, 1977), 144–145.

Jessie Benton Fremont. Far West Sketches. (Boston: D. Lothrop Company, 1890), 139.

CHAPTER 6

Mae B. Nattkemper. "Yosemite Honeymoon." *Yosemite Nature Notes*, vol. XXIX, no. 6 (June 1950): 57.

Allan Shields. "Guide to Tuolumne Meadows Trails." *Yosemite Nature Notes*, vol. XXXIX, no. 8 (Special Issue, 1960): 173.

CHAPTER 7

Frederick Law Olmsted. *The Yosemite Valley and the Mariposa Big Trees, a Preliminary Report, 1865.* Reprint. (Yosemite: Yosemite Association, 2009), 12.

Ibid., 23.

Stephen T. Mather, from U.S. Department of the Interior. *Report of the Director of the National Park Service to the Secretary of the Interior for the Fiscal Year ended June 30th, 1920 and the Travel Season 1920* (Washington D.C: Government Printing Office, 1920): 13–14.

CHAPTER 8

Mark Daniels. *Report of the Acting Superintendent of Yosemite National Park.* Department of the Interior, Yosemite, California: Office of the Superintendent, October 3, 1914.

Ibid.

CHAPTER 9

M. A. Badshah. From a speech given at the First World Conference on National Parks, India, 1962.

John Muir. *The Yosemite* (New York: The Century Company, 1912), 158.

CHAPTER 10

Ibid., 3.

Park visitor commenting on Nevada Fall, 1873. "Register," Albert and Emily Snow's La Casa Nevada Hotel Register, 1870–1891. CD #2, Yosemite Research Library.

Julia Parker, quoted in Mark Goodin. *Yosemite, The 100 Year Flood: Movement in Tides.* (Mariposa, CA: Sierra Press, 2003).

Charles Augustus Stoddard. *Beyond the Rockies: A Spring Journey in California.* (New York: Charles Scribner's Sons, 1894), 132.

CHAPTER 11

Joseph Grinnell and Tracy Storer. "Animal Life as an Asset of National Parks." Science 44 (September 15, 1916): 379.

John Muir. *Travels in Alaska.* (Cambridge, MA: The Riverside Press, 1915), 5.

PHOTOGRAPHS

All photographs are from the Yosemite Research Library Collection. Descriptions and photographer (when available) and reference numbers are provided.

ii: *Dancing Ladies on Overhanging Rock at Glacier Point*: Distant silhouette view of Kitty Tatch and friend dancing on the overhanging rock at Glacier Point, Yosemite, with distant view to northeast, circa 1890. YOSE005252

vi: *Yosemite Valley from near Tunnel View*, 1938, by Ralph H. Anderson. RL02954

x: *Visitors at the Foot of a "Big Tree,"* 1939, by Schwenk. RL3037

28: *Camping in Yosemite*: George Schaffer party, circa 1890. RL3472

43: *Camp Curry Early Days.* RL13874

56: *Early Trail Scene*: Nevada Fall in background, by George Fiske. RL012615

96: *Brown and Daulton Party*, 1880. YM17433

118: *Near View of the Six-story Ahwahnee Hotel, Yosemite Valley*, with two men standing in meadow in foreground, and Royal Arches, Washington Column, and Half Dome in distance. RL017344

129: *Yosemite Falls and Merced River*: Yosemite Falls and surrounding cliffs, with Merced River and meadows in foreground. RL000361

140: *Picnic Party in the Mariposa Grove*, 1940. RL3494

170: *Henry Washburn in the Mariposa Grove*, circa 1890. RL12782

189: *Badger Pass Ski House*, 1936. RL003263

204: *Hikers on the Side of Sentinel Dome*, 1940. RL6850

230: *Berry and Baldwin Party*, circa 1880, by Gustav Fagersteen. YM21983

250: *Wagon Driving Through Arch Rock.* RL19206

268: *Yosemite Ranger Force*, 1924, by A.H. Patterson. RL7838

297: *Holmes Brothers in a Stanley Steamer*, 1900. RL001876

298: *Bear*: copied September 1984 by Michael Dixon from an album belonging to Orville Orton. RL15377

311: *Ranger Club, Yosemite*. RL001638

318: *Bicycling Riders and Yosemite Falls*, 1938. RL06923

344: *Wedding Party in Wagon at Wawona Tunnel Tree, Mariposa Grove of Giant Sequoias*. RL04410

370: *Campfire Group near May Lake*, 1938. RL012758

INDEX OF AUTHORS AND TITLES

YOSEMITE
CONSERVANCY.

Providing For Yosemite's Future

Through the support of donors, Yosemite Conservancy provides grants and support to Yosemite National Park to help preserve and protect Yosemite today and for future generations. The work funded by Yosemite Conservancy is visible throughout the park, from trail rehabilitation to wildlife protection and habitat restoration. The Conservancy is dedicated to enhancing the visitor experience and providing a deeper connection to the park through outdoor programs, volunteering and wilderness services. Thanks to dedicated supporters, the Conservancy has provided more than $81 million in grants to Yosemite National Park.

yosemiteconservancy.org